DATE DUE

Midwest Politics

Midwest
Politics

JOHN H. FENTON
University of Massachusetts

HOLT, RINEHART AND WINSTON
New York · Chicago · San Francisco · Toronto · London

Dedicated to my Mother and Father

Preface

I wrote this book primarily because I enjoy American politics. Of course, there are other more sober reasons for the undertaking. The more serious reasons include the need to examine two-party politics in the United States in order to determine whether or not it contributes anything very useful to the republic. Are the political parties and the campaigns they wage for their candidates worth the cost to the citizenry? I hope that the following pages help answer this question.

I am indebted to a great many people for whatever merit my labors may have. The Social Science Research Council and the University of Massachusetts Research Council provided the financial wherewithal for the research and the recording of the results. I am grateful to former United States Senator Earle C. Clements and to Louis Harris and Associates for making available to me sample surveys of the voters in Ohio, Indiana, Wisconsin, and Minnesota. In each of the states scores of people gave freely of their time and their knowledge of the state's politics. Politicians and professors, in particular, must love to talk or are incredibly generous with their precious time. Whatever the reason, many thanks to all those who talked to me.

The individuals to whom I am most indebted for the completion of the book are Mrs. Doris Holden, who typed the manuscript and usually returned copy to me in a more readable form than the original, and Alan Merdek, who programmed my data for the automatic computer. Mr. Merdek is a mathematician but displayed a lively interest in the subject matter and consequently was able to provide me with more than mechanical advice and assistance. I also want to thank Professor Charles Adrian of Michigan State University and Professor David Mayhew of the University of Massachusetts for their helpful criticisms and suggestions. My thanks also to Professor Samuel J. Eldersveld and the Institute of Public Administration of the University of Michigan for the statistical information provided by them. Finally, I am grateful to the late Charles Winston, former Political Science Editor for Holt, Rinehart and Winston, whose encouraging response to an outline of the embryonic Midwest politics study motivated me to apply for foundation support.

It should be unnecessary to add that any errors of commission or omission in the manuscript are entirely the responsibility of the author.

J.H.F.

Amherst, Mass.
February 1966

Contents

Midwest Politics

Chapter 1

Introduction

A common complaint about studies of state politics is that they fail to devote enough attention to states with two competitive parties. The tendency, it is alleged, has been to seek out states that depart from the two-party norm rather than to analyze the norm itself. The force of the complaint was spent a bit by Duane Lockard's study of *New England State Politics* and by analyses of the politics of individual states, such as Leon Epstein's *Politics in Wisconsin* and Theodore Mitau's *Politics in Minnesota*. Nevertheless, it is true that until now no attempt has been made at a comparative state politics study of the nation's two-party heartland, the Midwest.

The inquiries into the politics of Michigan, Wisconsin, Minnesota, Ohio, Indiana, and Illinois contained in the following chapters represent an attempt to remedy this oversight. The six states were chosen for a wide variety of reasons, including their geographic location and their reputation for intensely competitive two-party politics. In addition, three of the states (Michigan, Wisconsin, and Minnesota) were rather widely represented as possessing programmatic or issue-oriented parties; and the other three states (Ohio, Indiana, and Illinois) were equally widely advertised as states with "traditional" or job-oriented parties, all of which made them even more interesting to the student of politics.

The expressed need for a study of two-party state politics contains the implicit assumption that there is something inherently useful and interesting about two-party politics. The literature of political science is replete with this assumption, for almost every textbook assumes that two-party competition

1

magically translates the wishes of the people into public policy. The rationale behind this position is that democracy places its faith in majority judgments in determining the direction of public policy, and two-party competition provides a mechanism by which an informed majority judgment may be expressed. More specifically, two-party competition, according to its exponents, is the very heart of democracy. It is the means by which information and meaningful debate and discussion of issues (the lifeblood of a democracy) are pumped to every part of the society. And after the debate and discussion of the issues, the people express a majority will concerning the issues through their votes for or against candidates. After the majority will has been expressed, the majority party assumes control of the government and proceeds to translate into public policy the programs it advocated in the election campaign. The minority party serves an equally useful function after the election through its criticism and surveillance of the performance of the majority party, thus assuring honesty, efficiency, and responsibility by the majority party while it is in control of the government.

The proposition that two-party competition "makes a difference" in the performance of government and generally in the direction predicted by the theorists has been fairly well established.[1] In a study of "Two-Party Competition and Governmental Expenditures," this writer concluded that two-party competition tends to inflate a state's expenditures for programs designed to reallocate goods and opportunities (that is, welfare and education expenditures). Even when the wealth and urbanism of the states were taken into account through a variety of statistical devices, the competitive states tended to spend more on welfare and education than the less competitive states.[2]

[1] Efforts to relate competitiveness to the performance of government include John H. Fenton, "Two-Party Competition and Governmental Expenditures," paper delivered at the September 1962 meeting of the American Political Science Association; Duane Lockard, *New England State Politics* (Princeton, N.J.: Princeton University Press, 1959), Chap. 3. A more recent attempt is a study by Richard E. Dawson and James A. Robinson, "Inter-Party Competition, Economic Variables, and Welfare Policies in the American States," *Journal of Politics*, vol. 25 (1963), p. 265. Early efforts to measure two-party competition in the states include Joseph A. Schlesenger, "A Two-Dimensional Scheme for Classifying the States According to Degree of Inter-Party Competition," *American Political Science Review*, vol. 49 (1955), p. 1120; and Austin Ranney and Willmore Kendall, "The American Party System," *American Political Science Review*, vol. 48 (1954), p. 477.
[2] The author's study of "Two-Party Competition and Governmental Expenditures" was, in a way, a preliminary exercise to the analysis of Midwest

It was apparent from the results of the study, however, that other variables besides the competitiveness of a state's politics contributed to the responsiveness of elected officials to the needs of the disadvantaged. Specifically, the competitive two-party states that were in the vanguard in their expenditures for welfare and education tended also to be states with a reputation for issue-oriented two-party politics as opposed to the more traditional job-oriented two-party politics. The six Midwest states conformed to this pattern in that Ohio, Indiana, and Illinois (job-oriented) ranked quite low in state expenditures relative to their wealth, whereas Michigan, Wisconsin, and Minnesota (issue-oriented) ranked high. The additional fact that the six states are contiguous geographically and have similar cultures added to their fascination for the researcher.

In large part, this study of Midwest Politics consists of an explanation of the many differences in the organization, functions, and performance of issue-oriented as opposed to job-oriented political parties. Not a great deal has been done in the way of distinguishing between job-oriented and issue-oriented

---

Politics. It established to the author's satisfaction that two-party competition was worth studying. The research involved, first, assigning a competition score to each state based upon the narrowness of the division between the two parties in the state legislature and in the vote for governor, 1946–1958. For example, if a state's parties divided, on the average, 50–50 in the state legislature and 50–50, on the average, in the gubernatorial elections, it would have a perfect score of 100. If, on the other hand, the divisions were 100–0, the competitive score would be zero. Next, the competitive scores were related to a variety of governmental expenditures and demographic data for the sake of determining whether or not two-party competition did make a measurable difference in the performance of state government. Happily for the fate of this book, the data showed that two-party competition had some effect independent of income and urbanism on the levels of welfare, aid to dependent children, and per-pupil expenditures. Multiple correlations ($R2$) showed that 55 percent of the variations in aid to dependent children from state to state were related to two-party competition plus urbanism plus the per-capita income of the state, and the partial regression coefficients indicated that 75 percent of the total relationship was attributable to the two-party competition variable; 63 percent of the variations from state to state in per-pupil expenditures were related to the three variables, and 32 percent were attributable to two-party competition; 35 percent of the variations in total welfare expenditures from state to state were attributable to the three variables, and 36 percent of the total relationship was attributable to two-party competition. The results were sufficiently significant for entering upon a study of Midwest Politics with the fairly confident assumption that two-party competition does indeed influence the degree to which governmental programs are aimed at providing a more equal distribution of goods and services.

two-party systems. Briefly, the traditional political parties are conceived to be groups that are primarily concerned with obtaining government jobs and privileges. The issue-oriented parties, on the other hand, are conceived to be groups of people who come together out of some common concern with public policy and a desire to do something about it. The important distinction between the two types of parties is that the people in the traditional parties are active in politics because they want a job, and issues are perceived as tools by which to secure the jobs, whereas the people in the programmatic parties are in politics not for the jobs as such, but because the job is seen as the means of securing the policy goals they regard as desirable.

Therefore, the preliminary research conducted before the intensive exploration of Midwest Politics led to the conviction that two-party competition has a measurable effect upon the performance of state government. It also led to the strong hunch that the kind of competition (job-oriented versus issue-oriented) also has an independent effect upon the character of the governmental services received by the citizen. The crucial question that remained was the differential utility of the two methods of organizing political parties in realizing the goals of American democracy; that is, promoting the general welfare within a context that protects the freedom of the individual.

In studying Midwest Politics, a guiding hypothesis was that two broad aspects of two-party competition must be present before the theoretical benefits of two-party competition may be fully realized: (1) a fairly equal division of the electorate between the two parties roughly along the lines of contemporary problems; and (2) a leadership of the parties that makes them distinct entities, competes at every level of government, advocates alternative approaches to the problems that concern the voters, and attempts to carry through after election by translating their proposed solutions to public problems into public policy. The chapters dealing with Michigan, Wisconsin, Minnesota, Ohio, Indiana, and Illinois are largely concerned with the degree to which each of these elements of two-party competition were present, the reasons for their presence or absence, and the consequences for the governments of the states.

The differing histories of the six states provide some preliminary insights into the reasons behind their political party patterns. Even though all six Midwest states had competitive two-party politics in the 1960s, the points in time at which the states' politics became competitive vary greatly. Vigorous two-party competition was a fairly recent development in Michigan, Wisconsin, and Minnesota, whereas it was a tradition dating from the very birth of Ohio, Indiana, and Illinois. A partial explanation for the differing political histories of the states may be divined from Table 1.1. The table tells numerically of the flow of people by wagon, boat, horse, and on foot into the several states. In 1850 the populations of Ohio, Indiana, and Illinois included a substantial proportion of people who followed the rivers and streams from the South to the Midwest. They came in search of land and settled, first, the bottomland, and then the hills of the southern portions of the three states. The Civil War was particularly painful to the transplanted Southerners and

Table 1.1

SECTIONAL ORIGINS OF THE POPULATION IN THE STATES OF THE OLD NORTHWEST, 1850

	NEW ENGLAND	MIDDLE STATES	THE SOUTH	THE NORTHWEST	FROM EUROPE
Ohio	66,000	300,000	150,000	—	200,000
Indiana	11,000	76,000	175,000	130,000	55,000
Illinois	37,000	112,000	138,000	110,000	110,000
Michigan	31,000	150,000	4,000	18,000	55,000
Wisconsin	27,000	80,000	5,000	23,000	107,000

Source: Ray Billington, *Westward Expansion: A History of the American Frontier* (New York: The Macmillan Company, 1949), p. 308.

many affiliated themselves with the Democratic party in the 1860s out of opposition to Abraham Lincoln's war.

The northern portions of Ohio, Indiana, and Illinois were originally settled largely by New Englanders. The New Englanders were Whig-inclined before the Civil War and also tended to oppose slavery with some fervor. They supported the Civil War wholeheartedly and found renewed reason in the political conflicts of the period to support the Republican party.

It was out of these two divergent streams of population settlement that the shape of two-party politics in Ohio, Indiana, and Illinois was molded. A great deal occurred in all three states after 1860, including the influx of new streams of immigrants from eastern Europe and the American South. However, the roots of two-party competition in the three states remained entwined in the rock of the Civil War.

There were few people who traveled directly from the South into Michigan and Wisconsin in search of land (Minnesota was not settled in 1850, but its subsequent settlement conformed to the Michigan and Wisconsin patterns). Most of the early settlers were Yankees or were from bordering states or were immigrants from Europe. Consequently, the reaction of the populations to the Civil War consisted of near-unanimous support for the Union forces against the Southern "rebels." The political result was a virtual one-party system in the three states from the Civil War and until the Great Depression. The one-party character of the states was further buttressed by the tendency of the newly arrived Scandinavians to join forces with Yankees in the Republican party.

However, the Scandinavians, joined by other disadvantaged groups, fought a continuing political battle with the dominant native elements within the Republican party. The disaffected elements within the Republican party were identified, variously, as Greenbackers, Populists, Progressives, Nonpartisan Leagues, and Farmer Laborites. After the New Deal, the Democratic party inherited the three states' history of protest movements, finally producing in Minnesota, Wisconsin, and Michigan viable two-party political systems.

Observers of the newly developed competitive parties in Michigan, Wisconsin, and Minnesota described them as programmatic or issue-oriented parties. Some welcomed the development enthusiastically as a means of realizing the goals of democracy. Others viewed it with alarm as being a threat to the stable foundations of American democracy.

In sum, the six states constitute something of a laboratory for an examination of the process by which traditional two-party politics and issue-oriented two-party politics affect the performance of state government. Ohio, Indiana, and Illinois are the archetypes of traditional two-party politics. On the other hand, Michigan, Wisconsin, and Minnesota are, perhaps, the first states that spring to mind when one thinks of programmatic or issue-oriented state politics. Minnesota with its farmer-labor tradition, Wisconsin with its La Follette progressives, and Michigan with Walter Reuther and the United Auto Workers Union typify to most Americans all that is good and bad about issue-oriented politics.

The following analyses of these six states should provide

guidance to students of politics concerning the virtues and vices of these alternative approaches to the government of men. In the field of political science as well as in the popular press, there has been much adulation of two-party competition, with little firm knowledge of its results. Similarly, many praise or condemn the political patterns in Minnesota, Wisconsin, and Michigan with a minimum of understanding of the products derived therefrom. It is hoped that the succeeding pages will help the citizenry in deciding whether the returns from various kinds of political competition are worth the cost and effort of securing and maintaining two viable and competitive political parties.

Part 1

The Issue-Oriented States: Michigan, Wisconsin, and Minnesota

The first group of Midwest states examined are contiguous geographically and have in common a history of two-party issue-oriented politics. It is significant that the issue-oriented two-party political form took root in Michigan, Wisconsin, and Minnesota at approximately the same time. In Michigan, the precipitant was the liberal-labor alliance in 1948 when the two groups joined forces to elect G. Mennen Williams governor of the state and simultaneously wrested control of the Democratic party from the faltering hands of job-oriented conservatives. In Minnesota, two-party issue-oriented politics began when the Democratic and Farmer-Labor parties combined in 1944. And in Wisconsin, the key dates in the formation of issue-oriented parties are 1946, when the Progressive party disbanded and Joseph McCarthy defeated Robert La Follette, Jr., in the Republican U.S. senatorial primary, and 1949, when the Progressives, Socialists, and Democrats joined forces in the Democratic Organizing Committee.

It could not have been entirely coincidental that such similar political events occurred within a space of a few years in three contiguous states. Thus, the analyses of the politics of the three states have an importance that transcends the immediate objective of providing an understanding of the politics of the individual states. The studies of the three states should provide insights into the processes by which waves of political change take place and might also provide useful insights into basic trends in American politics. In addition, the chapters on the three issue-oriented states, when placed beside the subsequent chapters dealing with three Midwest job-oriented states (Ohio, Indiana, and Illinois), should be useful in assessing the comparative public policy consequences of the two forms of political organization.

Chapter 2

Autos and Workers
in Michigan

In 1928 a look backward at the history of two-party politics in Michigan would have convinced the observer that Michigan had become a one-party state. The inexorable trend of voter loyalties was toward larger and larger Republican pluralities. Only four years later, in 1932, and then again in 1936, Michigan's people turned to the Democratic party, as did the voters of most other states. However, by 1946 it seemed to most students of politics that Michigan had returned to its dominantly Republican bias because of inept, corrupt, and conservative Democratic state politicians. The only important exception to Democratic ineptitude in the 1930s was the administration of liberal Democrat Frank Murphy, who was elected in 1936 as a result of the Roosevelt landslide.

Murphy was defeated in 1938 and departed the state for federal service. However, his two-year term left a mark on the state that was not immediately apparent. Even though Republicans won the governorship, 1938–1946, the Murphy period in Michigan history, 1937–1939, was vitally important to subsequent Democratic victories. While governor, Murphy, through his sympathetic attitude toward unions and particularly the sit-down strikes, played a very helpful if not an instrumental part in the victory that labor finally won over the motor companies. After Murphy, working people tended to associate pro-labor policies with the state Democratic as well as the national Democratic party. Murphy's importance, therefore, stems from his role in identifying the Michigan Democratic party with the economic well-being of workingmen. This party image contributed largely to Detroit's remaining a Democratic stronghold

11

after 1936, and was certainly vitally important in bringing to fruition the single most important event in modern Michigan politics—the emergence of a formalized labor-liberal Democratic alliance in 1948 that startled the state and the nation by capturing both the Democratic party and the governorship.

Political Organization in Michigan

After 1948, Michigan's politics was programmatic. And programmatic politics demands political organizations staffed by people whose primary concern is public policy rather than patronage. On the Democratic side, the liberal-labor coalition which dominated that party after 1948 was disinterested in jobs or spoils. Traditionally, a political party was an interest group composed primarily of people who (1) either wanted government jobs or sought to keep them, (2) wanted contracts or tried to keep them, and (3) managed or bossed political parties as a profession. In the nation's past, issue-oriented interest groups operated outside the framework of the political parties. For example, in West Virginia the United Mine Workers (UMW), while almost invariably supporting Democratic party candidates, always remained outside the party. The UMW influenced the selection of candidates and the policies adopted by Democratic party leaders, but was not a part of the party. The same situation prevailed in Illinois, Indiana, Ohio, and most other states. Political party leaders appealed to issue-oriented interest group leaders for their support on the basis of policies advocated and candidates nominated. However, the politicians' objective in advocating the policies was winning the jobs and spoils of government rather than translating specific programs into public policy. They were job-oriented rather than issue-oriented.

In Michigan, the new Democratic party leadership was issue-oriented rather than job-oriented. The party leaders entered into the hurly-burly of politics primarily out of concern with issues rather than out of a need for or desire for government jobs.[1] The central reason for the issue-orientation of the Demo-

[1] Theodore H. White, in *The Making of the President, 1960* (New York: Atheneum Publishers, 1961), pp. 137–139, has several interesting observations concerning the nature of Michigan's Democratic leadership and Kennedy's sensitive reactions to it. He characterizes Neil Staebler, Walter Reuther, and Governor G. Mennen Williams as "high-minded, yet hardknuckled." He also notes that "in the course of twelve years Neil Staebler,

cratic party leadership was that the United Auto Workers (UAW) was a part of the Democratic party rather than a separate interest group. Like the management of the auto companies in the Republican party, the union leadership was not content with simply influencing political parties. The union was part of the Democratic party.

The reasons for the domination of Michigan's Democratic party by a labor-liberal combination were to be found in developments of the 1930s and 1940s. It was Franklin Roosevelt's New Deal which made possible the organization of Detroit's auto workers. Specifically, the National Labor Relations Act with its provisions for collective bargaining made it virtually impossible for the auto companies to refuse to bargain with the unions. Consequently, the union leadership and the rank-and-file members identified their improved bargaining position with the national Democratic party.

The national Democratic party's policies toward minority groups and with respect to relief attracted the support of the auto workers, many of whom were periodically unemployed and were also members of Negro and other minority groups. In addition, a substantial number of the white as well as Negro workers had emigrated from traditionally Democratic areas in the South and were inclined to vote Democratic in Detroit. Consequently, virtually every political, social, and economic pressure pushed the Detroit auto workers in the direction of a Democratic vote after the New Deal.

More important, perhaps, than the Democratic bias of the members of the auto unions was the character of the union leadership that emerged in the 1930s and thereafter. Symbolic and representative of the UAW leadership was Walter Reuther, its president. Reuther's issue horizon extended beyond the traditional labor union concern with wages, hours, and working conditions. Most American labor unions did not try to participate in government. Rather, they concentrated their attention on "bread and butter" for the members of the union and security for the union itself through such measures as the union shop. They paid only marginal attention to issues of foreign and domestic policy that did not directly affect the welfare of their members or the organizational security of the union.

State Chairman and one of the most moral men in American politics, had built one of the most efficient citizen-politics organizations in the upper midwest. . . ."

Walter Reuther and the UAW leadership did not conform to the "bread and butter" approach of the AFL-CIO (American Federation of Labor and Congress of Industrial Organizations) leadership. Reuther wanted to participate in the government of the entire society. Consequently, the UAW leaders concerned themselves with all political policies, ranging from foreign aid to public health to the United Nations to park programs to tax and spending policies.

It is impossible to assign any single reason for the broad social and political horizons of the UAW leaders as compared to other labor leaders. As will be seen in the Ohio chapters, part of the explanation may be found by observing the differences between, say, steel workers and auto workers. Beginning with Henry Ford's $5-per-day salary policy, the auto industry attracted superior workers. The steel industry, in contrast, offered a notoriously unattractive type of employment and the workers tended to be the marginal members of the labor force. The leadership selected by the two groups of workers reflected these differences in the character of their members.

Interviews with United Steelworker officials and UAW leaders provided impressionistic confirmation of these observations. The Steelworker leaders were often semiliterate and showed little knowledge of or interest in political problems that transcended their immediate union problems. On the other hand, the UAW leaders were almost invariably well educated and regarded the union as a vehicle through which to work for a better world rather than just as a means of getting better pay for auto workers.

There were, of course, other reasons for the broad issue-orientation of the UAW leadership. For one thing, the UAW had good financial resources and held a dominant position in Detroit and Michigan. The smaller AFL craft unions did not enjoy the financial resources necessary to pursue political power. Perhaps even more important than financial resources was the difference between the position of the UAW in Michigan and the potential political power of unions in other states. The UAW dominated Michigan's labor movement, and consequently any increase in the political power of labor in the state automatically meant an expansion of the power of the UAW leadership.

Few, if any, unions in other states enjoyed such dominant power. Therefore, an increase in labor's political activity and power at the state or national level did not necessarily mean an expansion in the power of individual union leaders. On the contrary, it probably reduced the narrowly defined areas of political power enjoyed by union leaders. For example, Teamster Union officials in Ohio often received appointments to governmental positions as rewards for support of Republican candidates. If labor became issue-oriented in Ohio and became a part of a political party as in Michigan, it would reduce the political power of Teamster officials. There were similar situations in other states, such as arrangements made between Mayor Daley and trade union officials in Chicago concerning city jobs. Thus, where there were many unions, each union official had a vested interest in the continued diffusion of union power, for unity transferred power to a central labor body. The development of a unified labor approach to politics on an issue-oriented basis increased labor's power at the state level, but it also reduced the power of most labor leaders, with the exception of the few dominant and well-financed leaders like Walter Reuther.[2]

Paralleling the development of an issue-oriented labor leadership in Michigan was the emergence of a nucleus of liberal professional and business men and women. The existence in Michigan of groups of liberals whose aim was to reallocate power, goods, and opportunities in the society was not a unique situation. The Great Depression provoked doubts in the minds of men and women in every state concerning the virtues of the existing social and economic system. However, Michigan, in company with Minnesota and Wisconsin, was one of the few states where the liberals maintained their sense of identity after World War II.

In states such as Ohio there were few places where a liberal could obtain a job which was in harmony with his political philosophy. Intelligent and able liberals usually secured jobs in management and found themselves on the "other side" of the picket line from the working people. More important, however, in Ohio there was no cohesive group of liberals in a type of employment that might encourage liberal or left-wing political action.

In Michigan, on the other hand, the UAW provided a source of employment or patronage for liberals. The liberals in the UAW then interacted with liberals in the business community

[2] In 1963, the United Auto Workers had 1,056,000 members, the largest AFL-CIO union. Source: *World Almanac, 1964*, p. 725.

and the professions through organizations such as the Americans for Democratic Action. The liberals in Michigan, consequently, never felt homeless and powerless. Through the UAW they were in touch with a powerful organization with the potential to do something about the problems that troubled them.

In the 1930s and early 1940s, though, little developed politically from the liberal-labor relationships in Michigan. The Great Depression and the problems of organizing the auto industry absorbed most of the attention of the labor leaders. World War II followed close on the heels of the successful strikes against General Motors, Ford, and Chrysler and once again distracted the attention of the labor-liberal coalition from Michigan politics.

Even taking into consideration the distractions imposed by depression, organization, and war, political activity in Michigan did not seem to offer much promise of success. The Democratic party was dominated by conservative or middle-of-the-road politicians whose sole concern was jobs, and there was little chance of ousting them from their positions of political power. The alternative of a labor party was tempting, but Franklin Roosevelt's New Deal held the loyalty of most of the labor and liberal leaders and restrained them from a party-splitting political upheaval.

In 1941, however, the Michigan legislature enacted a strict merit system for the selection of state employees. The immediate reason the Republican legislature approved the law was that the most prolific source of state government jobs was controlled by the Democrats. Murry Van Wagoner was the elected Democratic highway commissioner and in this position had control of the distribution of jobs to Democrats. In 1939 he won control of the Democratic party organization by virtue of his patronage power.

The Republican legislature, by adopting the merit system law, robbed the Democratic leadership of its most important source of jobs. Thereafter, Democrats who were in the party simply for jobs tended to drift out of the party. In Detroit, there were fewer candidates for election as delegates to the Democratic District Convention in 1944 and 1946.

The Democratic party in Michigan, as a consequence, became moribund. The traditional job-oriented politicians lost interest in it because it was not a very useful means by which to get a job or a contract or a favor from government. Also, post-World War II prosperity reduced the attractiveness of government jobs. The fact that the Democratic party in Michigan was a vacuum did not escape the attention of politically knowledgeable labor and liberal leaders. The opportunity that the situation offered for seizure of the Democratic party by a labor-liberal coalition was discussed within the UAW and the Americans for Democratic Action (ADA). People such as Neil Staebler, Walter and Roy Reuther, and G. Mennen Williams met and talked about strategy and candidates.[3] It was finally agreed that Williams would be the candidate of the coalition and that the UAW would actively enter the Democratic party. On March 13, 1948, a state CIO-PAC (Congress of Industrial Organizations—Political Action Committee) conference adopted the following resolution:

Progressives and liberals within the Democratic party have often been outnumbered by conservative and reactionary elements. The PAC is unanimous in its opinion that the best way of supporting liberalism within the Democratic party, to conform to the national CIO policy, and to serve the best interests of Michigan labor, is to join the Democratic party. It is our objective in adopting this policy to remold the Democratic party into a real liberal and progressive political party which can be subscribed to by members of the CIO and other liberals. We therefore advise CIO members to become active precinct, ward, county, and Congressional district workers, and to attempt to become delegates to Democratic conventions.

The motor companies had already obtained an important place in the leadership of Michigan's Republican party. Beginning in 1940, the General Motors people, through Arthur Summerfield, a GM dealer, obtained control of the large Genesee County delegation to the Republican convention and the Ford people obtained control of the Wayne County delegation. By 1944, when one of Senator John Bricker's workers went to Michigan in search of support from delegates to the 1944 Republican National Convention, he was told that he was wasting his time. According to the Michigan Republican leader, "We like John Bricker for President, but the day before the convention we will all caucus and General Motors will tell us how to vote. If you want votes for John Bricker you'd better go to the General Motors and Ford people."

Republican Governor George Romney, a former president of the American Motor Company, was representative of the programmatic leadership provided by the motor companies in the

[3] This account of the emergence of a liberal-labor coalition in Michigan was drawn both from interviews and from the excellent study of Michigan politics by Stephen B. and Vera H. Sarasohn, *Political Party Patterns in Michigan* (Detroit: Wayne State University Press, 1957).

Republican party. Romney was a political moderate who was active in politics, in part because of beliefs he held concerning the policy content of good government. Similarly, organization men from the management of General Motors, Ford Motor Company, and other businesses participated in Republican politics because of philosophical beliefs they held concerning the proper role of government in American society. They were not interested in jobs for the sake of jobs. After all, their positions in the motor companies paid them much more handsomely than any political job. Similarly, petty spoils did not attract them. Rather, they were concerned with ideology, taxes, and spending programs. Generally, they held moderate political views which reduced themselves to a belief that we have a very good economic and political society and all it requires is improvement—not basic change.

The Liberal-Labor 1948 Revolt

In 1948, the UAW sought to obtain a political power position comparable to that of Ford and General Motors. The liberal-labor leaders enjoyed success that transcended their expectations. The strategy for the 1948 liberal-labor seizure of the Democratic party was worked out in conference between August Scholle, who was president of the Michigan CIO and head of the Political Action Committee, and Hicks G. Griffiths and G. Mennen Williams. Griffiths and Williams were both well-to-do and liberal. In addition, they enjoyed close relations with other liberals, some of whom were also wealthy. Most of the liberal leadership was provided by Griffiths and Williams, in consultation with liberals such as Noel P. Fox of Muskegon, Hickman Price of Ann Arbor, and Neil Staebler, who was a wealthy Ann Arbor businessman.[4]

These respected and respectable liberals provided the 1948 move to seize the Democratic party with money, but most important, they managed to identify the move with objectives and interests beyond those of labor. Tactically, the liberal contribution to the coalition was vital, for it served to undermine charges that the 1948 move was an effort by labor to seize control of Michigan government. The contribution of liberal votes or money was relatively unimportant. However, the names of G. Mennen Williams, Hicks Griffiths, and Neil Staebler made the coalition safe and relatively respectable in the minds of many Michigan voters.

[4] *Ibid.*, pp. 55–56.

The liberals, though, were not simply a façade for labor domination. In truth, they subsequently provided most of the ideological and formal leadership of the party. G. Mennen Williams was elected governor, and Hicks Griffiths and Neil Staebler succeeded one another as Democratic state chairmen. The importance of the liberals to the success of the coalition was never fully appreciated by labor until the events of 1960 and 1962, when labor attempted to seize formal control of the party and, according to some observers, thereby cost the Democrats the 1962 gubernatorial election.

Returning to the 1948 revolution in Democratic ranks, the liberal-labor coalition supported Williams in the Democratic gubernatorial primary and he won the nomination, largely through the votes provided in Wayne County. Just as important, about 1000 labor people and liberals filed for election to the Democratic district conventions in Wayne County, and 720 of them won election as delegates. Through the 720 votes in the district conventions, the labor-liberal coalition won control of four of the six Wayne County districts. As these districts elected representatives to the Democratic State Convention, the labor-liberals were able to monopolize the state delegate posts.[5]

In Michigan the representation to the state convention was based on the proportion that a district's vote represented of the total Democratic vote for secretary of state in the last election. Wayne County provided almost half the votes. Therefore, the liberal-labor delegates from the four Wayne County districts, in combination with fellow-travelers from other districts, dominated the Democratic State Convention. In 1949 Hicks Griffiths was elected state chairman and the labor-liberal people dictated most of the membership of the Democratic State Committee.[6] In spite of an attempted counter-revolution by traditional Democrats in 1950, the labor-liberal coalition maintained control of the Democratic party from 1948 and until the events of 1960 and 1962.

The most important role played by labor in the new coalition was getting out the Democratic-oriented vote in the Detroit area, and it did its job well. In most elections, if the Detroit vote were cast in large numbers, the Democrats had a good chance of winning the election, for the voters of the Detroit metropolitan area represented about 35 percent of the state's total vote and they were overwhelmingly Democratically inclined. For example,

[5] *Ibid.*, p. 56.
[6] *Ibid.*, pp. 56–58.

sample surveys found that 88 percent of the Negroes, 84 percent of the white people from the South, and 92 percent of the Polish people in Detroit were Democratically inclined. In addition, 85 percent of the CIO members and 74 percent of the AFL members preferred the Democratic party. Thus, the Democratic vote came from labor's rank and file.[7]

The political organizational activities of the unions were reflected in the membership of the Democratic State Central Committee after 1948. For example, one study of the Democratic State Central Committee in Michigan, 1949–1959, shows that 46.9 percent of its members were either blue-collar workers or officials of labor unions. However, the liberals dominated the top leadership group. The same study shows that only 15 percent of the Democrats' top leadership came from labor, and they were all officials and staff members.[8]

Almost all the liberal leadership of the Democratic party over the 1949–1959 period were "either self-employed or [had] employers who [were] not likely to penalize them for Democratic party activity."[9] Indeed, many of them were in positions where their employment exerted a positive push in the direction of Democratic party involvement (some were labor union officials and some were teachers in Democratic urban areas). Perhaps the most significant characteristic of the Democratic party leadership was the absence of professional politicians or government jobholders. In the Democratic State Central Committee, only 6.3 percent of the members were state government appointees and not one was on the Democratic party staff. In the top leadership group, however, 40 percent of the heads of families were officeholders or on the Democratic party staff.[10]

Programmatic Politics and Liberal-Labor Factionalism

The issue orientation of the liberal-labor leadership of the Democratic party, 1949–1959, is reflected in the composition of the party leadership, in the campaign documents of the party,

[7] The figures on party affiliation in Wayne County were obtained from Samuel J. Eldersveld *et al.*, *Political Affiliations in Metropolitan Detroit* ("Michigan Governmental Studies," No. 34 [Ann Arbor, Mich.: University of Michigan Press, 1957]), pp. 61–62, 63, 68, 93.

[8] Robert Lee Sawyer, Jr., *The Democratic State Central Committee in Michigan, 1949–1959* (Ann Arbor, Mich.: Institute of Public Administration, University of Michigan, 1960), p. 52.

[9] *Ibid.*, p. 51.

[10] *Ibid.*, p. 25.

and in the response to questions posed them with respect to their attitudes toward politics. The first category was discussed when it was shown that the leadership of the Democratic party is not an interest group concerned with jobs and patronage, but rather a leadership representing labor and other issue-oriented groups.

Perhaps the best indication of the programmatic character of the party was the "Michigan Declaration," a statement of party principles prepared with the help of professors at the state universities and issued in 1956. The declaration was a twentieth-century liberal document which emphasized an egalitarian approach to the problems of society and the importance of the government in securing these egalitarian objectives. For example, the declaration held that:

> So long as one human being is hungry and we can feed him and do not, so long as one person is naked and we can clothe him and do not, so long as one person is sick and we can minister to him and do not, so long as one worker or farmer is deprived of a just living and we can remedy it and do not, so long as one person is unwillingly illiterate and we can educate him and do not, so long as one nation is subjugated by another against its will and we can work for freedom and do not, the American task is not done.[11]

In dealing with the various problems of American society, such as civil liberties and civil rights, automation, economic policy, health, education, social security, agriculture, and natural resources, the document made clear in each case that the Democratic party did not rely on any "invisible hand" or "natural laws" to solve the problems, but rather upon positive actions of government through such measures as compulsory health insurance, social security programs, training programs for the unemployed, protection of small business against big business, and public recreation.[12]

In interviews with members of the leadership of the Michigan Democratic party, such persons as Staebler, Williams, and Swainson stated quite definitely that the Democratic party was a liberal vehicle. Similarly, in Sawyer's study of the Democratic State Central Committee in Michigan, it was found that the top and middle leadership perceived the Democratic party as a "liberal" vehicle.

The Republican party's issue-oriented state leadership re-

---

[11] *Ibid.*, p. 75.
[12] *Ibid.*, pp. 73–75.

mained relatively unchallenged after 1941. The Democratic leadership, however, suffered a traumatic internal fight between the liberal and labor elements of the party in 1960, the results of which remained uncertain in 1963. The precipitant of the factional fight was the retirement of Governor Williams after an unprecedented sixth term as governor. The candidates to succeed Williams were Secretary of State James M. Hare and Lieutenant Governor John B. Swainson.

James Hare was the heir-apparent to the gubernatorial nomination and most observers assumed that he would win. In 1958 Hare had led the Democratic ticket in votes received and was widely respected and liked by liberal Democrats. However, his identification was with the liberal wing of the party rather than the labor wing. Within the ranks of the leadership of the United Auto Workers, the Williams retirement brought to the surface some of the half-suppressed resentment at labor's lack of representation in the Democratic party's top leadership ranks. There was criticism of Hare's equivocal position on the sales tax and a widely accepted climate of opinion developed among labor leaders that Hare was "too conservative."

State Chairman Neil Staebler, however, headed off internecine warfare by securing a promise from the AFL-CIO, UAW, and liberal leaders that there would be an "open" primary without endorsements from either the party or factions of the party. By doing this, Staebler unwittingly provided Swainson with an advantage. For if it were not for Staebler's neutrality, Hare would probably have obtained the party's endorsement, which the liberals would have needed in order to work for his nomination.

The "no endorsement" promise was observed formally, but in fact the labor leadership at the local level worked hard for Swainson. In the summer of 1960 the writer attended a meeting of UAW leaders in Lansing where the topic was "How To Deliver the Union Vote for Swainson." The main purpose of the meeting was to emphasize that Hare was a conservative and that if he were elected governor labor would have less power in the Democratic party than it had under Staebler and Williams.

The labor leaders who worked for Swainson were successful in securing his nomination, to the surprise of many observers. The key to Swainson's victory was his top-heavy plurality in the UAW heartland, the Detroit metropolitan area, where he received 187,353 votes to only 115,205 votes for Hare in Wayne, Oakland, and Macomb Counties. Outside the Detroit metropolitan area, Hare's vote was 89,881 to 85,015 for Swainson. Hare carried virtually every county outside the state's metropolitan areas and won by lopsided margins in most low-income rural counties. However, the one-sided Swainson pluralities from the Detroit area decided the contest.[13]

Secretary of State Hare's success in low-income counties probably reflects the importance of patronage in low-income rural areas. The office of secretary of state in Michigan was one of the few offices which was able to employ people at the county level outside the merit system. In the low-income rural areas these political jobs were important, and Hare was able to build a fairly potent political organization. However, the low-income rural counties were also sparsely populated and Hare's advantage there was more than offset by Swainson's union support in the heavily populated metropolitan areas of the state.

In 1960 the full impact of this muscle flexing by the labor side of the liberal-labor coalition was not fully felt. In a display of party unity, Hare was renominated for secretary of state and all other incumbents were renominated. In the 1960 election Neil Staebler remained in his post as state chairman and the entire liberal-labor coalition worked hard for the Kennedy-Swainson ticket.

After Swainson's election, the strain of the 1960 fight began appearing, ·first, in the form of tiny tensions between Swainson and the liberals, and later in a widening gulf between them, as Swainson turned more and more to labor for political support and staff advice and virtually ignored the Williams-Staebler team of liberals. Some important liberals complained that Swainson never discussed policy decisions with them. They accused Swainson of consulting almost exclusively with the labor people.

In the 1962 Democratic convention there was a showdown between the liberals and labor when the Staebler liberals and the labor people supported opposing candidates for the post of state chairman. Through their bloc vote from Wayne County, labor representation won the day at the convention. However, they probably lost the 1962 gubernatorial election at the same time.

By virtue of the 1962 action at the Democratic State Convention, the Republican claim that labor ran the Democratic party was more plausible to moderate Michiganites. And when the Republicans nominated a political moderate for governor, many

---

[13] The coefficient of correlation between the percent Swainson vote of the total primary vote and percent urban by counties was .50, percent rural farm (−).36, and percent less than $3000 (−).60.

people, particularly in the medium-sized cities, turned to the Republican party. The result was the election of George Romney. After 1962 the liberal Democrats attempted to regain power within the party, and with some success. The UAW leadership appeared aware of its tactical error in 1962 and supported liberal Neil Staebler for the gubernatorial nomination in 1964. On the Republican side, the moderate political leadership triumphed in the person of George Romney and in the new state constitution adopted by Michigan's voters in 1963. The reapportionment of the state Senate seemed certain to reduce the power of the Republican conservatives and to increase the power of the Ford–American Motors "organization" moderate leadership in the party.

Political Opinions in Michigan

Given the issue-oriented leadership of Michigan's Democratic and Republican parties, one would expect the state's voters to also exhibit a great deal of interest in issues. The following discussion of the results of a sample survey of Michigan's voters in 1954 is designed to shed light on the issue positions of Michigan's voters. Most of the data are taken from a sample survey of Michigan's voters conducted by International Research Associates, Inc., in 1954 for the Congress of Industrial Organizations. The results showed that 46 percent of Michigan's voters were inclined Democratic, 20 percent neutral, and 34 percent Republican. It was further found that the big-city voters, worker and white-collar voters, young voters, low-education voters, and Catholic voters were markedly more Democratic than the rest of the state (see Table 2.1).[14]

Even more interesting were the findings concerning the issue positions of Michigan's voters. The most significant discovery was that a broad consensus existed in Michigan concerning most

---

[14] In the 1956 study of party affiliations in the Detroit area by Samuel T. Eldersveld *et al., Political Affiliations in Metropolitan Detroit* (p. 63), it was found that the percent Democratically inclined by ethnic groups (father's ancestors) in the Detroit area was as follows:

	% Democratic
England	40.5
Ireland	69.0
Germany	57.2
Poland	92.3
Southern Europe	80.0
Eastern Europe	83.0

Table 2.1

PARTY PREFERENCES OF GROUPS OF MICHIGAN VOTERS, 1954

GROUPS OF VOTERS	DEMO-CRATIC	NEUTRAL	REPUB-LICAN
State totals	46	20	34
Cities over 50,000 pop.	50	18	32
Small-city & rural (all other)	40	22	38
Upper income	37	17	46
Worker & white collar	55	19	26
Young voters (30 or less)	51	25	24
Women	42	22	36
Low education (grammar school or less)	53	14	33
College educated	33	21	46
Catholics	66	17	17

Source: "INRA State Poll, 1954, Michigan" (New York: International Research Associates, Inc.). Adapted from Appendix B.

issues. The New Deal and its programs were almost as widely accepted by Republican-oriented groups as by Democratic groups. Table 2.2 shows the results of the 1954 survey of the

Table 2.2

NET APPEAL OF ISSUES FOR MICHIGAN VOTERS, 1954

WOULD YOU FAVOR OR OPPOSE A CANDIDATE WHO:	% STATE	% DEMO-CRATS	% REPUB-LICANS	% BIG-CITY	% SMALL-TOWN & RURAL	% CATHO-LIC
Is a liberal.	(−) 6	(−) 4	(−) 7	(−) 4	(−)10	(−) 8
Is a conservative.	3	0	8	4	2	3
Favors higher pensions for old people.	82	89	80	84	86	86
Believes government should spend on public works programs to avoid unemployment.	70	78	62	70	72	74
Favors breaking off diplomatic relations with Russia.	9	10	7	11	4	12

Table 2.2 *(continued)*

NET APPEAL OF ISSUES FOR MICHIGAN VOTERS, 1954

WOULD YOU FAVOR OPPOSE A CANDIDATE WHO:	% STATE	% DEMO- CRATS	% REPUB- LICANS	% BIG- CITY	% SMALL- TOWN & RURAL	% CATHO- LIC
Believes we should withdraw from United Nations.	(−)58	(−)61	(−)54	(−)57	(−)59	(−)56
Believes government should cut spending and balance the budget.	41	36	52	40	45	40
Favors economic help to underdeveloped countries.	40	41	43	41	36	38
Is supported by the American Legion.	38	38	43	41	32	41
Believes we should encourage trade with Russia and China.	(−)37	(−)28	(−)47	(−)37	(−)38	(−)36
Is supported by Mc-Carthy.	(−)26	(−)32	(−)15	(−)27	(−)23	(−)21
Supports Eisenhower and program.	25	(−)19	79	21	32	8
Believes Taft-Hartley law should be changed in favor of labor.	25	51	(−) 8	29	13	41
Believes corporation taxes should be cut.	(−)23	(−)30	(−)12	(−)21	(−)26	(−)24
Is opposed to federal government spending money on health programs.	(−)21	(−)21	(−)13	(−)22	(−)20	(−)20
Believes Republican tax policy unfair to "little guy."	15	48	(−)31	17	11	23

Source: "INRA State Poll, 1954, Michigan," adapted from material, pp. 22–47.

attitudes of Michigan's voters toward issues. In reading Table 2.2, it should be remembered that the figures represent the balance between the pro and con positions of the respondents. For example, if 14 percent of the respondents said that they would favor a candidate who was a liberal, 20 percent said that they would oppose a candidate who was a liberal, and 66 percent regarded it as "immaterial," then the net appeal of the issue for the sample would be (−)6.

According to the table, Democrats, Republicans, big-city residents, small-town and rural dwellers, and Catholics were united in support of higher pensions for old people, public works programs to avoid unemployment, the United Nations, economic help for underdeveloped nations, corporation taxes, and a federal health program. All the groups named also shared a mildly negative reaction to the liberal label (66 percent said it was "immaterial") and, with the exception of the Democrats, a marginally favorable reaction to the "conservative" label on a candidate (71 percent said it was "immaterial"). Interestingly, the only groups that reacted favorably to the "liberal" label on candidates were Republican-oriented groups, such as upper-income voters and college-educated voters (not shown in Table 2.2). However, the small-city and rural voters reacted most vigorously against "liberals," followed by women and Catholics.

An unmistakable warning is contained in the data for both Democrats and Republicans. For the Republicans, the indication is clear that electoral success in Michigan lies in the Romney middle-of-the-road policy direction rather than in the Goldwater direction. Undeniably, Republican electoral disappointments between 1948 and 1960 came about mainly because of fear that the Republicans would undertake political change if elected, and not because of a desire for liberal experiments under the Democrats.

Largely because of the ultra-conservative Republican Senate, many Michigan voters feared that Republican victory would cost them social security benefits and protection against unemployment. If they had been certain that a Republican victory would mean more efficient and less wasteful administration of existing programs, they would have voted Republican, for there was a widespread feeling that the cost of government was too high. The loss of Democratic votes in Michigan's medium-sized cities (to be discussed in the following pages) indicated that the "no change" sentiment was in fact costing the Democrats votes. The residents of Michigan's cities were switching to the Republican ranks as they became convinced that the Republican party was "safe and sane." However, when Goldwater appeared on the ballot, these people tended to return to the Democratic ranks to protect the status quo.

The warning to the Democratic leadership in Michigan was that they must either do a better job of selling their liberalism or concentrate on holding the political middle. In the absence of a depression, the hope of selling liberalism was probably a forlorn one. The best hope of Michigan's Democrats was the continuing nomination by the Republicans of Goldwater-type candidates.

The Electoral Results of Michigan's Programmatic Politics

Figure 2.1 provides a graphic description of political developments in Michigan, 1948–1962, in the state's gubernatorial elections by showing the Democratic and Republican pluralities cast in the state and by sections of the state. Figure 2.2 shows the geographic location of Democratic and Republican voting strength in the gubernatorial elections, 1948–1962.

The 1948–1962 period begins with the election of G. Mennen ("Soapy") Williams as the liberal-labor Democratic governor after an uninterrupted string of Republican victories from 1938 through 1946. The Republicans assumed that 1948 was a "fluke" and confidently awaited 1950 for a return to the captaincy of the state. But, in 1950 Williams was reelected (helped by Republican factionalism) by about 1000 votes, after a recount. Williams narrowly won again in 1952 in the face of an Eisenhower landslide (assisted again by Republican division), and thereafter in 1954, 1956, and 1958 was reelected by landslide margins.

Figure 2.1 suggests an explanation for the Democratic successes in Michigan after 1948. The Williams election in 1948 was apparently a product of, first, the "usual" Democratic pluralities in Wayne County and the other urban counties, and, second, reduced Republican pluralities in outstate Michigan because of Dewey's unpopularity in rural areas and Truman's small-town electoral drawing power, and Republican dislike of incumbent Republican Governor Sigler. Before 1948 the potential Democratic vote in Wayne County had rarely been fully realized in state elections because of the conservatism of the Democratic gubernatorial candidates and a consequent failure of the UAW officials to work for their election. In 1948, however, the liberal-labor alliance was consummated in the person of pro-

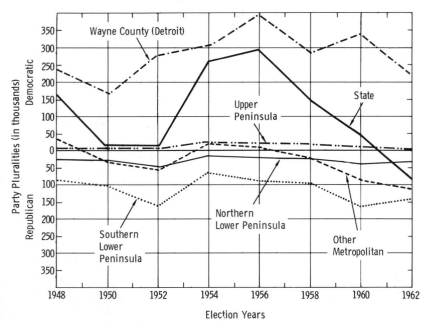

FIGURE 2.1   MICHIGAN VOTING TRENDS BY SECTIONS in gubernatorial elections, 1948–1962

Explanatory Note: The graph shows the margins or pluralities by which
the parties' candidates carried the state and sections thereof in gubernatorial elections 1948–1962. Referring to the solid line labeled "State," the
graph reveals that "Soapy" Williams (Democrat) carried Michigan by 160,
000 votes in 1948, barely squeaked through to victory in 1950 and 1952, and
won by more than 250,000 votes in 1954, 1956, and 1958. In 1960, the new
Democratic candidate (Swainson) won by 40,000 votes, and in 1962, Romney
(Republican) broke through to an 80,000 vote victory. The line with alternating dashes and dots traces the Democratic pluralities cast in Wayne
County (Detroit), and the other lines trace Republican or Democratic
pluralities cast in the respective sections of the state. Some impressions
derived from the figure are that the Democrats get most of their votes
out of Wayne County and the Republicans receive their pluralities from
the Southern Lower Peninsula. The political battleground is the group
labeled "Other Metropolitan," and the Republicans would appear to be
winning that tug-of-war.

labor "Soapy" Williams, and labor worked hard for his election.
After 1948 the UAW and its members learned that there was a
relationship between their economic well-being and their vote
for candidates for statewide office. In his legislative program as
well as in his administrative actions, Williams made evident his
desire to improve the position of working-class people. In addition, he astutely played to the sensibilities of minority groups
in Detroit, especially the Polish, through his appointments.
    The people in the United Auto Workers organization, as well

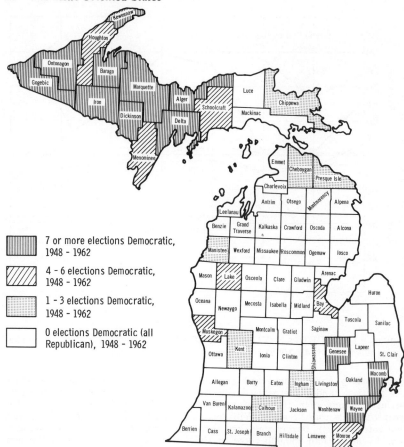

FIGURE 2.2   MICHIGAN GEOGRAPHICALLY REPUBLICAN even while Democrats win in gubernatorial elections, 1948–1962

Explanatory Note: The more heavily the counties are shaded in Figure 2.2, the more frequently the majority voted Democratic in the gubernatorial elections, 1948–1962. The predominance of white counties on the map demonstrates graphically the extent of Republican dominance at the county level even while Democrats were winning statewide in all but one of the gubernatorial elections, 1948–1962. The principal reason for Democratic victories in the face of Republican dominance at the county level was the large number of Democratic voters in only one county—Wayne County, which contains Detroit.

as rank-and-file workingmen, responded by bending even greater efforts for Williams' reelection. The results were dramatic. The pluralities cast in Wayne County for Williams soared after 1950 until they reached almost 400,000 votes in 1956. Williams' pluralities also increased in the far north Upper Peninsula of

Michigan, which was primarily a mining and lumber area where the unions were strong. In the remainder of the state, Williams' strength remained relatively constant, save in the more urban areas outside Wayne County.[15] In the urban areas outside Wayne County the Democrats lost strength after 1954, until by 1962 the Republican candidate, George Romney, won them by a wide margin. Romney's 1962 victory can be attributed largely to the pronounced defection of Michigan's metropolitan areas (excluding Detroit) from the Democratic standard. More will be said later concerning this development.

In the vote for all statewide offices, the Democratic party was Michigan's majority party by 1956. The 1956 and 1957 elections marked the death of Republican hegemony in the state. Prior to these elections Republicans had comforted themselves with the belief that "Soapy's" electoral strength in Michigan was the product of his personality and was not a reflection of basic party strength. However, when the Republicans lost every statewide office in the spring elections of 1957, even the personality illusion faded.

The Democratic party emerged triumphant in the off-year spring election of 1957 because the Democratic pluralities in Wayne County increased astronomically. For example, the plurality for the Democratic candidate for superintendent of public instruction (elected in odd-numbered years) increased from approximately 20,000 votes in 1949 to more than 140,000 in 1957. The increase in the off-year Democratic plurality in Wayne County was not a gradual development. It occurred at one stroke in 1955 when the Democratic vote in Wayne County almost doubled, and it was largely a product of improved Democratic organization.

Geographically, the Republican party was dominant in Michigan over the 1948–1962 period. As Figure 2.2 shows, Democratic strength was confined to the western half of the Upper Peninsula and the highly metropolitan Wayne County area, while most of the remainder of the state's counties were one-sidedly Republican. Fifty-seven of the state's eighty-two counties cast a plurality of their vote for the Republican candidate for governor in every election, 1948–1962.

The people of Wayne County and the western part of the Upper Peninsula tended to be Democratic because of the work-

[15] See Nicholas A. Masters and Deil S. Wright "Trends and Variations in the Two-Party Vote: The Case of Michigan," *American Political Science Review*, vol. 52 (1958), p. 1078.

ing-class character of the population and the pro-labor orientation of the Democratic party in Michigan, particularly after 1948. As a Republican leader explained it, the person who resides in a crowded city, lives in a rented apartment, and works on an assembly line tends to be a Democrat because he favors governmental activity oriented toward helping the disadvantaged person. He has little to lose from high taxes and a great deal to gain. In addition, he is psychologically and geographically distant from his employer, whereas he is in close touch with labor leaders. In addition, the fear of losing his job is always in the back of his mind, a fear that prompts him to support the party which is most likely to cushion the economic shock of unemployment.

Between 1948 and 1962, the people of Michigan's smaller cities and towns were inclined toward the Republican party. Some political leaders attributed the pro-Republican bias of the person who lived in the smaller towns to the "fact" that he was likely to own his home and was both psychologically and geographically close to his employer or other people in the business community, such as bank executives and members of the Chamber of Commerce. Because he owned property and tended to identify his economic interests with other property owners and was more subject to the influence of people in the business community, he tended to gravitate toward the party which pledged to minimize governmental activity. He also tended to fear labor unions and to dislike urban life, both of which he associated with the Democratic party.

Republican strength in the medium-sized cities was partially a result of residential patterns which reduced the cohesiveness of working-class people. In addition, people moving into the smaller Michigan cities tended to be natives with Republican voting histories. The Republican propensities of people living in medium-sized cities boded ill for the Democratic party in Michigan, for all indications pointed toward a continuing increase in the relative as well as the absolute size of their populations. One index of this development was the declining proportion which the Wayne County vote represented of the total vote cast in the state, even though Wayne County turnout remained high. In the gubernatorial elections, for example, the Wayne County proportion of the total vote declined from 40 percent in 1948 to 39 percent in 1950 and 1952, to 38 percent in 1954, to 37 percent in 1956, and to 36 percent in 1962. Over the same period, the percentage of the total vote cast by the next nine most urban and populous counties in the state increased from 27 percent in 1948 to 34 percent in 1962.

The evidence is indisputable that there is an extreme bipolarization of groups between the two parties in Michigan.[16] It is, perhaps, not overly repetitious to review some of the reasons for this bipolarization. The New Deal during the 1930s and the Frank Murphy administration in 1937 and 1938 succeeded in relating the economic self-interest of disadvantaged groups, such as the foreign-born, to the Democratic party. This was done, of course, through welfare and labor policies which resulted in dollars in their pockets. Similarly, the native American and more advantaged groups found that Democratic policies worked to their detriment by taxing away some of their income and funneling it to the less well-to-do. They turned to the Republican party.

In the years between 1938 and 1948 the state Democratic party did not effectively represent the interests of disadvantaged groups. Consequently, they, and particularly the groups representing them, such as the United Auto Workers, did not put forth any great efforts toward electing Democratic candidates for governor. However, beginning in 1948 with the election of "Soapy" Williams as governor, the relationship of the Democratic party with the economic well-being of low-income groups was reestablished. Initially, it was reestablished at the leader-

[16] Additional statistical confirmation of the extreme bipolarization of groups into the two political parties is provided by multiple coefficients of correlation between various political and demographic variables. In 1960 the relationship of John F. Kennedy's percent vote by counties with the percent Catholic plus percent rural farm of the counties was .83. In other words, the tendency in 1960 of Catholics to vote Democratic plus the tendency of farmers to vote Republican could be interpreted as accounting for about 69 percent of the variations in Kennedy's vote from county to county. The relationships of the 1960 and 1962 Democratic gubernatorial votes with the Catholic and rural-farm variables were also very close (.82 in 1960 and .78 in 1962), indicating that the Catholic-rural-farm dichotomy of Michigan's voters is a continuing phenomenon, which is not limited to a single election. The relationship of percent Catholic plus percent foreign-born and children of foreign-born with the Democratic vote (.79 in the 1960 presidential election and .71 in the 1962 gubernatorial election) by counties strongly indicates that Michigan's Catholics and foreign-born voted Democratic and the native Protestants voted Republican. The multiple correlations of the foreign-born plus rural-farm with the 1960 Kennedy vote (.73) and the 1962 Democratic vote for governor (.70) provide additional confirmation of the pronounced dichotomy of Michigan's voters along the lines of religion, place of residence, and family's length of residence in the United States.

ship level where liberals and labor leaders joined hands in the effort to elect Williams. However, the new bonds between the political party and low-income groups were soon impressed upon the consciousness of the rank-and-file throughout the state. This was done through both an intensive propaganda campaign by the unions and the objective performance in office of Williams, whose actions were designed to enhance the position of the disadvantaged. The result was two political parties which represented very different groups and, consequently, advocated policies which provided distinct alternatives to the voters.

Political Change in Michigan

We have observed the broad changes that occurred in Democratic and Republican fortunes between 1948 and 1962, as reflected in the state's gubernatorial elections. The purpose of the following pages is to look at political change more closely in an attempt to unearth the sources of, and reasons for, the changes. Figure 2.3 shows the geographic location of pronounced political change over the 1946–1962 time period.[17]

There were two political developments in Michigan over the 1946–1962 period that must be examined in order to understand the reasons for the political change that occurred. First, we must inquire into the factors that transformed the Democratic party into Michigan's majority party by 1957, when it held virtually every statewide elective office. Second, we must attempt to divine the reasons for the Republican victory in the gubernatorial election of 1962. In 1962 George Romney defeated incumbent Democratic Governor Swainson by about 80,000 votes, or 51.5 percent of the two-party vote.

We have already isolated the primary reason for Democratic successes in 1948 and thereafter. The central explanation is the huge Democratic pluralities returned from Wayne County (Detroit). As Figure 2.1 showed, these pluralities reached a peak in 1956, but they receded very little thereafter. Another part of the explanation for Democratic successes after 1948 was that the percentage Democratic vote improved in virtually every county of the state, as is shown in Figure 2.3. There were only twelve Michigan counties in which plus-Republican change occurred in

---

[17] Political change is measured by a line of regression computed for each county. The amount and direction of change represents the percentage-point difference between the two ends of the line. This measure of political change is a product of every election in the time series rather than the first and last elections.

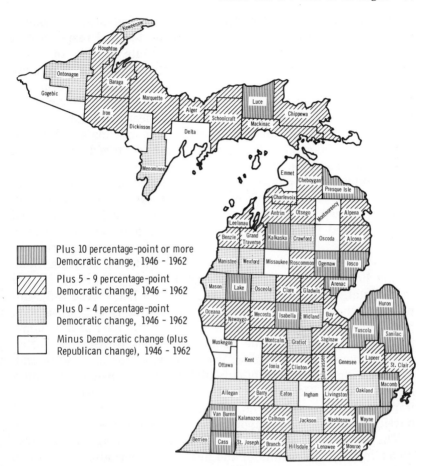

Plus 10 percentage-point or more
Democratic change, 1946 - 1962

Plus 5 - 9 percentage-point
Democratic change, 1946 - 1962

Plus 0 - 4 percentage-point
Democratic change, 1946 - 1962

Minus Democratic change (plus
Republican change), 1946 - 1962

FIGURE 2.3   MICHIGAN BECOMES TWO-PARTY STATE when Democrats gain ground throughout state in gubernatorial elections, 1946–1962

Explanatory Note: The map provides visual evidence of the extent of plus
Democratic change in Michigan, 1946–1962. The Democrats gained ground
almost everywhere in the state. Most of the exceptions were in the urban
counties of southern Michigan, where the Republicans tended to improve
their percentage slice of the vote. However, the Democrats did well in
Wayne County, where Detroit is located. The measure of change used in
the figure is along a line of regression for the elections. The advantage
of the technique is that the measure is a product of all the elections and not
just the first and last.

the gubernatorial elections, 1946–1962. Democratic fortunes improved throughout the state, first, because of Williams' attractive
personality, and, second, because of improved Democratic
political organization.

"Soapy" Williams lent respectability to the state's Democratic party. It was difficult for Republicans to successfully associate labor unions and radicalism with so respected and respectable a name and figure as "Soapy" Williams. While holding the office of governor, Williams shook at least half the hands in Michigan. He unfailingly attended county fairs and other local celebrations. His polka-dot bow tie and his friendly grin and handshake became common but precious currency at meetings of every kind in the state. Williams disarmed ardent Republicans and brought to the polls lukewarm Democrats who had stayed at home in despair of electing a Democrat.

The influence of political organization on the increased Democratic vote throughout Michigan should not be underestimated. Neil Staebler, the energetic state chairman, carefully planted and nurtured infant Democratic organizations in each county of the state. He persuaded local liberals and Democrats to interest themselves in the Democratic party by inviting them to his home in Ann Arbor, where they were charmed by the traditional, informal Staebler hospitality. They were duly impressed when introduced to Governor Williams and were soon persuaded that they could and would be a vital part of a dynamic political organization. The people recruited by Staebler often offered themselves as Democratic candidates for local office and, although almost invariably defeated, their presence on the ballot helped attract Democratic votes. Further, and perhaps most important, they served as officials in the polling places and participated in the all-important counting process.

The importance of taking part in the counting process was underlined by the results of the disputed gubernatorial elections of 1950 and 1952, when Williams won by narrow margins after recounts of the ballots. The recounts revealed that "counting errors" in rural Republican Michigan were almost invariably in favor of Republican candidates. The reason for the "errors" presumably was the absence of Democratic officials to audit the arithmetic of Republican counters.

Perhaps future political historians will find that the most significant development, 1946–1962, was the increased Republican vote out of Michigan's urban counties. Most of the twelve counties which registered plus-Republican gains during that period were urban counties with medium-sized cities located in them. These included Genesee (Flint, 1960 population 196,940), Ingham (Lansing, 1960 population 107,807), Kalamazoo (Kalamazoo, 1960 population 82,809), Kent (Grand Rapids, 1960 population 117,313), Muskegon (Muskegon, 1960 population

46,485), and Ottawa (Holland, 1960 population 24,777). The combined 1960 populations of these six urban counties was 1,370,000, or about 18 percent of the state's total population. In the 1962 gubernatorial election the metropolitan counties other than Wayne (Detroit) registered a Republican plurality of almost 120,000 votes (see Figure 2.1).[18]

Plus-Republican political movement in Michigan's medium-sized cities, 1946–1962, follows a pattern which, as we shall see, is repeated in other Midwest states. The workingman in a small or medium-sized city tends to be dissociated from any kind of community. He purchases a modest home, a car, a television set, and separates himself and his family from the larger community. The car accommodates only his family for weekend outings. Evenings are spent huddled around the television set. Economic calculations tend to revolve around taxes—especially income and property taxes. Thus, the small-town workingman is not reached by his labor unions. His economic concerns parallel the businessman's to a greater and greater extent. The result is a tendency to vote Republican in opposition to big government and taxes and in favor of the homilies represented by the home and the traditional respectability of the Republican party.

George Romney's 1962 election victory was partially a product of the long-term plus-Republican trend in the urban areas outside Detroit and partially a response to particular issues and situations which were peculiar to 1962, but which had a differential impact on urban areas. There were three such 1962 issues which helped Romney and hurt Swainson. The first was Swainson's veto of a bill which would have outlawed a Detroit income tax levied on both residents and non-residents. The voters in urban and suburban Oakland and Macomb Counties who worked in Detroit and consequently had to pay the Detroit income tax were particularly incensed at Swainson for vetoing the bill. The second and third factors were ill-defined but rather generally held feelings that Governor Swainson was inept and too closely identified with labor, and a companion notion that Romney was able, intelligent, and relatively free of the corrupting pressures of special interest groups (a rather curious situation in view of Romney's presidency of American Motors Corporation).

[18] The coefficient of correlation between percent urban by counties, 1960, and percentage point Democratic change, 1946–1962, was (−).33, which provides significant support for the observation that the cities are tending to move in a Republican direction.

In addition to the loss of votes in Michigan's medium-sized cities, the 1962 Democratic candidate for governor lost votes among the state's foreign people and Catholics.[19] A part of the explanation for this loss of votes was the return of some Catholics to the Republican party after voting for Kennedy in 1960. Another reason was the departure of Williams and Neil Staebler from positions of leadership in the state Democratic party. "Soapy" Williams had particularly cordial relations with Polish and other ethnic groups and was careful to cultivate them by attending their meetings and by appointing ethnic group leaders to political and governmental positions. Neil Staebler, the Democratic state chairman under Williams, also concentrated much attention on the state's ethnic groups. Staebler firmly believed that the party's electoral strength hinged upon the support of ethnic groups. Williams accepted an appointment as Assistant Secretary of State under President Kennedy and Staebler resigned as state chairman shortly after Swainson's election. In 1964 Staebler successfully sought the Democratic gubernatorial nomination in the belief that he could retrieve much, if not all, of the vote of the foreign-born population lost under Swainson. The single ray of comfort for the Democrats in 1962 was the continuing increase in the percentage vote received from the state's rural-farm Republican areas. The rural-farm areas remained Republican, but the margins by which Republicans won had been narrowed.[20]

Thus, in 1962 the Republicans increased their vote in the medium-sized cities and among Catholics and the foreign-born. The Democrats, on the other hand, maintained or improved their vote in the rural-farm sections of the state. The result was a Republican victory in the gubernatorial election by a margin of 80,000 votes.

Ideological Divisions of Michigan's Political Parties

The type of rural-urban division which existed in Michigan, 1948–1962, helped crystallize and clarify the issues between the two parties. For example, former Democratic Governor Swainson said that he was a Democrat because that party placed human

[19] A multiple correlation of the percent Democratic change, 1960–1962, with percent foreign-born and children of foreign-born plus percent Catholic by counties results in an R of (−).60.
[20] The relationship of percent Democratic change, 1960–1962, with percent rural-farm, 1960, by counties was .41.

rights above property rights. To substantiate his claim, Swainson ticked off a bill of particulars which included his and his fellow Democrats' support (against the opposition of Republicans) of legislation raising unemployment benefits, providing for smoke abatement, public housing, slum clearance, higher public assistance payments, and reducing the maximum penalty for forging checks.

Former Representative Van Peursem, the 1956 Republican Speaker of the House of Representatives, on the other hand, stated that property rights constituted one of the most important of the human rights. He pointed out that when government expands its activities and attempts to promote the welfare of one group it always finds it necessary to limit the freedom of another group. It was his position that this gradual growth of governmental powers and functions constitutes a menace to the rights of all the people.

Governor Swainson and Representative Van Peursem were important leaders of their respective parties and reflected quite faithfully the dominant if not the unanimous point of view of the elected representatives of the two parties. Such a sharp division in the legislature and elsewhere along party lines made for a lively political climate. In the 1954 session of the Michigan legislature the two parties divided along party lines on roll-call votes on approximately one-half of all controversial roll-call votes.[21] In the sessions after 1954, the number of party line votes remained high. Of principal interest, however, was the ideological consistency of the two parties in their votes. A good index of the ideological unity of the two parties was that the Michigan CIO, in its evaluations of the voting records of the two parties, gave the Democrats very nearly a 100 percent "right" grade for their votes on key issues. The Republican party, on the other hand, was a CIO dunce, rating a grade of almost 100 percent "wrong."[22]

The sharp division between the two parties at the legislative

[21] In 1954, in the state House of Representatives there were 123 controversial roll-call votes, and of these, 58 provided a partisan division. In the state Senate there were 80 controversial roll-call votes and 38 partisan divisions. A controversial roll-call vote in the House is one in which 9 or more votes are cast against the majority, or fewer than 60 votes are cast; in the Senate, where 3 or more votes are cast against the majority, or fewer than 20 votes are cast.

[22] See, for example, "The 1955–56 Session of the Michigan Legislature" (Lansing, Mich.: Michigan CIO Legislative Office). Also the *Michigan CIO News*, November 21, 1957.

level was brought about by the differing composition of the two parties. In most states both the Democratic and Republican parties owned rural and urban wings (or a business-community-oriented and labor-oriented wing), and thus the basic conflict over "who shall rule" was resolved primarily within the parties rather than between the parties. In Michigan, however, both parties were relatively clean of the corrupting influence of rival doctrines and met one another head-on with radically differing approaches to the problems of government. For example, on labor issues in which there was a partisan division in the 1954 state Senate, the Democrats had a cohesion score of 97 to the Republicans' 78.[23]

Consequently, both Republican and Democratic senators tended to vote as a bloc on partisan issues. It should be noted, however, that the urban Republican was subject to more conflicting pressures than the rural Republican. In terms of a party cohesion score, the urban Republican senator received a grade substantially below that for other Republican senators.[24] On both labor and agricultural issues, too, the urban Republicans ranked below the rural Republicans in party cohesion.[25] The tendency of urban Republicans to desert their rural brethren on key issues may be a harbinger of increasing factional difficulties between the two disparate elements of the party.[26] Certainly, the Republicans at the national level found it difficult to appease their rural wing while attempting to cultivate and develop their urban pastures.

[23] Cohesion score is based on Stuart Rice's "index of cohesion." See Stuart Rice, *Quantitative Methods in Politics* (New York: Alfred A. Knopf, 1928).
[24] For a statistical treatment of the record of the 1954 legislature, see Robert G. Scigliano, "Michigan Legislative Report, 1954" (East Lansing, Mich.: Governmental Research Bureau, Michigan State College, 1955). The material on the 1954 legislature was taken from Scigliano's study.
[25] Republican leaders, however, state that these figures mean little or nothing. According to them, urban Republicans vote against the party position only when they know that the Republican position will triumph without their support. With very few exceptions, according to Republican leaders, they can rely upon most Republican votes when they need them. Democratic leaders feel equally confident of the support of most Democratic legislators on key legislative issues. On labor issues the cohesion score of Democrats was 97 and that of Republicans 60 in the House and 97 and 78, respectively, in the Senate. On agricultural issues the cohesion score of Democrats was 54 and Republicans 71 in the House and 76 and 79, respectively, in the Senate.
[26] See Robert W. Becker *et al.*, "Correlates of Legislative Voting: Michigan House of Representatives, 1954–1961," *Midwest Journal of Political Science*, vol. 6 (1962), p. 384 ff.

The problems of the Republican party in Michigan paralleled, in some ways, the factional difficulties of the Democratic party in the Border States and the Deep South.

Relation between Political Patterns and the Programs of Michigan Government

After 1946 Michigan was one of the more competitive two-party states in the nation. In addition, as the earlier discussions made clear, its political competition was issue-oriented. Both the Republican and Democratic parties tended to be programmatic rather than job- or spoils-oriented. The management representatives from the auto companies who were active in the Republican party were not primarily interested in political jobs. Rather, they were concerned with influencing public policy in the areas of taxes and public services. In the main, these people were successful and not alienated from the status quo. Consequently, they were not proponents of radical change, but rather advocated better administration of existing programs and the maintenance of a tax program and governmental services that would attract industry.

The Democratic leaders, on the other hand, came from the ranks of labor or were ideological liberals from the business or professional communities. They were active in politics because they sought governmental policies that would promote the interests of the unions and of the working class. The ideological liberals were not so attached to the status quo as the auto people and were active in politics out of a desire to reallocate goods and opportunities in such a way as to produce a more egalitarian society.

The remaining question is the effect of these political activities on governmental services and programs. In general, the result was in the expected direction. Michigan's expenditures on welfare and education programs were more generous than in most other states. However, the level of expenditures was not so high as might have been expected, considering Michigan's reputation for liberal-labor leadership, because of the check placed on expenditures by the conservative state Senate. It will be interesting to observe the effect of the 1963 reapportionment of the state Senate on the level of expenditures.

Specifically, in 1960 Michigan ranked seventeenth among the states in its aid to dependent children payments, sixteenth in old age assistance, fourth in the estimated average salary of the instructional staff, twenty-third in per-pupil expenditures, and tenth in the state and local government per-capita expenditures. In terms of effort, Michigan ranked twenty-sixth (percent per-capita state and local tax revenue from own sources as a percent of per-capita income, 1959) compared to thirty-third for Indiana, forty-second for Ohio, and forty-fourth for Illinois.

Summary and Conclusions

Political prospects in Michigan after the 1962 and 1964 Republican gubernatorial victories were obscure. Prediction was made additionally hazardous by virtue of Michigan's adoption of a new constitution in 1963. The Democratic party opposed the new constitution and its adherents generally voted against it.[27] The principal reason for Democratic opposition to the new constitution was its retention of the area principle in drawing up districts for the state Senate (which was subsequently upset by the courts, resulting in Democratic majorities in the state House and Senate after the 1964 elections).

Another reason for Democratic opposition to the 1962 constitution was that it reduced the number of elected state officers from seven to four. The offices of governor, lieutenant governor, secretary of state, and attorney general remained elective, but those of the auditor general, treasurer, superintendent of public instruction, and highway commissioner became appointive. The Democrats were placed in an embarrassing position by the proposal because during Republican dominance of these elective posts they had advocated reducing the number of elective positions. However, by 1962 the Democrats were in control of all the positions, and the provisions for their appointment were certain to result in decreased Democratic dominance of the executive branch of state government. According to the newly adopted constitution, the auditor general was to be appointed by the legislature and thus would almost certainly be a Republican; the treasurer was to be appointed by the governor, and the superintendent of public instruction and highway commissioner were selected by independent commissions. The net effect of the new constitution was almost certain to be detrimental to the fortunes of Michigan's Democratic party. However, the negative

[27] There was a negative relationship between the percent "yes" vote for the constitution in 1963 and the percent Democratic vote for governor in 1962 of (−).75. Nevertheless, the constitution was approved by the voters by the narrow margin of 7424 votes out of 1,614,296 votes cast.

impact on the Democratic party of the new constitution may be offset by the court-imposed elimination of the area principle in redistricting.

The findings with respect to Michigan politics are similar to those which follow for Minnesota and Wisconsin. In all three states the Democratic party was an empty shell after World War II. In Michigan the United Auto Workers and the liberals united to fill the vacuum. They were able to capture the Democratic party relatively easily because, first, there was no large group of traditional Democrats whose reason for identification with the party was the Civil War; and, second, because the job-oriented, professional politicians had lost their interest in the party, partially because of the adoption of a merit system in 1941 and partially because of the prosperity attendant to World War II which reduced the attractiveness of government employment. Similarly, the Republican party was captured by issue-oriented, middle-of-the-road organization men, largely from the auto industry. They, too, found their path to power paved by the strict merit system law which tended to weaken the interest of the job-oriented politicians in the Republican party.

The immediate result of the issue-oriented turn of Michigan politics was victory for the Democrats. The reason was that the bulk of the population was Democratic-oriented and victory was easily obtained once their potential vote was organized. However, the long-term results would seem to assure Republican victory if the moderate leadership of the party maintains power. The reason is that Michigan voters, particularly in the medium-sized cities, do not desire new programs from government, but rather want both the continuation of existing programs and lower taxes. The Romney middle-of-the-road Republican leadership appears to be closer to this position of the electorate than the liberal-labor leadership of the Democratic party.

Barring depression, Michigan political trends indicate a continuing narrow statewide division between the parties, with Republicans and Democrats alternating in power in the governorship, but with the Republicans slowly drawing away from the Democrats, largely because of the plus-Republican trend in the medium-sized cities.

Chapter 3

Programmatic Politics
in Wisconsin

Before World War II, Wisconsin, like Michigan and Minnesota, was virtually a one-party state. In forty-two gubernatorial elections from 1857 through 1940, Wisconsin's Democrats won only four times. However, after World War II, Wisconsin was transformed from a dominantly Republican state into an issue-oriented, two-party state. The process by which this change occurred represents one of the more interesting passages in the history of American state politics.[1]

Before the Great Depression and World War II, the divisions on economic issues occurred within the Republican party rather than between the two major parties. The Republican division was between the stalwart or conservative Republicans and the Progressives or La Follette Republicans. From 1900 through 1913 the Progressive Republicans, led by Robert La Follette, Sr., dominated the Republican party and the politics of the state. The Progressive Republican vote in Wisconsin was in large part a vote of protest against "big business" and represented a de-

---

[1] This account of the history of Wisconsin politics was obtained from a large number of sources, including interviews. However, the most useful and important sources included Leon D. Epstein's "A Two-Party Wisconsin?" *Journal of Politics*, vol. 18 (1956), p. 427, and Epstein's *Politics in Wisconsin* (Madison: University of Wisconsin Press, 1958). Other very useful sources were Samuel C. Patterson, *"Toward a Theory of Legislative Behavior"* (unpublished Ph.D. dissertation, University of Wisconsin, 1958); Wilder Willard Crane, Jr., *"The Legislative Struggle in Wisconsin, Decision-Making in the 1957 Wisconsin Assembly"* (unpublished Ph.D. dissertation, University of Wisconsin, 1959); and David Walter Adamany, *"The 1960 Election in Wisconsin"* (unpublished Master's thesis, University of Wisconsin, 1963).

mand for economic reform. The vote cast for Progressives came from all elements in the state, but most consistently from Scandinavians and from the Socialist-leaning working class in Milwaukee.

The question that might occur to the reader is why storms of effective political protest occurred in Wisconsin but were largely absent in other states, such as Ohio, Indiana, and Illinois. There appear to be two principal reasons for the development of an issue-oriented vote in Wisconsin. First, the people and land in Wisconsin suffered from exploitation by big business to a degree that was not approached in most states. And, second, many settlers in Wisconsin never realized the promise of the frontier, whereas the frontiersmen in the Ohio, Indiana, and Illinois corn belt saw their most halcyon dreams realized as the corn grew high and the hogs grew fat on their rich land.

The problems of exploitation of land and people and of unrealized dreams of prosperity were all inextricably intertwined. In 1873 Chief Justice Ryan of the Wisconsin Supreme Court said the following:

> There is looming up a new and dark power. I cannot dwell upon the signs and shocking omens of its advent. The accumulation of individual wealth seems to be greater than it ever has been since the downfall of the Roman Empire. The enterprises of the country are aggregating vast corporate combinations of unexampled capital, boldly marching, not for economic conquests only, but for political power. For the first time really in our politics money is taking the field as an organized power. . . . Already, here at home, one great corporation has trifled with the sovereign power, and insulted the State. There is grave fear that it, and its great rival, have confederated to make partition of the State and share its spoils. . . . The question will arise, and arise in your day, though perhaps not fully in mine, "Which shall rule—wealth or man; which shall lead—money or intellect; who shall fill public stations—educated or patriotic free men, or the feudal serfs of corporate capital?"[2]

Robert M. La Follette heard Chief Justice Ryan's speech and never forgot it, for it seemed to him that much of what he warned against was an unhappy fact of economic life in Wisconsin. After 1874 and until La Follette's election in 1900, Wisconsin's railroad and lumber interests literally ruled the state, and the two interests were interlocked; that is, the same people controlled both. These interests dominated the political

---

[2] Wisconsin Writers' Project, *Wisconsin* (New York: Duell, Sloan & Pearce, 1941), p. 57.

parties by virtue of the money they provided for campaigns. Thereby, they were able to determine the identity of nominees for statewide office. The legislature was intimidated through the press or bought with money and free railroad passes.

By virtue of their political dominance, the railroads received large land grants from government to encourage them to extend their tracks into every section of the state. In return, they were required to pay few taxes and were virtually unregulated with respect to rates charged the shippers. The lumber companies, which received land from both the railroads and the legislatures, stripped the land of its forest cover. After the land was denuded, both the lumber companies and the railroads made strenuous efforts to sell the cutover lands to prospective settlers in order to maximize their profits.

Following is an appeal taken from one such attempt to sell cutover land to the land-hungry:

> This little booklet is written for the man who is hungry—hungry for a home of his own. For the man who has an unsatisfied appetite, which, gnawing away at his very being, has given him a craving to own a farm, or a piece of land he can develop into a farm home, and can call his very own. A place where he can live his life in his own way, untrammeled by any fear of an exacting landlord, where the factory whistle has no sinister meaning, where the pay envelope is exactly the returns of his own labor and brains. . . . To such a man the Soo Railway is offering a solution of his present difficulties.[3]

Many thousands who bought "cutover" Wisconsin land were doomed to the tragic toil of the frontier without reaping any returns from their effort. The growing season was short and the land was thin and barren. Consequently, they were bitter at the corporations which sold them the land, and they gave vent to their spleen through their ballots.

In 1900 they nominated and elected Robert La Follette governor of Wisconsin. Most important for the history of Wisconsin politics was the fact that they subsequently received a public policy return from their ballots. The La Follette Progressives, unlike reformers and Populists in some other states, translated their political program into public policy. In 1903 a primary election law was passed which removed the selection of Republican and Democratic candidates for office from the hands of railroad- and lumber-controlled political bosses. Subsequently, a civil service law was enacted which was designed to provide

[3] Larry Gara, *A Short History of Wisconsin* (Madison: The State Historical Society of Wisconsin, 1962), p. 190.

the people with honest and efficient administration of the laws, and anti-lobbying and corrupt practices laws were adopted. But in Wisconsin, reform did not stop with economy and efficiency. Instead, it extended to the reform of basic economic problems.

During the Progressive era, 1900–1914, laws were passed providing for strict regulation of railroads and public utilities, workmen's compensation, state control of corporation stock issues, a fixing of railroad fares, stricter regulation of insurance companies, a workable state income tax designed to shift the burden of taxation from the poor to the rich, regulation of the labor of women and children, a law designed to encourage cooperatives, a mothers' pension act, a minimum wage law for women and children, and a teachers' retirement fund. Other laws that were passed provided a system of vocational education for the people of the state and covered apprenticeship training and maximum hours of labor for women.

The most important feature of the period for the future of Wisconsin politics was that the people learned that there could be and was a relationship between their vote and their economic and social well-being. Unlike Ohio, Indiana, and Illinois, where such a relationship was rarely demonstrated and consequently the voters tended to cast their ballots in terms of personalities rather than issues, the Wisconsin people learned that politics was a means by which they could control their environment.

Numbers of the Progressive voters had learned of the relationship between politics and their welfare in Europe. Some were German Socialists in Milwaukee and Scandinavians in northern Wisconsin. The German Socialists had despaired of collective bargaining between unions and management in Germany because the class gap between worker and employee was too great to bridge. Therefore, they had turned to government as a means of securing wage increases and other reforms. In the United States they rejected the Gompers formula of "reward your friends" and plunged into politics directly. Similarly, the Scandinavians had behind them a tradition of class-oriented politics. Consequently, the Milwaukee Socialists and the Scandinavian farmers were unlike the Anglo-Saxon Kentucky mountaineer who saw in government only a threat to freedom. Rather, they saw it as a means by which they could secure their ends. The Kentucky mountain person sold his vote to the leaders of corporate wealth, for he saw little value in it. But the Wisconsin Scandinavians and Milwaukee Socialists used their ballots to elect candidates who promised to control the corporations.

In 1934, the Progressives despaired of reforming the Republican party internally and split off into a Progressive party. The new Progressive party won the gubernatorial elections of 1934 and 1936. The Progressives won again in 1942, but their candidate died shortly after the election and was succeeded by the Republican lieutenant governor. Over the entire period, 1934–1944, the Progressive vote suffered a secular decline and in 1946 its leaders disbanded the party and recommended to the party rank and file that they return to their Republican home.

The 1946 Republican senatorial primary (when McCarthy defeated La Follette, Jr.) marked the last important attempt of Progressives to seize control of the Republican party. In the 1946 primary, Robert La Follette, Jr., who in company with his brother Phil had inherited the mantle of Progressivism from his father, was opposed by Joseph McCarthy. The division of the electorate in the primary followed traditional patterns (see Figure 3.1). La Follette carried the northwest Scandinavians and wheat-growing section of the state, the largely low-income rural areas of central Wisconsin, and the liberal Madison area. McCarthy won in the higher-income counties. The only important departure from traditional voting patterns was McCarthy's victory in Milwaukee. Ironically, one explanation frequently given for La Follette's defeat in Milwaukee (and the state) in the 1946 Republican primary contest against Joseph McCarthy was the opposition to him by Communists. The Communist party controlled the Milwaukee and Wisconsin CIO in 1946 and opposed La Follette because of speeches he made which were critical of Stalin.

After 1946 and McCarthy's crusade against the political left, the more liberal Republican Progressives moved into the Democratic party, producing for the first time in the state's history a viable two-party system (compare Figures 3.1 and 3.2).

The pre-World War II Democratic party in Wisconsin was the state's most conservative party. In 1932 the Democratic party's candidate for governor, Albert G. Schmedeman, won election as a result of the Great Depression and the Roosevelt landslide. However, Schmedeman was no New Dealer. In 1933 he called out the National Guard in the milk strikes and in the Kohler strike. In both cases the National Guard was used to protect the interests of the business community. As a partial result, the Democrats lost the gubernatorial elections of 1934 and 1936 to Progressive Phil La Follette, when elsewhere "yellow dogs" were winning handsomely if only their shaggy coats were covered by the Democratic label.

Before the events of the 1930s, Republican voting strength was concentrated in the most Protestant and the most Scandinavian counties (compare Figures 3.3 and 3.4). On the other hand, Democratic candidates received their most enthusiastic support in the more Catholic counties of the state, and particularly in the German Catholic section in the Fox River Valley; that is, Appleton, Green Bay, and counties south of those cities. Therefore, the historic division between Wisconsin's two major parties was along religious and ethnic lines. Both the relatively prosperous and conservative Fox River Valley Germans and the low-income Irish and eastern European Catholics in the cities made common cause in the Democratic party, while the largely high-income Yankee Protestants and the somewhat less prosperous Scandinavian Protestants shared a political home in the Republican party. Consequently, the divisions between the parties had little or no relation to the important economic and other issues which faced Wisconsin's citizens between the Civil War and the Great Depression.

The period after World War II brought a combination of events which revolutionized the state's political party patterns. Perhaps the most important development in association with the abandonment of the Progressive party was the contest for the 1946 Republican senatorial nomination between Robert La Follette, Jr., and Joseph McCarthy. As pointed out above, La Follette's loss to McCarthy, followed by McCarthy's reactionary record in Congress, persuaded Progressives throughout the state of the impracticability of using the Republican party as a vehicle of reform. Consequently, the more liberal Progressives gravitated toward the Democratic party as the only viable alternative. The alliance of Democrats and Progressives in Wisconsin was made official in 1949 with the formation of the Democratic Organizing Committee (DOC), composed of liberal Democrats such as James Doyle of Madison, prominent Progressives such as Gaylord Nelson, and German Socialists from Milwaukee such as Daniel Hoan.

Another event which served to promote the uniting of Progressives, Socialists, and liberal Democrats was the erosion of the Democrats' traditional conservative support from the prosperous Catholic Fox River Valley area. This vote was lost partially because of the liberal New Deal policies during the 1930s and partially because of American involvement in another war with Germany under a Democratic administration. During the 1936–1942 period, the Democratic party was a weak third

Counties in which Robert LaFollette, Jr. received 53 percent or more of vote in primary contest with Joseph McCarthy

FIGURE 3.1   THE LA FOLLETTE COUNTIES in the 1946 Republican senatorial primary

Explanatory Note for Figures 3.1 and 3.2: The purpose of the two figures is to demonstrate graphically the degree to which the Progressives who voted for La Follette in 1946 joined the Democratic ranks thereafter. The shaded counties in Figure 3.1 are those carried by La Follette in 1946 by a rather substantial margin, and the shaded counties in Figure 3.2 are those which were won by the Democratic candidate for governor in 1962. The apparent correspondence between the two figures is verified by counting the counties that are shaded on both maps. La Follette carried 26 counties by 53 percent of the vote or more, and 16 of the 26 La Follette counties are also among the 27 Democratic counties in the 1962 gubernatorial election.

Counties in which Democratic gubernatorial candidate
(Reynolds) received plurality of vote

FIGURE 3.2   WISCONSIN'S DEMOCRATIC COUNTIES in 1962 gubernatorial election

party, trailing behind both the Progressive and Republican
parties. The Democratic party was, in effect, an empty shell
which was easily seized by the DOC and transformed from an
aggregation of patronage-hungry conservative politicians into
a progressive political force in the tradition of the La Follettes.

The changes in party affiliation that were induced by the
Great Depression and World War II were massive. The Republicans lost a large part of the Scandinavian vote in northwest

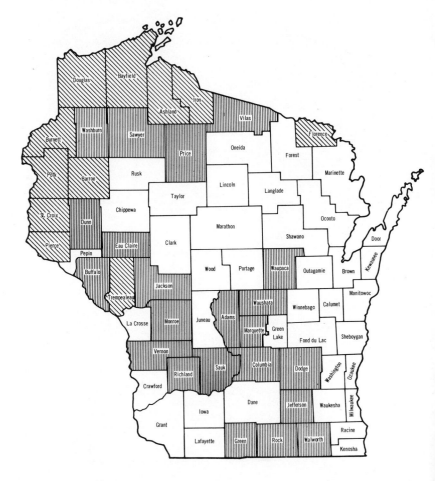

The Yankee Protestant counties: Counties 20 percent or less Catholic, 1957, and less than 10 percent Scandinavian, 1930

The Scandinavian counties: Counties 6 percent or more Scandinavian, 1930

FIGURE 3.3   WISCONSIN'S YANKEE PROTESTANT AND SCANDI-NAVIAN COUNTIES

Explanatory Note for Figures 3.3 and 3.4: The two figures are designed to demonstrate graphically the degree to which Republican voting strength prior to the New Deal was derived from a combination of native Protestants and Scandinavians. Figure 3.3 identifies the native (Yankee) Protestant counties and the Scandinavian counties. Figure 3.4 identifies the counties won by a substantial margin by the Republican presidential candidate in 1884 (Blaine). The 1884 election was chosen partially at random and partially because it was far enough removed in time from the demographic data to demonstrate the continuity over time of these relationships. Once

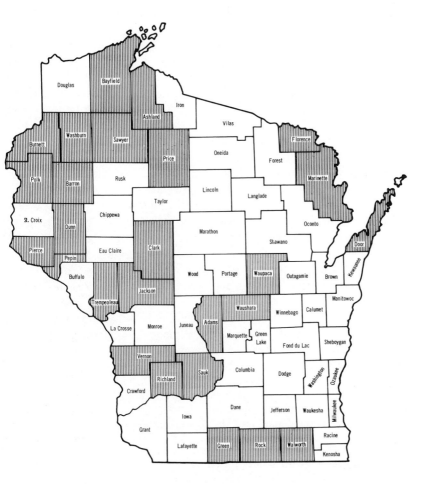

Counties in which Republican presidential candidate (Blaine) received 55 percent or more of two-party vote in 1884

FIGURE 3.4   WISCONSIN'S REPUBLICAN COUNTIES, 1884

again, the impression of a correspondence between the two figures may be verified by counting the counties that are shaded on both maps. The Republican presidential candidate in 1884 (Blaine) won 26 Wisconsin counties by 55 percent or more of the two-party vote, and 22 of the 26 Republican counties are also among the 33 counties designated as native Protestant or Scandinavian.

Wisconsin to the Democrats and replaced it with much of the conservative German Catholic vote in the Fox River Valley. However, the native Protestant voters remained firmly attached to the Republican party, and the Catholic vote (particularly in the cities) continued in the Democratic party, with the exception of the rural German Catholic vote.

After 1946 and through the 1962 gubernatorial election, the Democrats received most of their votes, percentagewise, in the northwest Scandinavian counties and in the metropolitan areas surrounding Milwaukee and Madison (Dane County). A third element in the post-World War II Democratic vote was the ballots cast by former adherents of the Progressive political faith (see Figures 3.1 and 3.2).[4]

Consequently, the post-Great Depression and World War II two-party division was along ideological, political, economic, and ethnic lines which were closely related to the issues facing Wisconsin voters. The conservative and relatively prosperous German Catholics and Yankee Protestants tended to congregate in the Republican party. On the other hand, the relatively liberal and, in many cases lower-income Scandinavian farmers, the Milwaukee and Madison working class, and the former La Follette Progressives were attracted to the Democratic party. Religious and ethnic political divisions, which were unrelated to twentieth-century issues and problems, had little influence on the 1962 two-party divisions. Most Wisconsin Catholics remained in the Democratic party, but they were largely the low-income eastern Europeans in the cities.

[4] The coefficients of correlation of Democratic Governor Gaylord Nelson's percentage vote in 1960 by counties with political and demographic variables provide additional confirmation of the generalizations concerning the sources of Democratic and Republican votes. The coefficient of correlation of Nelson's percent vote with percent Scandinavian was .58 and with percent German was (−).44. In other words, the Scandinavians voted for Nelson and the Germans voted against him, and herein lies much of the explanation for the results of the 1960 election. Of course, behind the Scandinavian and German votes rests the more basic political division over liberal and conservative policies. The vote for La Follette against McCarthy in 1946 was the most recent demonstration of this division. When Nelson's 1960 vote is related to La Follette's 1946 vote, the coefficient of correlation that results is .52. This rather conclusively nails down the assertion that the 1960 Democratic vote was, in very large part, a product of the movement of Progressives and most particularly Scandinavian Progressives from the Republican to the Democratic party. Perhaps the most significant fact revealed by the coefficient of correlation is that Wisconsin's Democratic party in 1960 was not exclusively a Catholic urban party. The relationship of Nelson's vote by counties with urbanism was only .12 and with rural-farm only (−).14, which indicates that his vote by counties had little to do with rural-urban place of residence. In addition, the relationship with percent Catholic was .25. The relatively small relationship of Democratic vote with Catholicism means that the Democratic vote came from many sources, including the Catholic vote.

The Organization of Wisconsin's Parties

In 1963 Wisconsin's Democratic and Republican parties were headed by extra-legal committees.[5] The Republican party's governing organization was the Republican Voluntary Committee, organized in 1925; and its counterpart, the Democratic Organizing Committee, appeared in 1949. Both organizations were founded to circumvent the legislation that the La Follette Progressives enacted for the specific purpose of weakening the parties. The Progressives benefited by a weak party organization because they were the rebels within the Republican organization. In addition, the money provided to finance a strong party organization almost invariably came from the business community and was used to promote conservative candidates and conservative policies. On the other hand, the Progressives had willing volunteer workers and, consequently, did not require large sums for their campaigns. Therefore, limitations on money spent on campaigns and on party organizational activity worked to the benefit of the Progressives.

Both parties established the extra-legal governing organizations in order to promote more effective political campaigns. Specifically, they were enabled to recruit a mass membership for their parties, which in turn ran the parties. In Wisconsin many citizens were card-carrying Democrats or Republicans after the creation of the party committees. Secondly, extra-legal organizations freed the parties from statutory restrictions and enabled them to order their internal affairs as they wished.

The 1949 Democratic Organizing Committee had objectives beyond improved campaign and political organization. The DOC represented a conscious effort to unify the urban New Deal Democrats, the former Milwaukee Socialists, and the Progressive dissidents. Not all Progressives responded to the call, but the DOC proved most successful in attracting former Progressives and other liberals from a wide variety of political backgrounds. Examples include Gaylord Nelson, whose family had been active in the Progressive party. In 1946 Nelson sought nomination as a Progressive Republican. In 1949 he was one of the organizers of the DOC. Subsequently, Nelson was elected governor in 1958, reelected in 1960, and in 1962 won election to the U.S. Senate. John W. Reynolds, elected as a Democratic governor in 1962, was

[5] See Frank J. Sorauf, "Extra Legal Political Parties in Wisconsin," *American Political Science Review*, vol. 48 (1954), p. 692, and Leon D. Epstein, "Party Activism in Wisconsin," *Midwest Journal of Political Science*, vol. 1 (1957), p. 291.

another Progressive Republican who helped form the DOC in 1949. Reynolds' father was elected attorney general in 1926 as a Progressive Republican and was Progressive party chairman in 1938.[6]

The DOC also attracted the support of liberal New Deal Democrats and Socialists. Daniel Hoan, a former Socialist mayor of Milwaukee, was an important figure who helped attract liberals and Progressives to the Democratic party. In 1944 he was the Democratic nominee for governor and helped provide a liberal bridge to the Democratic party for Progressives who were disillusioned with the Republican party after La Follette's defeat in 1946. Hoan was active in the DOC until his death in 1961. Andrew Biemiller, a former publisher of the Socialist party newspaper as well as a Socialist member of the Wisconsin House of Representatives, was elected to the U.S. House of Representatives as a Democrat in 1944 and also helped remake the Democratic party for Progressives, liberals, and Socialists.

Labor was also important in the Democratic Organizing Committee. Harvey Kitzman and Sam Rizzo of the United Auto Workers were elected to the party's administrative committee. Frank Wallick, an editor of the *CIO News*, became the editor of *The Wisconsin Democrat*, a Democratic party newspaper. In addition, union leaders served as county and district Democratic leaders. As a consequence, the powerful labor movement in Milwaukee almost automatically endorsed Democratic candidates for statewide office after 1949. The unions provided financial support, but their central function was the enlistment of "volunteer" workers for the Democratic party from among the ranks of labor.

The Influence of Personalities

By almost universal consent in Wisconsin, the most important single person in the building of Wisconsin's Democratic party was conceded to be William Proxmire. Proxmire studied at Harvard under John Gaus, who had formerly been a professor of political science at the University of Wisconsin. Gaus had been identified with the Progressives and was vitally concerned with the postwar shape of Wisconsin politics. He impressed Proxmire with the necessity of engineering a continuing coalition of liberal Democrats, urban and rural Progressives, and Socialists. Gaus

[6] This account of the DOC is drawn from interviews and especially from Adamany's unpublished Master's thesis, "The 1960 Election in Wisconsin," as well as the unpublished Ph.D. dissertations by Patterson and Crane.

feared that if this did not occur, the accomplishments of the Progressives (with which he identified himself) would slowly be erased by conservative Republican governors and legislators. Gaus had the same sense of mission about the "Wisconsin Idea" as Wright had concerning the need to blend Wisconsin architecture with its environment. In fact, in a sense the two missions were intertwined, for they both sought a society within which the life of man was adjusted in the happiest possible manner to the environment in which he lived.

In 1949 Proxmire settled in Dane County, a traditional center of Progressive political strength and the site of the state capital and the university. Subsequently, Proxmire was elected to the state legislature from a mixed rural and urban district and quickly built a reputation as an able and influential legislator. In 1952, when Democratic prospects for victory were dim, Proxmire volunteered to be the sacrificial goat in the campaign for the governorship against popular Walter Kohler. Proxmire received only 37 percent of the vote in the election, but succeeded in giving currency to his name. In addition, he initiated a long-term campaign to build Democratic party strength in every village and hamlet of the state.

Republican strength in the state was based upon that party's control of almost all local offices, which meant that in statewide campaigns the Democrats had little support at the local level in the small towns and hamlets of the state. Proxmire, by virtue of his campaigns throughout the state and through the force of his personality, made it respectable to be a Democrat in small-town Wisconsin. "Soapy" Williams and Neil Staebler proved to rural and small-town Michigan that the Democrat as labor racketeer or "drunken Irishman" was merely a stereotype. Hubert Humphrey did much the same job of lending luster to the Democratic ticket in Minnesota. And William Proxmire performed this important task for Wisconsin Democrats. Local Democrats were proud of their candidate and came out from "under rocks" to work for him and other Democrats on Election Day. In addition, they fielded local slates of Democratic candidates against Republicans, a state of affairs which shocked the Republican organization. By 1958 the Democrats were fielding 312 candidates for the state's 568 courthouse offices (compared with 259 in 1956), contested all but three assembly seats, and had at least a skeletal organization in all seventy-two counties. In addition, the paid party membership was 15,000.

It is somewhat difficult to isolate the reasons for Proxmire's popularity in Wisconsin. One of them was that people regarded him as an able public servant. If one must single out the most important causative agent in Proxmire's political success, it would have to be his reputation as a "maverick." The Wisconsin citizenry admired mavericks. They applauded La Follette when he attacked the "interests." They shook their heads in grinning delight when Joseph McCarthy charged that the Communists were running the State Department. They were equally happy with Proxmire when he repudiated the Democratic candidate for attorney general in 1956 as "unqualified," and supported an independent candidate. The Wisconsin small-town and rural person also grinned his approval when Proxmire read his "Declaration of Independence" to the state labor convention in 1957. The labor leaders were expecting Proxmire's thanks for the thousands of dollars and hours of work they had invested in his successful campaign for the recently deceased McCarthy's U.S. Senate seat in 1957. Instead, Proxmire told them that he would not be their man in Washington, and would represent "all the people." The labor leaders regarded the Proxmire remarks as a gratuitous slap in the face.

Perhaps the following comments by the owner of a small manufacturing plant outside Madison (taken from Lou Harris' 1958 public opinion survey) will provide the reader with some understanding of the psychology that induced many of Wisconsin's citizens to support with equal enthusiasm liberal La Follette, radical conservative McCarthy, and then liberal Proxmire:

> I have a lot of admiration for anyone who can stand up and make himself heard. The trouble with our statesmen today is that they aren't like that, they're too timid. We need a man like Franklin Delano Roosevelt running the country today. Or like Joe McCarthy. Now there was a guy. He was abrupt, probably even abusive, but he believed in what he had to say. Joe would even be on the nasty side, but I'm a lot like him myself. Damned if I won't make my point of view known; no sense in being timid. In a way Proxmire's like that. He's a little bit too radical, with ideas too much on the radical side. Ahead of his times, but maybe tomorrow his ideas will be accepted. My only worry is that he can be swayed by powerful influences. But I'll vote for him in spite of that because he seems to believe what he says.[7]

Along the same line, a dairy and potato farmer outside Antigo, Wisconsin, said the following:

> If only we had McCarthy today. There was a man with an awful lot of knowledge and experience. No one rates up to McCarthy today here in Wisconsin. He wouldn't sit around and let so many people take hand-

[7] Louis Harris and Associates "A Survey of the Issues in the Election in Wisconsin," July 1958, p. 16.

outs in this country. To my mind, the whole practice of unemployment compensation is unfair. It just leaves a lot of able-bodied men lying around collecting their compensation who won't go to work. No one like McCarthy today. Closest is Proxmire. The Republicans have done a pretty good job of running Wisconsin, but there's no harm in having a Democrat in and Proxmire is a young man with lots of get-up-and-go.[8]

Thus, the Democratic Organizing Committee enlisted the support of leaders of most of the liberal groups in the state, and Proxmire was influential in selling the coalition to the people of the state. The result was the development of a surprisingly well-organized Democratic party which competed with the Republican party for political office at both the local and state levels.

Three other names must be mentioned in this chronicle of Democratic party organization in Wisconsin. They are James Doyle, Gaylord Nelson and Pat Lucey. Many Wisconsin Democrats give Doyle the lion's share of the credit for persuading Progressives and Socialists to join hands with liberal Democrats in the DOC. Doyle was a liberal Democratic attorney in Madison and his influence was a product of his intellect and personal charm. Next is Gaylord Nelson, from a Progressive background, who was elected governor in 1958 and also developed a reputation as a maverick because he stood apart from his party on some issues, such as the sales tax. Nelson also cultivated a reputation as a sound and responsible politician with the press and with civic and business groups. This further contributed to the aura of respectability and acceptability which was cloaking (some claim smothering) the Democratic party. Patrick Lucey is last but very far from least in the listing of important figures in building Wisconsin's Democratic party. He was Proxmire's choice for Democratic chairman from 1958 to 1963 and must be given much of the credit for developing Democratic party organizations in each of the state's seventy-two counties. However, Lucey was constantly embroiled in intraparty battles, first with the Milwaukee Democrats over spoils and candidates and then with the party's liberals and former Progressives because of his support of Kennedy over Humphrey in the 1960 Democratic presidential primary. Consequently, he retired from the party chairmanship in 1963.

Democratic and Republican Factionalism

The schism within the Democratic party between the urban Democrats and the former Progressives was an omnipresent

[8] *Ibid.*, p. 5.

threat to party unity and effectiveness. But in spite of the intraparty feuds, which were usually between Milwaukee Democrats and Madison Progressives, the Democratic party remained relatively unified over the 1949–1963 period. The best evidence of unity was the party's electoral success. Another evidence of unity was the absence of bitter primary fights for nomination to important statewide office. Between 1948 and 1962, the Democrats had fewer primary contests in statewide elections than the Republicans, in spite of the fact that the Democrats did not endorse candidates, whereas the Republican convention endorsed candidates after 1925.[9]

Factionalism within the Republican party after World War II was on liberal-conservative lines, with the conservatives gradually assuming control of the party. The Republican party was divided along Progressive-Conservative lines from 1900 to 1946, but the weight of the Progressive element within the party pulled its leaders and candidates toward the left of the political spectrum. However, with the realignment of the two parties coincident with World War II and its aftermath, the Progressives exerted less and less influence in party councils.

Much of the Republican Progressive element left the Republican party in 1946 and thereafter, and many conservative Democrats moved into the Republican fold at about the same time. The Progressives departed the Republican ranks because of McCarthy and the liberalization of the Democratic party in the 1930s and 1940s. The conservatives left the Democratic party for much the same reasons; and, in addition, some of the conservative German Catholic Democrats found justification in World War II for their departure from the Democratic fold. The result was a polarization of the membership of the parties along ideological lines, and inevitably the Republican party leadership

[9] Several coefficients of correlation further confirm the evidence that the Democratic party was cohesive. The relationships of Democratic Governor Nelson's 1960 percentage vote by counties with the percentage vote for John F. Kennedy, 1960, and with the percent vote in 1962 for the Democratic gubernatorial candidate, John Reynolds, were both .92, which approaches a one-to-one relationship. That is, it indicates that the overwhelming majority of the voters who cast their ballots for Nelson in 1960 also voted for Kennedy in 1960 and Reynolds in 1962. The significance of the findings is that it indicates that the Democratic-Progressive coalition had cemented into a cohesive single political party in 1960 and 1962. John F. Kennedy was an eastern Irish Roman Catholic and John Reynolds was a Catholic from German Brown County, whereas Gaylord Nelson was identified with the La Follette Progressives. Nevertheless, the various elements of the Democratic coalition held firm and voted for all three candidates.

and candidates were forced to reflect the changed ideological complexion of their party. The nomination and election of Joseph McCarthy to the U.S. Senate in 1946 was both the expression of and the crystallizer of this polarization. Liberals who hesitated to leave their Republican home found their departure hastened by McCarthy, and subsequently liberals of all stripes found unity in their intense hatred of McCarthy. Similarly, conservatives within the Republican party found a rallying point in McCarthy, who symbolized to them the virtues and courage of conservatism.

In 1956 the Republican party moved further to the right when it refused to endorse Senator Alexander Wiley in the Republican primary against ultra-conservative Glenn Davis. The reason for the refusal to endorse Wiley was his failure to defend McCarthy during the censure debates in the U.S. Senate. Wiley was nominated and reelected, but only after a bitter campaign that alienated both conservative and liberal Republicans from their party. The conservatives were bitter at Governor Walter Kohler, a moderate Republican, who supported Wiley. The liberals were alienated from the party because of the nature of the fight against Wiley and the fact that much or most of the party leadership supported Davis.

Consequently, the Republicans had the worst of all possible worlds in the following years. In 1957 the conservatives bolted the party when Governor Kohler contended with Proxmire for McCarthy's U.S. Senate seat and helped elect Proxmire after another bitter Republican primary battle between Kohler and conservative Glenn Davis.

In 1958 the Republican State Convention was once again dominated by conservatives. The convention endorsed right-to-work and a sales tax in addition to endorsing a conservative candidate for U.S. senator, Roland J. Steinle. Steinle was nominated, but in 1958 the liberals bolted the party and the Democrats carried both the Senate seat and the governorship. After his 1958 defeat, Steinle refused to congratulate Proxmire and denounced the Democrats as seeking to "sovietize the U.S."

In 1963 the conservatives were in firm control of the Republican party. The state chairman was Talbot Peterson, the president of the Valley Iron Works, located in Appleton, Wisconsin. He was a former friend of McCarthy's and reflected his political views. He and other influential Republican leaders supported Goldwater and insisted upon the nomination of ultra-conservatives. Peterson and other Republican leaders regarded the nomination of conservatives on the Republican ticket as an issue of principle. They were ideologically oriented rather than election-oriented. Peterson was less interested in winning elections than in promoting his public policy positions. He frankly stated in an interview:

> I am not a politician. I am a conservative. We are tired of politicians who coddle the unions and the Communists in order to get votes.

In a sense, the ideological complexion of the Republican party leadership was a product of Progressive reforms. As there were few patronage jobs and little in the way of contracts to be obtained from government, the Republican party had few professional politicians performing the traditional brokerage job of reconciling the claims of conflicting interests in order to win elections. Instead, the party was dominated by businessmen who used the party to promote their own ideas of the general interest without regard to the claims of other groups, because they had little to gain from compromise. After all, they were not after jobs or contracts. All they wanted was "good government"; that is, low taxes and a minimum of government regulation of their business enterprises.

The Democratic party, ironically, was the moderate party in Wisconsin. The reason was the desire of men such as Proxmire and Nelson to keep their political jobs, and these people led the Democratic party, rather than businessmen or union leaders. Although the union leaders were influential in the Democratic party, their power was not at all comparable to the influence exerted by businessmen in the Republican party.

Political Change in Wisconsin

In examining political change, after World War II and through 1962, it should be remembered that the period begins with a Democratic party which was a somewhat uneasy coalition of traditional Democratic elements and the Progressives.[10] At this time the Democratic party remained a minority party. By the end of the period through a gradual accretion of voting strength, the Democrats pulled even with the Republicans in their statewide vote and won the gubernatorial elections of 1958, 1960, and 1962, as well as both U.S. Senate seats.

Democratic gains over the 1946–1962 period were general

[10] For an interesting account of political change in Wisconsin see Andrew R. Baggaley, "Patterns of Voting Change in Wisconsin Counties, 1952–1957," *Western Political Quarterly*, vol. 12 (1959), p. 141.

throughout the state. The reasons for the widespread increase in the Democratic vote, that is, improved organization, Proxmire's popularity, Republican factionalism can be found in earlier pages. However, the most pronounced plus-Democratic change occurred in the northwest corner of the state where most of the state's Scandinavian farmers live, and in the center of the state, which is also primarily farm country. On the other hand, the Republican vote remained relatively untouched in the southern portion of the state and in the German Catholic country in the Oshkosh-Appleton-Green Bay area. The metropolitan counties generally failed to register important plus percentage-point Democratic change (the cities of La Crosse, Madison, Belmont, Racine, Kenosha, and Green Bay are all in counties wherein plus-Democratic change was least, 1946–1962).[11] However, the actual vote increase in the heavily populated cities was important to the Democratic party.

The data indicate, then, that the most dramatic gains enjoyed by the Democratic party, 1946–1962, were, first, the increase in its rural-farm vote and, second, the continued movement of the Scandinavian and Progressive elements into the Democratic party over the period as a result of disenchantment with the increasingly conservative Republican party. Thus, the political reaction chain set off by McCarthy's defeat of La Follette in 1946 left an enduring mark on political change in the state. The polarization between the two parties of liberal and conservative elements continued, 1946–1962. The Democrats lost much of their conservative German Catholic support and gained the liberal Progressive rural vote.

The end result of this polarization of the Wisconsin electorate was the creation of a two-party, issue-oriented political system in the state. It would be useful now to inquire briefly into the

[11] Coefficients of correlation provide statistical support for the generalization concerning the causative factors behind degrees of plus-Democratic change. The relationship of percentage-point Democratic change along a line of regression, 1946–1962, by counties with percent urban was (−).31, with percent Catholic was (−).03, and with percent German was (−).08. However, there was a .53 relationship with percent rural-farm, a .29 relationship with La Follette's 1946 percent vote in the Republican primary, a .37 relationship with percent families earning less than $3000, and a .21 relationship with percent Scandinavian, 1930. The coefficients of correlation, then, indicate that the Democrats enjoyed their most pronounced increases in Scandinavian low-income, rural-farm, Progressive counties; and the Republicans did best in the higher income, more urban, conservative, and German Catholic counties. It should be remembered, however, that the Democrats gained almost everywhere in the state, and the Democratic vote gains, numerically, in the cities were an important part of the total.

result of a sample survey of political opinions of Wisconsin voters to see whether or not the issue-oriented character of Wisconsin politics is stamped on the opinions of the voters.

Political Opinion in Wisconsin

In the first part of the twentieth century, Wisconsin was known as a liberal state. During the La Follette period, Wisconsin produced the first statewide primary election law, the first complete labor code, the first workmen's compensation law, and the first unemployment compensation act in the nation. In the 1960s Wisconsin's voters appeared to remain committed to the liberal side of the political fence despite their electoral flirtation with Joseph McCarthy. For example, in a poll conducted by Senator Proxmire and reported in the *Congressional Record* on September 18, 1961, Proxmire found that 60 percent of Wisconsin's voters supported health insurance tied to social security; 63 percent were in favor of federal aid to education; and they approved a nuclear test ban agreement with Russia by a margin of four to one.[12]

In attempting to isolate the particular attitudes which reflect or are responsible for "liberal" legislation in Wisconsin, it is useful to compare the opinions of Wisconsin's voters with those of the people of relatively conservative Ohio and Indiana. For this purpose, the results of polls conducted by Louis Harris in 1958 in all three states were compared. In the final analysis, the attitudes in the three states which account for their varying degrees of liberalism and conservatism appear to be those toward taxes, governmental expenditures, and the relative emphasis placed upon the income and expenditure sides of the family budget. In addition, there was a profound difference in the ability of people in the three states to successfully relate their attitudes toward issues to the public policy performance and positions of candidates for elective office.

Before looking at the statistical differences in attitudes toward issues, let us attempt to get the flavor of the differences by lending an ear to the complaints of people from the states. The following quotes are taken from Harris' 1958 studies of opinions in Ohio and Wisconsin. First, we will hear from a forty-eight-year-old office worker in Milwaukee, Wisconsin:

---

[12] *Congressional Record*, Senate, 1961, p. 18755.

Nobody's hiring. There are a lot of cutbacks and closing down of plants that have affected a lot of my friends. Somehow we've got to create more jobs. I don't think taxes being cut will help. We're already in a hole, so taxes won't do us any good now. They should have done it before. Maybe in the future they could put some kind of sales tax on tourists coming into the state so we could have better social security or unemployment benefits without raising our own taxes. I don't think the Republicans have been on their toes. I wouldn't have liked to see Davis running with all the Milwaukee industrialists in back of him. I know Steinle and I'd vote for him, but the Republicans haven't done anything to help people in my position or the working class of people. There's too much worrying about taxes the big business boys have to pay.[13]

Compare the reactions of the Wisconsin voter to issues and candidates with the following opinions of a thirty-two-year-old housewife living in Toledo, Ohio, who, although posessing liberal views, was unable to relate her attitudes to the public policy positions of candidates:

Schools are the biggest problem. They are overcrowded and there is not enough teachers to take care of them. I think the solution is to pay teachers higher salaries. Then the good kids in college today would look forward to be teachers when they get out. Then here in Toledo, our traffic situation should be improved. I think the Expressway is one way to solve our problem. I cannot see why people cannot see that our travel time would be so much shorter. A mistake they have made on the Craig Memorial Bridge was to have a bridge that cost that amount of money. They should have had a high level bridge. I thought the purpose of the Expressway was to save time. The Bridge will hold up traffic for as long as one hour sometimes. That was a real waste of money, I think.

Now I want to make clear that Ike has helped out in lots of crisis situations, like the Far East, for instance. He kept us from getting into more wars like Korea. So I'm glad for him. But I do think it would be better if he would stay in his office more and see to what has to be done and not have someone else do his work for him, like that Adams.

Now I think Bricker [conservative Republican] has been pretty good. Right offhand, golly, I find it hard to think when you ask me about him. I cannot see that he has made us go backward in any way. Oh, yes, he has done a good job of keeping expenses down when he was Governor. Now O'Neil [moderate Republican], I feel, has done an excellent job in pushing for older people for social security benefits. He has the people in mind. He has done a lot to curb our gambling situation, too. On Lausche [conservative Democrat], I think he did a wonderful job in state government and he got other cities to working that way, too.

When O'Neil took over from Lausche, there were certain problems

[13] Louis Harris and Associates, "An Analysis of the Race for U.S. Senator," July 1958, pp. 6–7.

that he seemed to solve easier than Lausche did. He did good with the older people and seemed to have the people completely at heart. I have nothing against DiSalle [liberal Democrat]. I think from all I've heard that he is also quite a wonderful person and he has the people at heart when he does anything. I wasn't of voting age when DiSalle was in. But he does think of the people of Toledo, I'm told. I think O'Neil is younger and his ideas are more for the upcoming citizens of Ohio. So I'll vote for O'Neil over DiSalle. Just like I'll vote for Bricker because I just feel I know him more and feel better with him in there. If Young [liberal Democrat] was better known to me, maybe I'd vote for him. But why change if you like the people in there now?

Why am I going to vote Republican? Well, I'm not really. I'm voting for the man. Now if you asked me who I'd vote for for President, I'd say for a Democrat, and even though I'm a Protestant, I like that Kennedy fellow. But here in the State it all depends on the man.[14]

The principal points dramatized by the quotes from citizens of Wisconsin and Ohio are (1) the relatively more liberal and more sophisticated views of the Wisconsin person, and (2) the superior ability shown by the Wisconsin voter to successfully identify the candidates for political office whose positions on public policy issues most closely correspond to his own. Both of these points will be explored in more detail and supported by statistics from the Harris study.

In his 1958 study of Wisconsin, Harris found less of a demand for a tax cut than in most other states. For example, he discovered that only one person in twenty in Wisconsin wanted a cut in federal income taxes. This was a smaller percentage concerned with the income tax than Harris had found in any other state. Also, only one in twenty was opposed to a state sales tax, and about one in ten complained that the property tax was too high. Overall, in Wisconsin only about one person in ten complained that taxes in general were too high.

Furthermore, few Wisconsin voters supported the notion that governmental services should be reduced in order to make a tax cut possible. In 1958 Harris found that only 4 percent wanted a cut in social security; 23 percent favored reducing the contribution to the United Nations; 37 percent wanted a cut in the farm program; only 14 percent thought it was possible to save tax money through a reduction in defense expenditure. The single item wherein the majority (57 percent) felt that budget cuts were desirable was in economic aid to foreign countries. Here the attitude was not necessarily based on a desire for

[14] Louis Harris and Associates, "A Study of Issues and Candidates in Ohio," September 1958, pp. 13–14.

economy; rather, it was the product of a belief that such spending should be shifted from the needy abroad to the needy at home.

When asked to assign a reason for the 1958 recession, only 2 percent of Wisconsin's voters blamed it on taxes and 5 percent on unions. However, a full 31 percent of Harris' Wisconsin sample blamed big business. Finally, 70 percent of Wisconsin's voters were deeply concerned about the recession, unemployment, low wages, and high prices; and 20 percent were upset because they thought milk and crop prices were too low. In Indiana and Ohio, on the other hand, there was much more concern about taxes than in Wisconsin. In Indiana, 51 percent felt that taxes were too high, and 40 percent of the Ohioans shared this feeling.

But perhaps the most interesting finding of the Harris pollsters was that Wisconsinites tended to vote for Democratic candidates if they held liberal views, whereas in Ohio (and to a lesser extent in Indiana) the vote tended to be based upon personalities rather than on issues. As Harris commented in his study of Ohio political views:

. . . we found in this survey . . . an almost complete lack of associating economic self-interest and the real problems in people's lives with their vote for statewide offices in Ohio. This utter disassociation of self-interest with votes being cast is unquestionably, in our judgment, the root cause of the failure of the Democratic party. While a good deal of it can be blamed on the orientation of non-partisanship that voters may have been conditioned to under Lausche regimes, it is also indicative of the failure—up to now—of Democratic candidates to relate issues of voter concern to either party or personal identification.[15]

At this juncture, the remaining question is why Wisconsin's people had differentially liberal attitudes and were better able than the voters of other states to relate issues to candidates and to political parties. The answer to the query resides in a mélange of the history of the state, the groups that settled it, the farm and labor organizations that emerged, and the political personalities who articulated, dramatized, and responded to the needs of the people as expressed by their ballots.

The two most important factors in the history of Wisconsin that account for its political sophistication are the exploitation it suffered from railroad and lumber companies and the immigration into the state of large numbers of politically alert Germans and Scandinavians. The exploitation generated a climate of pro-

[15] *Ibid.*, p. 14.

test to which the Germans and Scandinavians responded by forming organizations designed to remedy these ills. They took the form of a Socialist movement and strong trade union movement in Milwaukee and militant farm organizations and the Progressive party outstate.

Personalities, of course, appeared who articulated and crystallized the protests. Of these, La Follette was the most important. Others included Chief Justice Ryan, who wrote opinions upholding the constitutionality of reform legislation in the late nineteenth century, providing the reformers with much of their rationale for legislation; and Victor L. Berger (in company with Eugene Debs), who organized the powerful Socialist movement in Milwaukee. These people, along with many others, directed and focused the feelings of Wisconsin's less well-to-do into programmatic parties and political movements which offered solutions to their problems.

Wisconsin's Politicians "Deliver"

But a central factor in explaining the issue-oriented nature of Wisconsin politics is that Wisconsin's politicians "delivered" for the voters when elected. When Wisconsin's voters were unhappy about the excesses of big business and expressed their protest through their votes, they got legislation which strictly regulated railroads, insurance companies, and lumber companies. When they became upset with corruption in state government and voted for the candidate who promised to remedy the evil, they got a strong civil service law and one of the most honest state governments in the nation.

Again and again this same pattern of protest-leadership-action repeated itself in Wisconsin's history. Let the voters be disturbed about the party bosses, and the successful reform candidate succeeded in obtaining a primary election law; let them turn their eyes to hills denuded of their forest cover and to polluted rivers, and their candidate gave them an effective conservation program; when the workers bemoaned their insecure lot, their candidates procured for them the nation's first unemployment compensation and workmen's compensation laws.

Now it must be emphasized that none of Wisconsin's effective political action occurred in a vacuum. It required, first, the climate of protest; second, groups which were cohesive and informed; third, personalities who mobilized the groups and translated their protests into public policy. For example, Wisconsin's Scandinavians were politically sophisticated. As a consequence, they tended to join the Farmers' Union, which championed the cause of the common farmer. The Farmers' Union, in turn, kept the Scandinavians informed of the identity of their political friends and enemies, which in Wisconsin in the 1950s and 1960s meant that it told them to vote Democratic. The result was that in 1958 Harris found that 70 percent of the farmers in his sample intended to vote for the liberal Democrat, Proxmire.

The result was an electorate in Wisconsin which was relatively well informed concerning the issues and the candidates, and which, through experience, had learned that something happened when they voted for a liberal candidate that did not happen when they voted for a conservative candidate. The relationship between their economic self-interest and their vote was demonstrated for them time and time again.

Look back again at the woman in Ohio who voted on the basis of personalities. She said: "In Ohio, somehow we just vote for the man. Now if you asked me who I'd vote for for President, I'd say for a Democrat. . . ." What she was really saying was that at the state level in Ohio she had never found that there was any significant relationship between voting Democratic or Republican and her self-interest. It was her experience and the experience of her parents and friends that "it doesn't make a hell of a lot of difference whether we vote for a Democrat or Republican. Consequently, we vote for the man." On the other hand, her comment would indicate that at the national level she and those around her had detected some meaningful difference in the performance of the parties and their candidates.

In Wisconsin, however, the voters learned through happy or sad experience that it made a great deal of difference which party controlled the Statehouse. When the Progressives were in power, legislation was enacted which affected the life of every person in the state. When conservative Republicans were in power, programs designed to help the less well-to-do tended to contract and tax policies were oriented toward holding the "bite" on the wealthy at something of a plateau. This experience under the Progressives left its mark on Wisconsin politics and in 1963 the old identification of liberal with Progressive had been transferred to the Democratic label.

Table 3.1 contains the results of a sample survey conducted by Louis Harris and Associates in Wisconsin in 1958. The results of the survey generally confirm the foregoing observations con-

Table 3.1

SAMPLE SURVEY OF VOTER OPINION IN WISCONSIN*

	PERCENTAGE OF VOTERS FOR PROXMIRE, DEMO- CRATIC CANDIDATE FOR U.S. SENATOR
By areas of the state:	
Milwaukee	58
Other big cities	47
Farmers	71
Rest of state	57
By income level:	
Upper income	36
Middle income	61
Lower income	65
By nationality origin:	
German background	50
Other western Europe	48
Polish background	79
Other eastern Europe	75
By age groups:	
Under 35	67
35 to 44	62
45 to 54	53
55 to 64	46
65 and over	40
By sex:	
Men	62
Women	52
By religion:	
Catholic	69
Protestant	47
Statewide preferences	58

---

*Source: Louis Harris and Associates, "An Analysis of the Race for U.S. Senator," July 1958, p. 12.

cerning voting behavior in Wisconsin. The table reveals that William Proxmire, the 1958 Democratic candidate for U.S. senator, received most of his support from Milwaukee, farmers (largely liberal Scandinavians), middle- and lower-income people, eastern Europeans, and Catholics. On the other hand, the

Republican voters were mainly concentrated among the conservative Germans and other western European people, upper-income voters, and Protestants.

Governmental Expenditures in Wisconsin

We turn now to the measurable effect of competitive politics on the performance of state government in Wisconsin. The period analyzed is 1946–1960, when two-party competitive politics emerged in the state. However, the long history of Progressive versus stalwart Republican competition probably had more of an effect on state government in Wisconsin than the more recent two-party politics. Undoubtedly, though, they are inextricably intertwined, for the Democratic party in Wisconsin was, in 1962, the torchbearer of the Progressive philosophy.

Over the 1946–1958 period, Wisconsin ranked twenty-fourth among the states in terms of the narrowness of the two-party division in the legislature and in the vote for governor.[16] The reason for Wisconsin's relatively low ranking was the rather large Republican majorities in the state legislature.

In its expenditures on state programs, though, Wisconsin ranked high among the states. Its welfare programs were particularly generous. In 1960 Wisconsin ranked sixth among the states in per-recipient aid to dependent children payments, twelfth in aid to the blind, and sixth in old age assistance payments. In 1960 it ranked nineteenth in per-pupil expenditures and twenty-first in the estimated average salary of the instructional staff. It ranked eleventh in its per-capita state and local tax revenue, and twenty-first in effort; that is, the proportion that the per-capita tax revenue represented of per-capita income. This rank is extremely high for a prosperous industrial state. The only industrial states ahead of Wisconsin in effort were California and Massachusetts.

The indication, then, is that even though two-party competition is an element affecting levels of state governmental expenditures, it is far from the sole determinant. In Wisconsin the struggle between elements of the business community and the less well-to-do within the Republican party was primarily responsible for the relatively high level of governmental services and expendi-

---

[16] The measure of two-party competition by states consisted of the sum of the lesser average percent gubernatorial vote and average two-party division in the state legislature. For example, if the average divisions were 52–48 and 53–47, respectively, the score would be 95.

tures. The Progressive-stalwart Republican factional fight was institutionalized into a two-party division of forces after 1946, and the effect was a continuing emphasis on programs designed to reallocate goods and services from the prosperous to the less fortunate members of the Wisconsin community.

Summary and Conclusions

Between the Civil War and 1900, Wisconsin was virtually a one-party state, and the dominant Republican party was controlled by the railroads and lumber interests. The exploitation suffered by Wisconsin's land and people during the period left a legacy of land denuded of its forest cover and a people embittered at the excesses of the business community. In 1963, when an eighty-year-old former Democratic leader in Minocqua, Wisconsin was asked why he was a Democrat, he talked for hours about misdeeds perpetrated by the lumber companies.

In 1900 this bitterness bore fruit in the nomination and election of Robert La Follette as a reform-minded, Progressive Republican governor. La Follette and his Progressive Republican followers translated his reform program into public policy. From 1900 until 1934 the battle between the business community or the conservative Republicans and the Progressives took place within the Republican party, with the two factions alternating in public office. The Democratic party was impotent, conservative, and patronage-oriented.

In 1934 the Progressives broke from the Republican party and formed a third party. After suffering several successive electoral defeats, the Progressive party leaders decided in 1946 to disband the party and to return to their Republican home. However, in the 1946 Republican primary the Progressives were not greeted with the traditional fatted calf. On the contrary, Robert La Follette, Jr., the Progressive Republican candidate for U.S. senator, was defeated in the primary by Joseph McCarthy, the candidate of the conservative Republicans. Consequently, many Progressives gravitated into the Democratic party in 1946. Between 1946 and 1962 the Democratic party became the majority party in the state, electing the governor in 1958, 1960, and 1962 (see Figure 3.5), and two Democratic senators in 1958 and 1962. The source of Democratic votes was, primarily, disillusioned Progressives. In addition, the Democrats attracted the votes of people from rural Wisconsin who were unhappy with the Benson farm program. Over the 1946–1962 period, the Democrats did

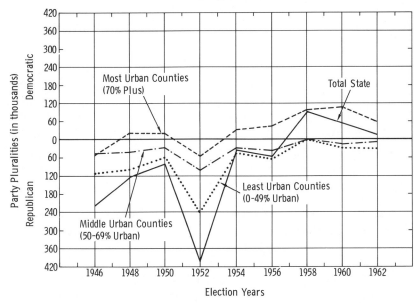

FIGURE 3.5 WISCONSIN VOTING TRENDS BY SECTIONS in gubernatorial elections, 1946–1962

Explanatory Note: The graph brings home the secular nature of plus Democratic change and its universal character, 1946–1962. It also serves to emphasize the very pronounced improvement in the Democratic vote cast in the least urban counties. The solid line designated "Total State" traces the size of Republican and Democratic pluralities in the nine elections. It shows that the Republican candidates won by sizable but slowly declining pluralities from 1946 to 1956. In 1958, the solid line jumps upward to the Democratic side of the plurality line and remains there through 1962. The dotted line identifies the pluralities cast by the state's rural counties. The rural counties were so one-sidedly Republican in 1946 that the Democratic candidate had little or no chance of victory, but by 1962 the rural counties were dividing their votes almost 50–50 between the candidates of the two parties. The division of the vote in the medium-sized cities ("middle urban") was almost unchanged, 1946–1962; and the vote out of the big cities provided the Democrats with the pluralities that brought victory, but the increase in Democratic pluralities in the metropolitan counties, 1946–1962, did not approach the change in the rural counties.

less well, percentagewise, in the urban than they did in the rural sections of the state, partially because of the defection of conservative Catholic Germans.[17] The net impact of the political change, however, was in bringing about Democratic gains throughout the state and the emergence of two-party, issue-

---

[17] See Leon D. Epstein, "Size of Place and the Division of the Two-Party Vote in Wisconsin," *Western Political Quarterly*, vol. 9 (1956), p. 138, for an interesting account of the vote in Wisconsin cities.

oriented politics. And votewise the Democratic gains in the cities were crucial to their electoral victories.

Thus, the Progressive and former Socialist vote out of Milwaukee, Madison, and other cities which was transferred to Democratic candidates in ever-increasing numbers after 1946, and the former Progressive rural vote which also gravitated toward the Democratic party after 1946, resulted in an unprecedented string of three Democratic victories, 1958–1962, in the gubernatorial elections. In 1964, unpopular Democratic Governor John Reynolds was defeated at the same time that Lyndon Johnson and other Democrats were winning landslide victories in Wisconsin.

The final political product in Wisconsin was a state that was extremely competitive, where the two parties tended to take rather sharply divergent positions on issues, and a state government that was almost painfully honest and had one of the nation's most generous welfare programs, most ambitious conservation programs, and a generally high level of governmental services. Judgments concerning the desirability of Wisconsin's style of politics and government depend upon one's ideological biases. However, regardless of political values, it is difficult to deny that the performance of Wisconsin's government generally corresponded with the informed wishes of the electorate. And this comes close to a good working definition of a democratic form of government.

Chapter 4

The Professors and Women
in Minnesota Politics

In 1962 the Democratic-Farmer-Labor candidate for governor of Minnesota won by 91 votes. The people who elected the Democrat were largely Scandinavians in the countryside and working-class people in the cities.[1] The 1962 Republicans were, in the main, the more well-to-do in the cities and the native Protestants. In 1857, at the state's constitutional convention, the division between the two parties was very nearly as narrow. At that 1857 convention there were fifty-nine elected Republican delegates and fifty-five elected Democratic delegates. If the origins of the delegates are any index, the 1857 Republicans were dominantly of New England and New York extraction, whereas the Democrats were from the Old Northwest and the Middle States and, perhaps, were sons and daughters of people from the South. In terms of statistics, 44 percent of the Republican delegates were from New England compared to only 23 percent of the Democrats. On the other hand, 23 percent of the Democrats were from the Old Northwest compared to 8 percent of the Republicans.

In 1857 the Republican party was the liberal or radical party and the Democrats were the conservatives. In a League of Women Voters pamphlet, the 1857 Democrats are described as "mainly astute, experienced, practiced and conservative, suspicious of the radical Republicans." On the other hand, the Republicans were "for the most part politically inexperienced, idealistic, naïve, radical. They were small farmers, small merchants, lawyers, ministers. Great believers in the popular

---

[1] "Scandinavian" refers to people from Norway, Sweden, Finland, and Denmark.

referendum, they wanted more democracy than existed anywhere. They were anti-slavery and prohibitionist."[2]

By 1962, the ideological complexion as well as the ethnic composition of the parties had changed. The Democratic-Farmer-Labor party was the political vehicle of the liberals and the Republican party was identified with experience and caution and conservatism. The events that produced the ideological and ethnic changes in the parties are (1) the settlement pattern of the state, (2) the changes that occurred in the ideological complexion of the national Democratic and Republican parties, and (3) the events that stirred the nation and Minnesota in the 105 years between 1857 and 1962.

After 1857 Minnesota was a dominantly Republican state. In fact, between 1860 and 1930 it was very nearly a one-party state.[3] After becoming a state in 1858, Minnesota never cast a plurality of its vote for a Democratic candidate for President until 1932, when it gave Franklin Roosevelt 600,000 votes to 360,000 for Herbert Hoover. The vote at the state level was almost as monotonously Republican. In thirty-five gubernatorial elections after 1858 and through 1928, the Republicans won thirty times to only five victories for the Democrats, three of which were won by John A. Johnson, 1904–1909, a magnetic figure whose personality enabled him to attract votes from all segments of Minnesota's population.

Minnesota's one-sided voting behavior after 1857 was a result of the state's massive support for the Union in the Civil War and the influx of literate, liberal, and Lutheran Scandinavians who affiliated themselves with the anti-slavery, anti-liquor, anti-Catholic Yankees in the Republican party.[4] They approved of a Republican party which, in its 1855 platform, "denounced the Kansas-Nebraska Act as a 'violation of the plighted faith of the South.' It branded the Fugitive Slave Act as unconstitutional; upheld the principle of the supremacy of Freedom and free institutions over our whole country; and called for the

[2] League of Women Voters of Minnesota, *The State You're In* (Minneapolis, Minn., 1958), p. 15.

[3] This account of Minnesota's political history was derived from many sources, including interviews. However, I am particularly indebted to Arthur Naftalin's interesting unpublished Ph.D. dissertation, "A History of the Farmer-Labor Party in Minnesota." Other very useful sources were Theodore C. Blegen, *Minnesota: A History of the State* (Minneapolis: University of Minnesota Press, 1963); and Federal Writers Project, *Minnesota*, Works Progress Administration (1938).

[4] Blegen, *Minnesota, A History of the State*, p. 217.

'enactment and enforcement of a Prohibition Liquor Law' and demanded 'Free land in limited quantities to actual settlers.' "[5]

The Scandinavians rejected a Democratic party which supported slavery, was the political home of Catholics, and was anti-Prohibitionist. It seemed the very embodiment of evil to the liberal Protestant Scandinavians. All their instincts attracted them to the Republican party, which was dominated by Yankee Protestants and promised to use government in a crusade to stamp out the twin evils of slavery and liquor.

One writer has said that

> Minnesota owes more to Scandinavians than to any other one foreign group. They came from countries where illiteracy was extremely low. Their traditions were of thrift, respect for both intellectual and physical effort, and interest in government, and they combined to an unusual degree love of individual freedom and talent for cooperating with their neighbors.[6]

Further, they, above all other immigrants in Minnesota, were delighted with their adopted home. They wasted few fond backward looks at their homelands. They integrated quickly and discarded their native dress and customs and tongue for the American standard which had been stamped upon the state by its early Yankee settlers.[7]

The Scandinavians embraced the Yankee Republican politics as well as their values. By the latter part of the nineteenth century, 70 percent of Minnesota's population was first- or second-generation immigrant and half of the immigrants were Scandinavians. When this vote was combined with the eastern or Yankee vote, it placed the Republican party in an overwhelmingly dominant position.

Even though Minnesota's Democratic party fared poorly, 1858–1930, it, too, attracted partisans from out of the stream of immigrants entering the state. The Germans, and particularly the German Catholics, leaned toward the Democratic party even though they were opposed to slavery. The Irish, and after 1890 the eastern European immigrants, also tended to affiliate with the Democratic party. Their Democratic predilections were a

[5] *Ibid.*, p. 217.

[6] Federal Writers Project, *Minnesota*, p. 77.

[7] The Scandinavians and particularly the Norwegians brought to the United States a political sophistication lacking in some other groups. See Angus Campbell and Henry Valen, "Party Identification in Norway and the United States," *Public Opinion Quarterly*, vol. 25 (1961), p. 505.

result of the antiforeign and anti-Catholic bias they detected in the Republican party.[8] In addition, the Germans liked their beer and looked askance at the prohibitionist fervor of the Yankee and Scandinavian Republicans.

The Democrats won few counties in most elections and fewer statewide victories before the Great Depression and Franklin Roosevelt. But the politics of the state were not so placid as the statistics would indicate. The farmers and laborers and especially the Scandinavians were stirred into flaming discontent with existing economic and political institutions at least once a decade after the Civil War. The Grangers and the People's Anti-Monopoly party in the 1870s, the Farmers' Alliance in the 1880s and 1890s, the Progressives in the early 1900s, the Non-Partisan League after 1915, and the Farmer-Labor party in the 1920s all attracted numerous supporters.

The platforms of the parties of protest varied all the way from the mild reform planks of the Grangers to the socialist proposals of the Non-Partisan Leaguers. The complaints of the farmers and laborers and particularly the Scandinavian wheat farmers revolved around the difficulty of making both ends meet. They tended to blame their economic plight on the warehouse and commission merchants and the railroads; specifically, they were unhappy about unfair grading, improper dockage, dishonest weighing, and exorbitant railway charges.

Until 1918 the Republican party was responsive to the complaints of their rural adherents, and the Scandinavians maintained their allegiance to the party. For example, in 1885 a state-enforced system of grading and inspection was established by state law under a Republican governor and legislature, albeit in response to pressure from Granger legislators; in 1871, 1874, and again in 1885, legislation was enacted under Republicans regulating railroad, freight, and elevator charges; and from 1901 to 1905 it was Republican Governor Van Sant who successfully prosecuted the Northern Securities Company, a giant scheme to monopolize control over the railroads engineered by James J. Hill, J. Pierpont Morgan, Edward H. Harriman, and other financial interests. It was also during Van Sant's administration that Minnesota adopted a direct primary law. Labor, too, achieved many of its goals under Republican governors and

[8] For example, in the 1884 presidential election the Democratic candidate received a plurality of the vote in only twelve of the state's eighty-seven counties, and eleven of the twelve counties were among the twenty counties which were 30 percent or more Catholic according to the 1957 Census of Religious Bodies.

legislatures. In 1885 a State Board of Labor Statistics was created; in 1895 a child labor law was adopted, and in 1913 a workmen's compensation act was passed.

Thus, the Republican party was a reasonably liberal political instrument in the nineteenth and early twentieth centuries in Minnesota. It was not the exclusive political instrumentality of the wealthy and, albeit with much pushing, it responded with remedial legislation when its Scandinavian adherents evinced sufficient concern about economic or social problems.

In 1918, a Republican governor departed from the successful Republican tradition of neutralizing protest movements by adopting many of their programs. Instead of embracing or at least sympathizing with the protests of the Non-Partisan League adherents in 1918, Republican Governor J. A. A. Burnquist launched a bitter frontal attack upon them. In statements similar to those made by Senator Joseph McCarthy and Vice President Richard Nixon after World War II, he indicted the Non-Partisan League as "a party of treason," thereby permanently alienating from the Republican party much of its Scandinavian support, for the wheat-growing Scandinavians in western Minnesota were the most enthusiastic proponents of the program of the Non-Partisan League.

The Non-Partisan League and Farmer-Labor Party

The Non-Partisan League was first organized in North Dakota in 1915 by A. C. Townley, a native of Minnesota. It was inspired by "the Wisconsin Idea" and the personality and program of La Follette. It was quite successful in North Dakota and soon spread to the wheat-growing and Scandinavian area of western Minnesota. In 1918 its platform included support of World War I (a defensive reaction to the "treason" charge hurled at Non-Partisan League leaders), demanded the establishment of state-owned packing plants, elevators, and flour and pulp mills. It also called for a system of state-financed rural credits and a tonnage tax on iron ore. In essence, it was a mildly socialistic program designed to meet the farmers' complaint that the middleman was gouging all the profits out of the price paid by the consumer for the fruit of his toil.

The Non-Partisan League supported a full slate of candidates in the 1918 Republican primaries, all of whom were pledged to support the League platform. Governor Burnquist and the regular Republican organization reacted violently to the attempted takeover of the Republican party by the Non-Partisan League.

In addition, most business interests and the state's newspapers were violently opposed to the League.

Governor Burnquist established a Minnesota Commission of Public Safety which purportedly was created to ensure the patriotic behavior of Minnesotans, but in reality was a campaign arm of Burnquist, the regular Republicans, and the business community. It was a Gestapo-like organization which had agencies in every county and township and had attached to it an 8000-member home guard. The primary function of the Commission of Public Safety was to harass Non-Partisan League candidates and break up their meetings. The excuse for their activity was the alleged antiwar position of League leaders and members. The basic causative factor behind the repression was fear of socialism stimulated largely by the successful Communist revolution in Russia.

Judge John F. McGee of Minneapolis was chairman of the Commission of Public Safety. The following statement by Judge McGee should give the reader some appreciation of the political repression which characterized the activities of the Commission of Public Safety. According to Judge McGee:

> A Non-Partisan League lecturer is a traitor every time. In other words, no matter what he says or does, a League worker is a traitor. Where we made a mistake was in not establishing a firing squad in the first days of the war. We should now get busy and have that firing squad working overtime.[9]

In truth, some leaders of the Non-Partisan League were vulnerable to charges that they were unenthusiastic about World War I. The League candidate for the Republican nomination for governor was Charles Lindbergh, the father of the "Lone Eagle," a former U.S. representative, 1907–1917, and a known opponent of American involvement in the war. Further, A. C. Townley and Robert La Follette, who campaigned for the party, made antiwar statements. The issue, though, was largely irrelevant to the purposes of the League. The organization was primarily a reform movement and most of the leaders and members were mainly concerned with remedying existing economic evils. The charges of treason stunned the Scandinavian members of the League and helped attract to its rolls Germans who were antipathetic to the war and who suffered persecution during the war.

Lindbergh lost the Republican primary to Burnquist, but the

[9] Arthur Naftalin, "A History of the Farmer-Labor Party in Minnesota" (unpublished Ph.D. dissertation, University of Minnesota, 1948), p. 53.

Scandinavian and German adherents of the League were unwilling to accept the verdict at the polls. The farm and labor supporters of the League slate met on August 24, 1918, and decided to enter a Farmer-Labor ticket in the general election. The Republican governor, J. A. A. Burnquist, won the 1918 election, but at the cost of permanently rearranging Minnesota's political spectrum. In the 1918 election Burnquist received 166,515 votes to 111,948 votes for the Farmer-Labor candidate. The Democratic candidate for governor ran a poor third with 76,793 votes. In state elections the Democrats were destined thereafter and until 1944 to occupy third place in the state's politics, with the center of the political stage held by the Farmer-Labor and Republican candidates and the battles between them.

The 1918 election caused a radical reshuffling of groups associated with the parties. Scandinavians and like-minded progressives moved out of the Republican party by the thousands and numbers of Germans deserted the Democratic party, both groups going into the Farmer-Labor party. The Democratic party retained the loyalty of most Catholics. The Republican party was left as the nativist party and thereafter was dominant only in those areas with few Scandinavians or Catholics (see Figures 4.1 and 4.2).[10]

---

[10] Statistical confirmation of the generalizations concerning the composition of the parties after 1918 may be derived from several coefficients of correlation. The simple coefficient of correlation of the 1942 percent Farmer-Labor vote by counties with the 1930 percent Scandinavian of the total population by counties is .48. There is no German variable to work with because of the small percent born in Germany in the state in 1930 (most Germans were second or third generation by 1930). However, the next best thing to a German variable is the relationship between the 1942 Farmer-Labor vote in the gubernatorial election and the Henrik Shipstead vote in the 1946 Republican primary. Shipstead was an old Farmer-Laborite senator and an arch isolationist foe of American involvement in World War II. The relationship between Shipstead's 1946 vote and the 1942 Farmer-Labor vote was .48. However, there was absolutely no relationship between Shipstead's vote and percent Scandinavian (−).07. A reasonable inference from the evidence is that the other large proportion of the 1942 Farmer-Labor vote was the German vote which was also cast for isolationist Shipstead in 1946. This corresponds with the impressionistic evidence of scholars, such as Theodore C. Blegen in *Minnesota: A History of the State*, Arthur Naftalin in his "History of the Farmer-Labor Party," and George H. Mayer in *The Political Career of Floyd B. Olson*, all of whom state that the Farmer-Labor party, although consisting of many elements in the state, was primarily a coalition of Scandinavians and Germans. The relationship between the percent Democratic vote for governor in 1942 by counties and the 1957 percent Catholic of total population by counties is .54.

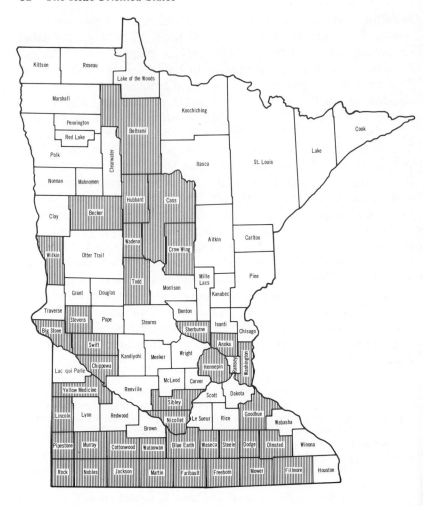

Native Protestant counties: Counties less than 2.5 percent Catholic, 1957, and less th
10 percent Scandinavian, 1930

FIGURE 4.1   MINNESOTA'S NATIVE PROTESTANT COUNTIES

Explanatory Note for Figures 4.1 and 4.2: The two figures provide visual
evidence of the degree to which Minnesota's Republican party receives its
vote from the native Protestants. The shaded counties in Figure 4.1 are
those in which there are few Catholics or Scandinavians, and the counties
in Figure 4.2 which are shaded are the state's most Republican counties in
the gubernatorial elections, 1946–1962. A count of the counties that are
shaded in both maps shows that the Republican candidates for governor,
1946–1962, won 41 of the state's 87 counties in 7 of the 9 elections; and 24
of the 41 Republican counties are also among the 38 native Protestant
counties as identified in Figure 4.1. In percentage terms, 44 percent of the
state's counties are "native Protestant," whereas 59 percent of the Republican counties are "native Protestant."

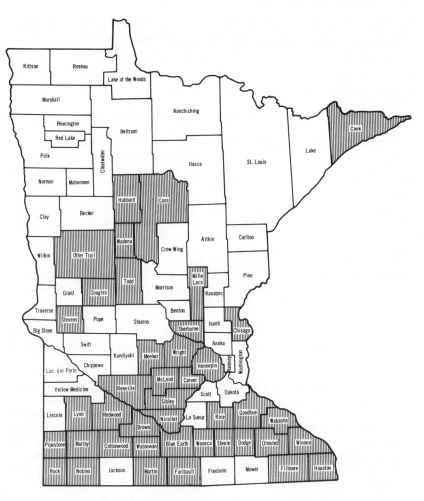

Counties in which Republican gubernatorial candidates received a plurality of the vote in 7 of 9 elections, 1946 - 1962

FIGURE 4.2   MINNESOTA'S REPUBLICAN COUNTIES in gubernatorial elections, 1946–1962

During the relatively prosperous years, 1920–1928, the Republicans managed to maintain their hold on the state government, but the 1929 depression cost them their grip on the state government and their position of dominance in the politics of the state.[11] The Farmer-Labor party that assumed power in

[11] Farmer-Labor strength at the ballot box, however, was displayed through the election of Shipstead in 1922 as U.S. senator, and the election of several U.S. representatives, 1920–1928.

Minnesota in 1930 with the election of Floyd B. Olson as governor was unique in the annals of American political history. In many ways it was akin to the British Labor party, both in its organizational structure and its socialist ideology. According to one student of the Farmer-Labor party:

> The structure of the new association reflected orthodox socialistic doctrines of political organization. The primary unit was the local Farmer-Labor club, which consisted of active reformers in the village or township who were willing to pay annual dues of three dollars. . . . Once a local club was chartered it represented the reformers in the area regardless of its geographical relationship to regular ward and precinct divisions.
> The constitution also permitted economic organizations such as local labor unions or farmers' cooperatives to affiliate with the Association upon payment of a two percent per-capita tax. Like the Farmer-Labor clubs they were entitled to participate in county conventions. These in turn endorsed candidates for local office, passed resolutions advising the parent body of rank-and-file sentiment, and selected delegates to the biennial convention of the Farmer-Labor Association which stood at the apex of the pyramid.[12]

The Farmer-Labor Association was frankly socialistic. In the declaration of principles contained in its constitution it was stated that

> . . . 'every person is entitled to an opportunity to earn a living, and should be secure in the enjoyment of fruits of his or her toils.' To implement these rights, the following steps were advocated: (1) a union of 'all persons in agriculture and other useful industry' to promote the economic welfare of the wealth producers; (2) the abolition of private monopolistic privilege and its replacement by a system of public ownership to increase the total wealth of society and abolish unemployment.[13]

The 1934 platform of the Farmer-Labor party perhaps best expressed the socialist objectives of the party and was, by far, the most radical platform by a major party in the history of American politics. Governor Floyd Olson, the Farmer-Labor governor, had said: "Now I am frank to say that I am not a liberal . . . I am what I want to be—I am a radical. I am a radical in the sense that I want a definite change in the system."[14] The 1934 platform was a blueprint for securing a definite change in the system.

[12] George H. Mayer, *The Political Career of Floyd B. Olson*, (Minneapolis: University of Minnesota Press, 1951), p. 38.
[13] *Ibid.*, p. 37.
[14] Naftalin, "A History of the Farmer-Labor Party in Minnesota," pp. 240–241.

The platform stated:

We therefore declare, that capitalism has failed and immediate steps must be taken by the people to abolish capitalism in a peaceful and lawful manner and that a new sane and just society must be established; a system where all the natural resources, machinery of production, transportation and communication shall be owned by the government and operated democratically for the benefit of all the people and not for the benefit of the few.[15]

The platform included some fifteen planks which were designed to secure the party's aim of abolishing capitalism. The means included laws to provide farmers security of tenure on their land regardless of mortgages; cooperative marketing and purchasing agencies; state-owned mines, state-owned water power, state-owned transport and communication, state-owned banks, state-owned packing plants, and state-owned public utilities.

In practice, however, the Farmer-Labor party was a reform organization rather than a radical socialist party. Olson was politically embarrassed by the 1934 platform and spent most of the campaign watering down its more radical planks. Olson's programs as governor were New Dealish rather than socialistic and included conservation, old-age pensions, prohibition of the injunction in labor disputes, expanded welfare programs, improved state highways, the income tax, and a halt to mortgage sales of farm lands.

Governor Olson died of cancer in August of 1936 after winning election by large margins in 1930, 1932, and 1934. He is revered in Minnesota as "a crusader for social justice," and liberal Minnesotans still measure governors by the yardstick provided by Olson. His importance in Minnesota political history lies in the fact that he campaigned for reform and after election worked hard and successfully to translate the reforms into public policy. Through Olson, Minnesotans rediscovered that there was indeed a relationship between their economic welfare and their votes. Farmers who voted for Olson were rewarded by legislation which forbade foreclosure of mortgages on their land. Labor union members were rewarded for their votes by laws forbidding the use of labor injunctions in strikes.

Olson's death marked the apex of Farmer-Labor power. Thereafter, the party declined rapidly as an independent political force. In 1936 Elmer Benson and the entire Farmer-Labor party swept to a landslide victory, due partially to the wave of emotion following Olson's death. But Benson proved to be a singularly

[15] *Ibid.*, p. 244.

inept governor. During his short two-year term he and his administration reduced the Farmer-Labor party to the status of a weak minority party. In the 1938 Farmer-Labor gubernatorial primary Benson's opponent (Hjalmar Petersen) accused him of corruption and pro-Communism. Although Benson won the primary by a narrow margin, the party was left irretrievably divided by the battle.

The Republicans nominated Harold Stassen in 1938. Stassen was a liberal Republican who promised to eliminate both corruption and Communism in government. In the primary and general election he was supported by liberal Minnesotans such as Edward J. Thye of Dakota County, who later succeeded Stassen as governor and served in the U.S. Senate. Thye's reasons for working for Stassen against Benson reveal some of the basic causes of the fall of the Farmer-Labor party.

Thye was president of a milk cooperative association in 1938. He was a political liberal and sympathized with the aspirations of labor, but a series of strikes by truck drivers in Minneapolis seriously affected the operation of the cooperative and raised doubts in his mind concerning the probity of the union officials. For example, the union insisted that the cooperative employ an extra Minneapolis truck driver on its runs into Minneapolis. Thye subsequently learned that the union was dominated by Communists and received Benson's support. Therefore, Thye decided that "something had to be done." The "something" proved to be support for Stassen against Benson.

Stassen won easily in 1938 over Elmer Benson and the Stassen Republicans assumed uninterrupted control over the state government from 1938 through 1954. Stassen was succeeded by Thye as governor and Thye by Luther Youngdahl in 1946, when Thye was elected to the U.S. Senate. Each promised liberal reform government, and Minnesota's voters were rewarded by a civil service system that largely cleansed state government of political corruption, and were additionally rewarded by well-financed welfare, conservation, and mental health programs. The end of liberal Republican control of Minnesota's government was engineered by Harry Truman when he appointed Luther Youngdahl to a federal district judgeship in the summer of 1951, leaving the Republican party leaderless.[16] The new Democratic-

[16] Michael Amrine, in *This Is Humphrey* (Garden City, N.Y.: Doubleday & Company, Inc., 1960), maintains that Humphrey was behind the Youngdahl appointment because of his desire to get Youngdahl out of the state and thus weaken the Republican party.

Farmer-Labor party took advantage of the leadership vacuum in Republican ranks and won the 1954 gubernatorial election after a brief two-year term in office for Youngdahl's Republican successor, C. Elmer Andersen. After 1954 the Democratic-Farmer-Labor party became the state's dominant party.

Political Organization in Minnesota

In 1962 most Minnesota politicians agreed that their state had "programmatic" parties. By this they meant that both parties were issue-oriented rather than primarily job-oriented. In other words, most active Minnesota politicians wanted to win elections in order to translate certain political programs into public policy. The first question, then, is why and how Minnesota politics became issue-oriented; second, the effect of this kind of politics on the opinions of the voters; and, third, the results of programmatic politics on the performance of state government.[17]

In discussions of political organization, a comment frequently heard in Minnesota was that the professors ran the Democratic party and the League of Women Voters dominated the Republicans. This was, of course, an exaggeration, but it successfully draws attention to the unusual professional backgrounds of Minnesota's political leaders. In the Democratic-Farmer-Labor party, an unusually large proportion of the U.S. congressmen and other party leaders were former professors, such as Hubert Humphrey, Eugene McCarthy, Representative John Blatnik, Mayor of Minneapolis Art Naftalin, and State Chairman George Farr. The Democrats also had a feminine contingent including National Committeewoman Geri Joseph; Eugenie Andersen, ambassador to Bulgaria; and Dorothy Jacobson, an assistant to Freeman and a former professor.

The leadership of the Republican party, on the other hand, tended to be matriarchal. Mrs. F. Peavey Heffelfinger, former national committeewoman; Mrs. Wright W. Brooks, former district chairman in Minneapolis; and Mrs. Russell Lund, Republican national committeewoman, were all extremely important personalities in the Republican party with the alleged ability to affect the nomination or defeat of Republican hopefuls. The Republicans also had college professors serving in positions of

[17] I am particularly indebted to Professor G. T. Mitau of Macalester College for the several hours during which he recounted the recent history of Minnesota politics for me, and to his very useful book, *Politics in Minnesota* (Minneapolis: University of Minnesota Press, 1960).

leadership, including Ralph Fjelstad of Carleton College, who was vice-chairman of the Republican party.

It was, perhaps, no exaggeration to say that the professors ran the Democratic-Farmer-Labor party, for Hubert Humphrey was Mr. Democrat in Minnesota. And although it did constitute an overstatement, it remained true that women, and particularly former members of the League of Women Voters, exercised an unusual degree of leadership in the Republican party. The question is why these people were in power in Minnesota rather than the more familiar political figure, such as a Mayor Daley of Chicago, a Frank McKinney of Indiana, or a Ray Bliss of Ohio.

A partial explanation for the presence of so many professors in Minnesota politics is the location of the University of Minnesota in Minneapolis and the impact on the parties of activist professors, including Hubert Humphrey and his followers in the graduate school. A strict civil service law also helps explain the prominence of issue-oriented professors and women in Minnesota politics. The civil service law was passed under Governor Stassen as a reaction to corruption in the 1930s during the Farmer-Labor period of power. According to George H. Mayer, spoils were the undoing of the Farmer-Labor party, for this diverted the party from issues and resulted in leadership passing from the hands of the party purists to professional spoilsmen who paid only lip-service to the Farmer-Labor program.[18] It should be added that before the Farmer-Labor party won control of state government in 1920, the Republican party organization also used spoils as an effective organizational tool.

After the Stassen civil service law, there was little reason for the job- or contract-seeker to spend time or money on politics. In the absence of the professional government job-hunter, the professors and the women moved in to fill the vacuum. Much of the new leadership came from these two groups because professors have a flexible time schedule and middle-class women have the spare time (combined with motivation) to devote to politics. Few businessmen can leave their enterprises frequently enough to provide a party with effective leadership, and besides, most businessmen regard politics as relatively unimportant in comparison with making the goods and providing the services which enable the society to survive (and, not-so-incidentally, making money). Professors, on the other hand, and particularly political science professors, can rationalize their political activity

[18] See Mayer, *The Political Career of Floyd B. Olson*, pp. 278–279.

in terms of the additional knowledge they secure which they can impart to their students. Similarly, women rationalize it in terms of making the world a better place for their families. In reality, though, politically active women are often engaged in a crusade for expanded political and economic power for women. Most women are not fully aware of this reason for their activities, but when questioned they sometimes half-laughingly, half-defiantly confess it.

Hubert Humphrey and Issue-Oriented Politics

Equally important for an understanding of Minnesota political organization is the process by which the issue-oriented political figures secured power and the means by which they maintained it. Power is a peculiarly slippery element in American politics for both the practitioner and the student. Some of the people who possess power are not fully aware of it, and others who think they are powerful are the executive assistants of the power elite. It should shock no one, then, that the voters are often confused concerning the loci of political power, for they not unnaturally accept the sincere protestations of the powerful of their disinterest in politics and the equally convinced and convincing claims to influence and power of the satraps. In Minnesota, however, the visible possessors of formal political power also exercised authority in practice. This is in contrast with a state such as Ohio where formal political power was vested in a governor, but the real power rested in a newspaper editor or publisher or bank president or all three.

Minnesotans generally conceded in 1963 that Hubert Humphrey was the most powerful figure in the Democratic-Farmer-Labor party. Most other prominent Democratic-Farmer-Labor leaders were associated with Humphrey and enjoyed their power largely or in part through him. Some of these were U.S. Senator Eugene McCarthy, Ambassador Eugenie Andersen, Mayor of Minneapolis Arthur Naftalin, former Governor and in 1963 Secretary of the U.S. Department of Agriculture Orville Freeman. Humphrey and the people around him obtained or seized control of the Democratic-Farmer-Labor party in 1948.

When the Farmer-Labor and Democratic parties joined forces in 1944, Humphrey was a political science instructor at Macalester College in St. Paul. The year before, 1943, he had lost the mayoralty election in Minneapolis. He was respected and liked by political and labor figures as a result of his handling of the campaign, and thereafter he was able to persuade leaders on both the Democratic and Farmer-Labor sides that political survival demanded a merger. He spoke both as a political scientist and as a practical politician. In addition, he had a most persuasive personality and was blessed by a peculiarly fortuitous set of circumstances for a merger: the losses to the Republicans after 1938 and the continued third-party status of the Democrats. Humphrey was generally conceded to be the most influential single individual in arranging the Democratic-Farmer-Labor merger.

The merger meant the joining of urban Irish and Polish Catholics and rural Scandinavian Lutherans. It also brought together some rather extreme left-wing elements from the Farmer-Labor party with relatively conservative middle-class Democrats. Humphrey and the people around him fancied themselves a middle ground between the two elements of the Democratic-Farmer-Labor party.

The left-wing elements obtained control of the Democratic-Farmer-Labor Association, which was the continuation of the old Socialist-oriented Farmer-Labor Association. The Humphrey, or right-wing, elements obtained control of the Democratic-Farmer-Labor state central committee, enjoying a three-to-one majority there largely because of the representation from the Minneapolis–St. Paul area.

The right-left division within Democratic-Farmer-Labor ranks was climaxed and terminated by the Henry Wallace Progressive candidacy in 1948. The left wing of the party, led by former Farmer-Labor Governor Elmer Benson, sought Democratic-Farmer-Labor convention endorsement of pro-Wallace candidates for governor, U.S. senator, and other statewide elective offices. In addition, they hoped to nominate Henry Wallace as the Democratic-Farmer-Labor candidate for President, thus freezing Truman out of Minnesota.[19]

The Humphrey-led right-wing forces dominated the convention by virtue of their control of the state central committee. From this vantage point they read the left-wingers out of the party and refused to seat pro-Wallace people in the convention. The pro-Wallace people then held a separate convention and

[19] This account of the 1948 left-right schism in the Democratic-Farmer-Labor party was obtained from interviews with Professor G. T. Mitau of Macalester College and from his article entitled "The Democratic-Farmer-Labor Party Schism of 1948," *Minnesota History*, vol. 34 (Spring 1955), p. 187.

endorsed candidates for the Democratic-Farmer-Labor primaries and nominated a slate of electors pledged to Wallace. Following their rump convention, they went to court and claimed that their convention was the true Democratic-Farmer-Labor conclave and that their presidential electors should be declared the Democratic-Farmer-Labor party's presidential electors, thereby making Wallace the party's presidential candidate. They based their claim on the refusal of the Democratic-Farmer-Labor convention to seat the left-wing delegates. The court denied their petition.

The Humphrey Liberals Gain Control of the Democratic-Farmer-Labor Party

The convention was the major test of left-right strength in the state and the Humphrey-led right wing emerged triumphant. The 1948 popular primary following the conventions was a second test of the power of the two factions with right- and left-wing candidates opposing one another for the Democratic-Farmer-Labor nominations for U.S. senator, governor, and other offices. The right wing won five of the seven contests and was victorious by a wide margin in the senatorial and gubernatorial contests. Hubert Humphrey defeated his left-wing opponent, James M. Shields, for the Senate nomination by 204,175 to 25,051 votes, and Charles Halsted, the Humphrey or right-wing candidate, received 80,901 votes to 37,004 for his left-wing opponent, Walter E. Johnson, in a contest for the gubernatorial nomination involving five candidates.

The pattern of the vote in the 1948 Democratic-Farmer-Labor primaries is interesting, and analysis of it is important for an understanding of subsequent developments in Minnesota politics. In the primary, Humphrey did least well percentagewise in the Scandinavian counties (always remembering that Humphrey led his left-wing opponent virtually everywhere in the state), which also tended to be the counties that supported the left-wing Farmer-Labor Governor Benson in the 1938 primary where the issues were Communism and corruption. On the other hand, Humphrey's percent vote tended to be largest in the more urban and more Catholic counties, as well as in the more Republican counties.[20] Therefore, in the 1948 primary the right wing or

---

[20] Simple coefficients of correlation also support the generalizations concerning the sources of Humphrey's voting strength and weakness in the 1948 primary. The negative correlation of Humphrey's percent vote by counties with percent Scandinavian is (—).56; with the 1962 percent

Humphrey wing of the Democratic-Farmer-Labor party drew much of its support from the Republican or conservative sections of the state as well as among Catholics. The left-wing candidates, on the other hand, enjoyed their most pronounced electoral success in the Scandinavian and Democratic-Farmer-Labor strongholds that were traditional left-wing centers of voting strength. In the general election Humphrey became the first Democratic-Farmer-Labor candidate to win major statewide elective office and Harry Truman also carried the state. Republicans won the governorship and the minor statewide elective offices, but the Democratic-Farmer-Labor party had made its first major inroad into Republican monopolization of elective office.

The Humphrey position was vindicated by the results of the 1948 general election. He, along with other Americans for Democratic Action right-wing liberals, had made the Democratic-Farmer-Labor party respectable in the eyes of middle-class property-owning Minnesotans. Humphrey and the Democratic-Farmer-Labor leadership in Minnesota were thereafter identified as occupying a middle-of-the-road position between Republican conservatives and left-wing farmer-laborites, socialists, and communists. Within Minnesota, the Democratic-Farmer-Labor leadership capitalized handsomely on their liberal anti-Communist position. Between 1948 and 1954 the Humphrey people consolidated their hold on the Democratic-Farmer-Labor party, and that party's proportion of the vote steadily increased until in 1954 Orville Freeman, a Humphrey liberal, won the governorship. After 1954 the domination of the party by the Humphrey forces was complete, as evidenced by the invariable electoral success of Humphrey-backed candidates in the Democratic-Farmer-Labor primaries.

The improved Democratic-Farmer-Labor leadership and the increase in the Democratic-Farmer-Labor vote were accompanied by the disintegration of Republican leadership in the state. After Harold Stassen's landslide victories in the 1938, 1940, and 1942 gubernatorial elections, the Republican party appeared to be resuming its accustomed role of providing the state with

---

Democratic-Farmer-Labor vote for governor it is (−).46; and with the 1938 percent vote for left-wing Farmer-Labor Governor Benson it is (−).53. On the other hand, there is a positive relationship between Humphrey's 1948 percent vote in the Democratic-Farmer-Labor primary and percent urban by counties (.22) and with percent Catholic (.15), as well as with percent Republican in the 1962 gubernatorial election (the other side of the correlation coin for the above negative relationship with percent Democratic).

political leadership. In 1942, however, Stassen went to war and subsequently left the state in order to seek the Presidency. Edward Thye, who succeeded Stassen, was elected to the U.S. Senate in 1946 and thereafter directed much of his attention to Washington. Luther Youngdahl followed Thye in the governorship and provided the Minnesota Republicans with the same kind of political leadership as they had enjoyed under Stassen and Thye. But in 1951 Youngdahl accepted a Democratic appointment to the federal district court. If, as rumored, Humphrey arranged the Youngdahl appointment to the federal bench in order to deprive the Republican party of leadership, it was a singularly successful piece of Machiavellian strategy. Thereafter, and through the 1962 election, the Republican party was without strong statewide leadership that could hold its several factions together.

In Minnesota, it was said in 1962 that there were two Republican parties. The first was centered in the state legislature and primarily in the person of Ray Dunn, a strongly conservative member of the Minnesota House of Representatives. Dunn and his fellow conservatives yearned for a Republican party in the image of Robert Taft. The Republican leadership outside the legislature searched for another liberal Republican in the image of Stassen or Youngdahl. Both formulas were tried by the Republicans but without much success. In 1958 a conservative Republican was nominated as the Republican candidate for governor, but he was overwhelmed by Freeman, who won by almost 200,000 votes. In other years liberal Republicans were nominated, and in 1960 Elmer L. Andersen won election as a liberal Republican. However, he disappointed the state and the Republican party in particular by his failure to grasp the reins of power firmly, and in 1962 the Democratic-Farmer-Labor party returned to power.

Political Change in Minnesota[21]

It is impossible to understand the 1960 political preferences of Minnesotans without some knowledge of the political history of the state. The modern political history of Minnesota begins with the election of 1918 and the permanent severance of much

---

[21] The measure of political change referred to herein is along a line of regression for each county of the state. Consequently, it is a product of all the gubernatorial elections, 1944–1962, and not just the first and last elections in the time series.

of the Scandinavian vote from the Republican party, which is a tale already told. The second important event was the election of Franklin Roosevelt in 1932. Franklin Roosevelt's liberal New Deal lent a new luster to the Democratic party for Farmer-Laborite Scandinavians. In 1932 and 1936 the Farmer-Labor party and Floyd Olson in particular supported the election of Franklin Roosevelt. Although the liberal Farmer-Laborites remained suspicious of the Catholic conservative Minnesota Democrats, the Roosevelt period served to make the party more palatable to them. Further, they developed the habit of voting Democratic in national elections, which helped make possible a marriage of the two parties.

After 1932 and the New Deal, the low-income Scandinavian grain farmers tended to vote Democratic in presidential elections while most Catholic Democrats remained associated with the party. The conservative Germans moved in a Republican direction as did higher-income dairy and livestock farmers.[22]

This indicates why it was possible to combine Minnesota's Democratic and Farmer-Labor parties in 1944. The principal element in the Farmer-Labor party (Scandinavian grain farmers) was already voting Democratic in national elections. Moreover, it was increasingly evident to both Democrats and

[22] Donald V. Webster, in a seminar paper at the University of Massachusetts, analyzed the political behavior of people in thirty-six rural-farm Minnesota counties in the presidential elections, 1932–1960. Nineteen of the counties had no urban population. The criteria by which the remaining seventeen counties were selected were counties more than 40 percent rural-farm and counties wherein the production per farm was more than $30,000 or which had an urban population of less than 25 percent. Webster found that fifteen of the thirty-six counties had given the Democratic candidate for President the majority of their vote in from six to eight elections, 1932–1960; seventeen in three to five elections, and four in zero to two elections. On the average, the fifteen most Democratic counties were the lowest income, largest percent Catholic (18.8), smallest percent German (5.6), and highest percent Scandinavian (17.7). In addition, all six of the predominantly grain counties were among the most Democratic fifteen counties, while three of the six "mixed" counties, two of the thirteen "livestock," and two of the eleven "dairy" counties were among the fifteen most Democratic counties. The most Republican counties, on average, were the highest income, smallest percent Catholic (15.7), largest percent German (8.6), and smallest percent Scandinavian (9.9). Not one of the Republican counties was a "grain" or "mixed" economy county. All were either livestock or dairy. All figures were 1960 except percent Catholic, which was a 1957 figure. The categories of Catholic and Scandinavian, by the way, are mutually exclusive, for the coefficient of correlation between the two variables is (−).51.

Farmer-Laborites that with the three-party division in the state the Republicans would remain in control of the state government. Finally, the more conservative elements in the Democratic party had deserted to the Republican banner, making the Democratic and Farmer-Labor parties more alike ideologically.

In the gubernatorial elections of 1938, 1940, and 1942, the political divisions of the state remained virtually unchanged. The Republican party won by a wide margin, the Farmer-Labor party was second in votes received, and the Democratic party lagged far behind as a weak third party. In the last three-party election in 1942, Harold Stassen (Republican) received 409,800 votes, Hjalmar Petersen (Farmer-Labor) 299,917 votes, and John D. Sullivan (Democrat) only 75,151 votes.

In 1944, largely through the efforts of Hubert Humphrey, a formal alliance of the two parties took place. In the 1944 election Democratic-Farmer-Labor candidates for statewide elective office appeared on the ballot for the first time. Edward J. Thye, the Republican candidate for governor, received 701,185 votes to 430,132 votes for Byron L. Allen, the Democratic-Farmer-Labor candidate. This defeat at the polls, however, did not completely still the merrymaking at Democratic-Farmer-Labor headquarters on election night, for the balloting indicated that the merger of the parties at the leadership level was also consummated at the level of the rank-and-file voters. By and large, the more liberal portion of the Farmer-Labor voters joined Democrats in casting their ballots for Democratic-Farmer-Labor candidates in 1944.[23]

The Farmer-Labor vote that followed its leadership into the Democratic party was by and large the left wing of the party, whereas those who moved into the Republican party or did not vote in 1944 were largely in the party's right wing. This is

[23] The coefficient of correlation between the percentage increase in the Democratic to Democratic-Farmer-Labor vote, 1942–1944, and the 1942 Farmer-Labor percentage vote was .59. The relationship of the percentage Democratic to Democratic-Farmer-Labor increase, 1942–1944, with percent Scandinavian, 1930, was .71. This means that Farmer-Labor voters tended to follow their leaders into the new Democratic-Farmer-Labor party, and that the liberal Scandinavian elements of the Farmer-Labor party were particularly prone to move into the new party. Evidence of the tendency of Democratic voters to remain in the Democratic-Farmer-Labor party is the .22 relationship of the 1944 percentage vote received by the Democratic-Farmer-Labor candidate for governor with the 1942 percent Democratic vote for governor. The relationship of the 1944 Democratic-Farmer-Labor vote with the 1942 Farmer-Labor vote was .48.

indicated by the avalanche of votes received by Democratic-Farmer-Labor candidates in 1944 from the same sections of the state that supported the left-wing Governor Benson in the 1938 Farmer-Labor gubernatorial primary. However, the 1944 Democratic-Farmer-Labor increases over the 1942 Democratic vote were much more modest in the strongholds of conservative Farmer-Laborites, such as Henrik Shipstead. Shipstead was a right-wing isolationist Farmer-Laborite before his affiliation with the Republican party in 1946, and much of his branch of the Farmer-Labor party transferred to the Republican party in 1944.[24]

In the years 1944–1962 there was a secular increase in the percentage vote received by the Democratic-Farmer-Labor party in every county of the state. The new party succeeded in erasing the Catholic image of the Democratic party in voters' minds and was equally successful in blurring the radical left-wing perception of the Farmer-Labor party. The result was an increase in voter strength that reached into every corner of the state and affected the political loyalties of almost every group of voters.

Reference to voting data indicates, however, that plus Democratic-Farmer-Labor change, 1944–1962, was most pronounced in the northwest Scandinavian rural-farm areas and in the low-income rural sections in central and western Minnesota. The percentage Democratic-Farmer-Labor increase was least pronounced in the urban sections of Minnesota. However, in terms of votes the increases in the cities were a significant contributing factor to Democratic-Farmer-Labor electoral success.[25]

[24] The bipolarization of liberal and conservative Farmer-Labor voters in 1944 is further confirmed by three coefficients of correlation. The simple correlation of the plus-Democratic to Democratic-Farmer-Labor change, 1942–1944, with the 1938 left-wing vote for Benson is .76. Secondly, the relationship between the 1942–1944 Democratic to Democratic-Farmer-Labor change and the 1946 vote for Shipstead in the Republican senatorial primary is (−).20. Thirdly, the relationship between the 1942–1944 Democratic to Democratic-Farmer-Labor change and the vote for Hubert Humphrey in the 1948 Democratic-Farmer-Labor primary when he opposed a left-wing candidate is (−).49.

[25] Multiple correlations provide statistical support for the generalization concerning the character of plus-Democratic-Farmer-Labor change, 1944–1962, in Minnesota. The multiple correlation (R) between Democratic-Farmer-Labor percentage-point change by counties in gubernatorial elections, 1944–1962, with percent rural-farm plus percent earning less than $3000, is .62.

Reasons for Political Change

The explanation for this pattern of political change has two parts. First, the Democratic and Farmer-Labor parties very nearly realized their full potential of urban votes in the 1930s. Labor organizations gave unreserved support to both the national Democratic party and to the state Farmer-Labor party. Most of this vote was left wing and followed the parties' leadership into the Democratic-Farmer-Labor party. In the rural-farm areas many Protestants were reluctant to enter the Democratic party. Further, some farmers had moved into the Republican party in 1938 because of disillusionment with the Farmer-Labor party, but returned to the Democratic-Farmer-Labor party in the 1950s out of disagreement with policies pursued by Secretary of Agriculture Ezra Taft Benson under President Eisenhower. The evidence that Catholics did not dominate the new Democratic-Farmer-Labor party, that it was ideologically moderate, and that its senators and representatives opposed Secretary of Agriculture Benson's farm program and supported high, rigid price supports, induced many low-income farmers to enter the Democratic-Farmer-Labor party.

In 1948 the Democrats and Farmer-Laborites realized the first fruit of their alliance when Truman and Humphrey carried the state. In 1954 Orville L. Freeman, the Democratic-Farmer-Labor gubernatorial candidate, won the governorship and was reelected in 1956 and 1958. In 1960 Kennedy carried Minnesota, but Freeman lost to Republican Elmer L. Andersen. But in 1962 the Democratic-Farmer-Labor party returned to power in the state when Karl F. Rolvaag, a long-time lieutenant governor, won by 91 votes in a disputed election.

It is useful to examine the 1960 presidential vote and the 1960 and 1962 gubernatorial vote in some detail, because they provide insights into the sources of Democratic and Republican strength in the state and may provide clues to the future political behavior of the people of the state. In 1960 John F. Kennedy carried Minnesota with 779,933 votes to 757,915 for Richard Nixon, a margin of 22,018 votes. In the same 1960 election, Orville Freeman was the Democratic-Farmer-Labor candidate for governor, and he lost to Elmer L. Andersen, the Republican candidate, by almost the same margin as Kennedy's plurality; that is, 22,879 votes.

Examination of the election results reveals, first, that there was a close relationship between the vote received by the vic-

torious Catholic Democratic presidential candidate, Kennedy, and
the unsuccessful Protestant Democratic-Farmer-Labor candidate
for governor, Orville Freeman. The coefficient of correlation
between their votes was .91, which conclusively demonstrates
that the two candidates tended to be strong or weak in the same
counties. On the other hand, the differences in their strength
seem largely attributable to the differential reactions of Catholics
and Scandinavian Lutherans to the two candidates.[26] In effect,
in 1960 the coalition between the Democratic and the Farmer-
Labor parties held together better for Kennedy than for Freeman. The difference in support was largely due to the failure of
the former Democrats to vote for Freeman, whereas the Farmer-
Labor side of the party supported both candidates.[27]

In 1962 the Democratic-Farmer-Labor party returned to
power in Minnesota, when Karl F. Rolvaag won by a very few
votes. The narrow Democratic victory in the 1962 gubernatorial
election resulted from improved support for the Democratic-
Farmer-Labor candidate from both sides of the coalition.[28] The
differences in the votes received by the three Democratic-Farmer-
Labor candidates would appear to be a result, first, of the support
Kennedy attracted from Catholics and old-line Democrats; second, the alienation of some Catholic and conservative Democratic
votes by Freeman because of his support of several strikes and
particularly his use of National Guardsmen to close packing-

[26] The relationship between Kennedy's vote and the proportion of Catholics
by counties is not nearly so close in Minnesota as in the other Midwest
states studied. However, a significant positive relationship did exist in the
1960 presidential election (.39), and it helps explain Kennedy's victory.
Kennedy also received some of the Lutheran Scandinavian vote, the coefficient of correlation of his vote with percent Scandinavians by counties
being .27. On the other hand, there was absolutely no relationship of Freeman's vote with percent Catholic by counties (.07). Freeman fared better
among Scandinavians than Kennedy (.47), but the difference was not of
the same dimension as the differential support provided by Catholic voters.
There is additional evidence that suggests that the Catholic vote for
Kennedy contributed to his victory. The simple correlation between the
percentage-point change in the Democratic vote by county, 1956–1960,
and the percentage Catholic by county is .81. The same operation using
the elections of 1948 and 1960 produced a simple correlation of .60.
[27] When a multiple correlation is run of Kennedy's 1960 vote by counties
with the 1942 percent Democratic plus the 1942 percent Farmer-Labor vote
for governor, the result is an R of .71. When the same operation is performed with Freeman's 1960 vote, the R is only .63.
[28] A multiple correlation of the 1962 Democratic-Farmer-Labor percent
vote for governor by counties with the 1942 Democratic plus-Farmer-Labor
votes results in an R of .72, slightly higher than Kennedy's.

house plants which attempted to operate in spite of the strike. In 1962 much of the old-line Democratic support returned to the Democratic-Farmer-Labor party and, in addition, Rolvaag received support among Farmer-Laborites because of his family's long identification with that party.[29] Finally, Rolvaag had friendly relations with Irish Catholic politicians from St. Paul. One observer described them as "the Irish Mafia."

The main problem of Minnesota's Democratic-Farmer-Labor party in the 1960s was to hold both ends of the coalition together. In the 1960 and 1962 gubernatorial elections, the side of the political marriage most likely to stray next door was the Democratic. The reason was the relative liberalism of the Democratic-Farmer-Labor party and the comparative conservatism of the 1942 Democrats. Given the conservative bias of the Democrats, it is not surprising that some found the Republican candidate attractive. In Minnesota, the Republican party in 1960 was a relatively moderate, middle-of-the-road party, and in most elections the choice was not between a reactionary and a liberal but between a middle-of-the-road Republican and a liberal.

On the other hand, the loyalty of the Farmer-Labor voters is understandable, for they had no viable alternative but to support the Democratic-Farmer-Labor candidates. The old Farmer-Labor party was to the left of the Democratic-Farmer-Labor party and its adherents had no candidate with a chance of winning to whom they could have turned if they were dissatisfied with the Democratic-Farmer-Labor candidate. Consequently, most of them swallowed their ideological and religious discomfort at Kennedy's candidacy and voted for him because of Nixon's right-wing political position. If they had had a meaningful alternative to the left of Kennedy, they might have deserted the Democratic-Farmer-Labor party in large numbers.

This discussion of the departures of groups allied to the Democratic-Farmer-Labor party from the party reservation should not obscure the fact that most of the voters of both parties were quite constant in their political loyalties in the 1960 and 1962 elections. The interrelationships of the votes cast by counties in the three elections were massive. In every case the coefficient of correlation was in excess of .90. This is as near to a one-to-one relationship as one finds in the social sciences, and is conclusive evidence that Minnesota had developed a strong

[29] Rolvaag's father wrote *Giants in the Earth*.

two-party system with the overwhelming majority of the voters associating themselves rather definitely with one of the two parties.

It is particularly safe to generalize with respect to party cohesion on the basis of the 1960 and 1962 elections because the strains on party allegiance were unusually pronounced. In the 1960 presidential election the Catholic German Republicans and the Lutheran Scandinavian Democrats were strongly tempted to vote on the basis of religious rather than political convictions. The fact that so many remained loyal to their political faith in the face of religious and ethnic prejudice is a striking testimonial to the hold both parties had on the affections of their adherents.

Political Opinions in Minnesota

Minnesota politics was sharply competitive beginning in 1918 with the creation of a Farmer-Labor party and continuing through 1962. In addition to its competitive complexion, the state's politics was distinguished by the programmatic orientation of its candidates and parties. According to the bulk of the nation's political scientists, the "democratic" competitive character of the state's politics should produce both an informed citizenry and a government responsive to the wishes of the citizenry and staffed by honest public servants. Political scientists are often scoffed at by cynics, but in this instance they seem close to the truth, although, as the following discussion indicates, the "truth" is much more cloudy than the bright white sometimes painted by the teacher.

In discussing the results of a sample survey taken of Minnesota's voters in 1958, Lou Harris commented:

> We are singularly struck by the fact that people who are concerned with mental hospitals are by and large keenly aware of what Governor Freeman has done to improve conditions. Much the same is the case with retarded children. It is unusual to find an electorate that has such a high degree of awareness of things having been done which directly relate to them and their families. We ran into some 13 families which had retarded children and felt they had been helped by the Governor's program. This high degree of "relating" of governmental programs with live and active need is indeed an accomplishment in the art of governing.[30]

The ability of many Minnesota (like Wisconsin's) voters to relate a candidate with specific governmental programs that

[30] Louis Harris and Associates, "A Study of the Election for Governor and United States Senator in Minnesota," September 1958, p. 28.

concerned them markedly differentiates Minnesota from Ohio. In Ohio, as will be seen in the next chapter, few voters were able to make the connection between a candidate's performance and services provided them by government. Although several variables enter into this difference between the states, such as different economies and different immigration patterns, the principal cleavage between the citizens of the two states was in their experience with government. Minnesotans had a long experience of demanding particular reforms from candidates and enjoying the return of effective governmental action to cope with the problem after the candidate's election. In Ohio the candidates have seldom discussed issues, and the voters have lost the ability to connect a candidate with performance. Basically, then, the difference between the states rests in the conditioning of the voters through variant experiences with the promises and performance of candidates and political parties.

Perhaps the informed flavor of the issue-conscious Minnesota voter can be captured through the following words of a forty-seven-year-old German Catholic wife of a mail carrier living in Minneapolis:

We need more schools more than anything. And we also need more mental hospitals real bad. Now I'd say that Ike [Republican] has done pretty good. But Humphrey [Democrat] has been excellent. Freeman's [Democrat] been good, too. He's worked hard for mental health, and, as I've said, that's important all right. Then our state taxes haven't gone up, so that's good. And Freeman's honest.

Senator Thye [Republican] has done an excellent job, too. He backed our pay raise for mail carriers. You see, he has the average person in mind. So I'll vote for Thye against McCarthy [Democrat]. He's done a good job. And has a bit of experience behind him. He writes a beautiful letter. Now, McCarthy seems honest and he's interested in the good of the state and the government. And he's a Catholic, which means something to me. Still and all, Thye's been too good to us to change.

I'll vote to keep Freeman in as Governor, too. He's done a pretty good job. And he's a good family man, intelligent with a wonderful education. He seems to know politics pretty good. I don't know anything about MacKinnon [Republican].

Now old age security must be raised. They should make some sort of low-cost housing arrangements for them. Like having the ground floor for the very old.

The only thing that could make me change my vote on Thye is if I heard that McCarthy was being discriminated against because he's a Catholic. That would be a terrible thing.[31]

31 *Ibid.*, p. 12.

Two features of the interview stand out: the woman's ability to identify candidates with particular governmental actions, and her non-partisanship. She was obviously not party-oriented at all, supporting Republicans Eisenhower and Thye and Democrats Freeman and Humphrey. For her, the performance and personality of the candidate were more important than party membership.

This candidate- rather than party-oriented turn of the Minnesota voter's mind was one of the interesting features of Minnesota political opinion uncovered by the Harris pollsters. Harris observed:

> To a degree, the shifts of tides in Minnesota political fortunes have been according to political party dominance. Yet the state has been singularly affected by the impact of personalities. The farm vote in the state is up for grabs in each election and Minnesota's voters have demonstrated quite clearly their voting independence.[32]

It is hardly surprising that a portion of Minnesota's voters were inattentive to party labels and tended to fasten on the candidate and his personality. In the space of thirty years, the people of the state had watched, applauded, and voted for Floyd Olson, a Farmer-Labor governor; Harold Stassen, a Republican governor; and Hubert Humphrey, a Democratic-Farmer-Labor U.S. senator. Each of these leaders demonstrated a quick sensitivity to the needs of the people and responded with appropriate governmental programs. Many voters concluded, whether consciously or not, that the key to performance in office was the candidate and his program and personality rather than his party affiliation. However, it remains true that in 1960 and 1962 most Minnesotans voted according to party rather than personality or religion.

It should not be concluded from the evidence so far presented that the genius of Minnesotans has magically wrought the ideal citizen voter. There were dark and irrational sides to some Minnesotans' opinions which reflected religious, ethnic, and other biases that had little relation to the objective political world in which they lived. For example, one resident of Goodhue County said:

> I do feel strongly about a man's religion in running for important office. Around here, we Swedish Lutherans feel we want Protestants for high office. For myself, I don't want to see the Catholics take over.

[32] *Ibid.*, pp. 3–4.

Feeling is real high. I know Senator Thye and Governor Freeman are Protestants, and I'm for them. I just don't know what McCarthy's religion would be.[33]

On the other hand, one Irish Catholic housewife from DeGraff made the following observations:

There should be some way of collecting money from people on old age assistance. I own some property and we rent to some of those people. There is no way of getting to their government checks to collect the rent. Then there should be a law against strikes. These unions are nothing but a bunch of Communists. This grain strike should be outlawed. If they can't clean themselves up then we should have strict legislation. I'm also against Freeman's unemployment compensation extension. He has made crooks out of a lot of people who would have found work otherwise. Freeman has been radical with his spending program and he says he's cutting taxes; he really hasn't if you look closely and examine it.

Now Thye doesn't do enough or he keeps too quiet about what he does do. So I'm for that wonderful Irishman, McCarthy. He's a wonderful man, you know. I hate to vote Democratic, but I think he's just what we need. Thye has some goodness and dignity in him. But he's really getting stale from being there too long. McCarthy is a very intelligent conservative. It's too bad he's not a Republican, but he has my vote. The only thing I hold against him is the crowd of Democrats he's surrounded by.

I never heard of this other man, but I wouldn't vote for Freeman. I can't stand the man, period.

A man's religion won't make any difference to me, but any Irishman named McCarthy will.[34]

Minnesota's voters, then, did not differ markedly from the crowd at the neighborhood bar or the group at the League of Women Voters meeting. Some were issue-oriented; some were influenced by their religious affiliation or wealth or lack thereof or ethnic affiliation; some were personality-oriented. The Minnesotans deviated from the norm only in the relative number of them who had the ability to identify the candidate whose programs or actions in office served their particular interests.

Governor Freeman, for example, concentrated on the problem of reckless driving while in office, cracking down particularly on reckless teen-age drivers. In his 1958 poll, Harris found that 11 percent of Freeman's voters were concerned with reckless driving, whereas only 5 percent of MacKinnon's supporters mentioned the issue. On the other hand, Governor Freeman sup-

[33] *Ibid.*, p. 10.
[34] *Ibid.*, p. 19.

ported generous education, welfare, and conservation programs which were expensive. Consequently, MacKinnon, his conservative Republican opponent, made a major issue of spending and taxes. Harris found that 71 percent of the voters for MacKinnon, compared to 47 percent of Freeman's backers, mentioned state taxes as a problem that bothered them. The farmers demonstrated a similar political sophistication. In 1958, no fewer than 39 percent of conservative MacKinnon's backers, compared to 18 percent of liberal Freeman's, wanted to cut price supports, whereas 35 percent of those planning to vote for Freeman wanted increased price supports, compared to 14 percent of those for MacKinnon.

The way in which issues, candidate appeal, and group affiliation all affect voting behavior may be seen by turning to Table 4.1. The table gives the percent of a sample of Minnesota's voters who supported liberal Protestant Democrat Orville Freeman for governor and liberal Catholic Democrat Eugene McCarthy, who hailed from St. Paul, for U.S. senator. It would appear from the evidence contained in the table that each of the variables listed had an affect on the preferences of the people polled.

According to the Harris poll, women were more likely than men to vote for Freeman. On the other hand, women were much less likely to support McCarthy than men, possibly because religion is a more salient concern for women than men. By age groups, there is a stepladder effect in Freeman's support, with 71 percent of the younger voters, 50 percent of the middle-aged, and 48 percent of the oldest for Freeman. In McCarthy's case, though, the stepladder collapses in the center with only 47 percent of both the youngsters and oldsters for McCarthy, while 57 percent of the middle-aged registered their intent to vote for him. There was a stairstep relationship of income level with intent to vote for both Freeman and McCarthy. The poor were most likely to vote for Freeman and McCarthy, middle-income people next most likely, and the well-to-do were squarely in the Republican camp. McCarthy's vote was behind Freeman's among the poor and middle-income groups, but led Freeman among the well-to-do. Speculation is fruitless here, unless name association had some affect on wealthy voters.

St. Paul (Ramsey County) led all other counties in the support its people gave to both Democratic candidates. St. Paul was Catholic, traditionally Democratic, and the district represented by McCarthy in the U.S. House of Representatives. The West Central counties were almost as enthusiastically for Freeman

Table 4.1

PERCENT OF MINNESOTANS FOR PROTESTANT LIBERAL DEMOCRAT FREEMAN AND CATHOLIC LIBERAL DEMOCRAT McCARTHY BY VARIOUS GROUPS AND STATE, SEPTEMBER 1958

AREA	PERCENT FOR FREEMAN	PERCENT FOR MC CARTHY
State	58	50
Men	55	54
Women	61	46
Age Groups		
21–34	71	47
34–49	58	57
50 and over	48	47
Income Level		
Upper middle	36	41
Lower middle	62	50
Lowest 20%	71	60
Area of State		
Hennepin County (Minneapolis)	57	49
Ramsey County (St. Paul)	65	67
Southeastern counties	52	45
South Central counties	60	52
West Central counties	64	41
Rest of State	49	44
Religion		
Protestant	53	40
Catholic	69	70
Trade union workers	68	66
Farmers	64	49
Ethnic Groups		
Swedish	52	38
Norwegian	64	42
Irish	56	57
German	58	58

Source: Louis Harris and Associates, "A Study of the Election for Governor and United States Senator in Minnesota," September 1958, p. 53.

(64 percent) as St. Paul (65 percent). But the same West Central counties ranked last among the six designated areas of the state in their support for McCarthy (41 percent). The West Central counties were Scandinavian Lutheran centers and a

traditional stronghold of the Farmer-Labor party. It would seem that in 1958 many of the old Farmer-Laborites were reluctant to vote for a Catholic Democrat. The statistics on the vote by religious and ethnic groups confirms this observation. Catholics were overwhelmingly for Freeman (69 percent) and even more enthusiastic about McCarthy (70 percent), while a majority of Protestants (53 percent) intended to vote for Freeman, but only 40 percent supported McCarthy. Among ethnic groups, the Norwegian Lutherans were the strongest backers of Freeman (64 percent), while the Irish Catholics were McCarthy's most faithful followers (57 percent).

The reader should not conclude from the data in Table 4.1 that Protestants were necessarily more affected by their religion in casting their votes than Catholics. On the surface, this would appear to be the case, for Catholics divided in about the same proportions in their support for Protestant Freeman and Catholic McCarthy, while Protestants were much less likely to vote for Catholic McCarthy than for their fellow Protestant, Freeman. However, it should be remembered that Freeman was a popular incumbent governor who was well known throughout the state, and that his opponent, MacKinnon, was conservative and virtually unknown. On the other hand, McCarthy was an obscure U.S. representative from St. Paul who was virtually unknown outside the city limits, whereas his opponent, Thye, was a well-known, popular, Scandinavian, liberal U.S. senator. Under these circumstances, Freeman's lead over McCarthy was predictable. The only surprise is that McCarthy outdistanced Freeman among Catholics.

Finally, trade union members and farmers were both strongly on Freeman's side. Trade union members were almost equally pro-McCarthy, but only 49 percent of the farmers expressed their intention to vote for McCarthy. One reason for the difference in the support for McCarthy between farmers and trade union members is that many union members were Catholics and residents of St. Paul, McCarthy's home, while most of the farmers were Protestants, and Senator Thye was a fellow Lutheran farmer.

Thus, political opinions and resultant political behavior in Minnesota were a product of a very complex mixture of interrelated and interacting variables. In 1958 the person most likely to vote for Freeman was an impoverished young woman who lived in St. Paul, attended the Catholic church, and belonged to a trade union. It would be unlikely, but it would help if she were

Norwegian. On the other hand, the person most inclined to vote for McCarthy would have been a low-income, middle-aged Irishman with his home in St. Paul. He should also have belonged to the Catholic church and a trade union.

In spite of the complexity of Minnesota politics, certain facts come through rather clearly. These facts include the history of issue-oriented politics in the state and, consequently, a voting public which was better attuned to the performance of its candidates than in most states. In addition, the leadership of the parties was seen to be issue-oriented, partially because of the absence of patronage in the state. The question to which we turn at this point is whether the issue-orientation of its political leadership and the voting public has had a measurable impact upon the performance of government.

Government's Performance in Minnesota

The data indicate that issues in Minnesota politics have indeed resulted in relatively high levels of expenditures and taxes. Minnesota spends more and taxes more than most other states. In the fields of mental health, welfare, and education, in particular, the state ranks among the leaders in the nation.

Before reciting some comparative statistics, it should be noted that it is difficult to compare Minnesota with other states relative to two-party competition. The reason is that state law forbids party designations on the ballot for candidates for the state legislature; consequently, it was formally a non-partisan legislature. As no measure of two-party competition in a state can be called complete without including state legislatures, it was impossible to construct a score for Minnesota that would be comparable to other states. However, it can be noted that the divisions between the two parties in the gubernatorial elections have been quite close since World War II, and the trend has been in the direction of an ever-narrower division. In 1960 and 1962 the victorious candidates for governor won by extremely narrow margins.

In the state legislature, although there were no party divisions, there was a liberal-conservative division. In each session of the legislature, liberals and conservatives canvassed and selected candidates for leadership posts in the House and Senate. After the non-partisan legislature was created in 1913, the conservatives controlled the Senate in every session. The conservatives generally controlled the House until the period of Democratic-

Farmer-Labor victories in the 1950s. Table 4.2 reveals that the conservatives dominated the state Senate by nearly two-to-one majorities in every session, 1957–1963. In the House of Representatives, however, the liberals had a majority in 1957, 1959, and 1961, but the conservatives regained control in 1963.

The conservative caucus in the legislature followed the philosophy its name demanded, and was largely independent of the party label of the incumbent governor. It opposed the program of Farmer-Labor Governors Olson and Benson, Republican Governors Stassen, Thye, and Youngdahl, and those of Democratic Governors Freeman and Rolvaag with non-partisan vigor. An unanticipated result, according to Charles Adrian in his unpublished study of Minnesota's non-partisan legislature, has

Table 4.2

LIBERAL-CONSERVATIVE   DIVISION   IN   MINNESOTA   STATE LEGISLATURE

	1957	1959	1961	1963
House				
Conservatives	63	59	58	80
Liberals	71	72	73	54
Independent	—	—	—	1
Senate				
Conservatives	48	43	43	43
Liberals	19	24	24	24

been a shift of leadership and power from the legislature to the governor. The governor of Minnesota proposes and the legislature approves or vetoes. Consequently, the legislature has had no program of its own save opposition. In this leadership vacuum, the governor preempted representation of the interests of the people. Therefore, the legislature frequently found itself in the painful position of opposing the will of the voters of their districts. Consequently, they have usually yielded when the governor applied sufficient pressure.

In the years both before and following World War II, Minnesota had an extraordinarily issue-oriented and competitive politics. The result was the initiation by state and local governments of extremely generous programs, particularly in those fields where the effect of the program was to reallocate goods and opportunities. The high level of expenditures commands attention because Minnesota was not a wealthy state. In 1960 it ranked twenty-fifth among the states in per-capita personal income ($2074 per person).

In June of 1960 Minnesota ranked seventh among the states in average payments for general assistance ($72.82 average per recipient); seventh in old age assistance ($88.73); fifth in aid to dependent children ($45.31); and ninth in aid to the blind ($95.33). Minnesota's education program was also well financed, and it was therefore an extremely literate state. In 1959–1960 it ranked twelfth in per-pupil expenditures in average daily attendance ($404 per pupil) and eighth in literacy, with only 1.5 percent of its population fourteen years of age and over unable to read and write.

The dividends to the state and the nation of its ambitious state welfare and education program included a reasonably healthy and literate population. The best available measure of this return to state and nation is the percent of Selective Service registrants disqualified by the mental test. In 1958 Minnesota ranked eighth on the happy end of the rejection scale. By way of comparison, only 5.8 percent of Minnesota's Selective Service registrants failed the mental test, compared to 58.5 percent in South Carolina, 16.0 percent in Illinois, 10.9 percent in Ohio, 10.3 percent in Indiana, and 33.4 percent in Kentucky.

The Minnesota taxpayer's pocketbook suffers as a consequence of the expenditures. In terms of effort, Minnesota ranked twenty-first in the nation in fiscal year 1961. During that fiscal year, Minnesotans paid $54.43 in state taxes for every $1000 of personal income. Ohio, Indiana, and Illinois ranked among the last eight states by this measure of effort.[35]

In summary, Minnesota's political leadership, political opinions, political competition, and governmental programs all make a logical pattern. The state has a history of issue-oriented politics, originating in the protests of farmers and small businessmen against exploitation by big business. The voters found that political protest paid, for when they demanded action their candidates generally provided programs designed to erase the reasons for their grievances.

In 1944 the division in the state between liberals and con-

---

[35] The eight bottom states in state taxes per $1000 of income, 1961, were Indiana, Ohio, Missouri, Connecticut, New Hampshire, Illinois, Nebraska, and New Jersey.

servatives was formalized in the traditional two-party form. The liberals captured the Democratic party in 1944 because it was an empty shell—a weak third party trailing far behind the Republican and Farmer-Labor parties. The Democratic-Farmer-Labor party obtained power in 1954, partially because of its success in persuading old Farmer-Laborites that the new party was genuinely liberal and partially by convincing moderates that it was not a radical Communist or Socialist party.

The result is apparent in the expenditure statistics for the state. Programs in welfare and education were generally in the top quartile of all the states in dollars spent, and the generous expenditures occurred in a state that ranked only twenty-fifth in per-capita income.

The payoff, in part, has been a largely literate and healthy population. Conservatives fear that another payoff will be the loss of industry to low-tax, cheap-labor states.

Summary and Conclusions

Perhaps the most interesting finding concerning Minnesota politics is that place of residence had little influence on the vote in 1960 and 1962. There was no significant relationship between percent urban and percent rural-farm and the Democratic or Republican vote in 1960 and 1962. This means, of course, that a person in the city was almost as likely to vote Republican (or Democratic) as the voter on the farm.

This finding was surprising because most students of politics are accustomed to equating an issue-oriented vote with a rural-urban division of the vote. Supposedly, the urban voter is concerned with smoke abatement, urban redevelopment, civil rights, and unemployment, and the farmer has no interest or concern with these issues. Consequently, so the theory goes, the urban voter casts his ballot for the liberal candidate who promises to use government to help solve such problems, whereas the farmer votes for the conservative who discounts the importance of the issues emphasized by the liberal.

In Minnesota, political divisions were not along urban-rural lines. Rather, they tended to follow ethnic, occupational, and income lines. For example, the Scandinavian low-income grain farmer was most likely to vote Democratic, whereas the Yankee or German high-income dairy or livestock farmer voted Republican. Just which of the variables was most important in determining voting behavior is difficult to determine, for they are intertwined. However, it would seem that the ethnic variable is very important, because when income and occupation are held constant, the Scandinavians emerge as the more Democratic of the groups.

The political future in Minnesota almost certainly contains continued intense two-party competition. In the period after the 1944 marriage of the Democratic and Farmer-Labor parties, the state's farmers tended to shift in fairly massive fashion to the new Democratic-Farmer-Labor party. The Democratic-Farmer-Labor party also enjoyed political gains over the 1944–1962 period in the cities, but they were small, percentagewise, in comparison with the rural-farm increase.

Figure 4.3 demonstrates graphically the vote payoff of the trends in Minnesota politics, 1944–1962. The figure reveals that the Republican candidates for governor won in each of the 1944–1952 elections, largely because of the substantial Republican pluralities registered by the nonmetropolitan portions of the state. In 1954, however, the Republican margin in the less urban parts of the state dropped from 191,000 to 10,000, while in the cities (Minneapolis–St. Paul and Duluth metropolitan areas) the Democratic margin increased from 31,000 to 79,000 votes. After 1954 the secular trend was for the Democratic margins in the cities to fall, which was balanced by improved Democratic fortunes outside the metropolitan areas. Finally, in 1962 the Democratic plurality out of Minneapolis–St. Paul and Duluth was less than in 1952, when the Republicans carried the state by 161,000 votes. However, because of the improved Democratic vote in nonmetropolitan Minnesota, the Democrats carried the state by 91 votes.

The indication, then, is that the Republican party has an opportunity to make inroads into Democratic-Farmer-Labor strength in the cities. The diminishing Democratic strength in the urban areas of other Midwest states, 1936–1960, indicates that there is some common factor at work in urban localities which is pushing voters toward the Republican party. Part of the reason, without a doubt, is the increase in home ownership in the cities with an attendant sharpening concern with taxes, an issue on which liberal Democrats are vulnerable to Republican charges of waste and extravagance with public funds.

In Minnesota, the urban vote is not so decisive as in some other states. The "bread-and-butter state" remained in 1960 a rural-oriented place. The proportion of Minnesota's 3,413,864 people who lived in urban areas was 62 percent in 1960, but the

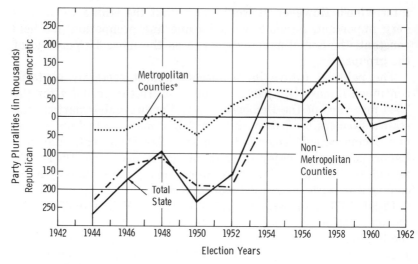

* Anoka, Dakota, Hennepin, Ramsey, St. Louis Counties

FIGURE 4.3   MINNESOTA VOTING TRENDS BY SECTIONS in gubernatorial elections, 1944—1962

Explanatory Note: The graph is a visual aid in appreciating the dimensions of Democratic-Farmer-Labor (DFL) vote gains in Minnesota's gubernatorial elections, 1944–1962, and the sources of the gains as between the cities and the countryside. The bottom half of the graph indicates Republican pluralities, and the top half DFL pluralities. The solid line traces the pluralities received by Republican and DFL candidates. It shows that the Republicans carried the state by margins ranging from about 95,000 to 270,000 in the elections from 1944 through 1952. In 1954 the DFL candidate (Freeman) won by 65,000 votes, and the DFL party won three of the four elections from 1954 to 1962. The line with alternating dashes and dots traces party pluralities in the state's nonmetropolitan counties. The improvement of the DFL vote in the less urban counties, 1944–1962, is staggering. In 1944, the Republican gubernatorial candidate won by 235,000 votes, and by the 1954–1962 period the nonmetropolitan counties were dividing their votes almost evenly between the parties. The party pluralities registered by the "metropolitan counties" is traced by the dotted line. The metropolitan vote fluctuated less over the period than the nonmetropolitan vote, but the DFL margins tended to increase there too over the period. In fact, it was the metropolitan counties that provided DFL candidates with their victory margins in 1954, 1956, and 1962.

state remained a predominantly food-growing or food-processing center. Consequently, the Republican party faced the problem of increasing its attractiveness to Minnesota's farmers. The problem may be insoluble for Republicans, for the national Republican party seemed unable or unwilling to develop a program designed to satisfy Minnesota farmers.

The Minnesota Republican dilemma represented a national

Republican opportunity, for the Democratic farm program was not popular with urban people even in Minnesota. For example, when Lou Harris polled Minnesotans in 1958, he found that 26 percent of the population favored high price supports and 26 percent opposed them. But he also found that the issue which worried Minnesotans most was high prices, and many urban voters made the obvious connection between high prices and high price supports.

Despite the trends, the future holds little promise for immediate dramatic Republican gains. Polls taken by the *Minneapolis Tribune* indicated that most of the state's voters identified their interest with the Democratic-Farmer-Labor party. Even in the absence of poll results, the fact that there were two Democratic-Farmer-Labor senators, and a Democratic-Farmer-Labor governor in 1962 and 1964 testified to that party's popularity. However, the division between the two parties remained so narrow that relatively minor differences between the candidates on issues or in their personalities or ethnic or religious associations often meant the difference between victory or defeat for a party.

Part 2

The Job-Oriented States: Ohio, Indiana, and Illinois

In the preceding discussion of three issue-oriented, two-party states, it was found that a variety of variables contributed to the emergence of programmatic politics, including: (1) strict civil service systems which very nearly eliminated political patronage at both the state and city levels; (2) the reduction of one party to an empty shell by virtue of repeated defeats at the polls; (3) the existence of well-organized interest groups in the society with both the will and the nerve to seize control of the moribund party; and (4) the division of the electorate between the two major parties along lines related to mid-twentieth-century political, economic, and social problems.

Attention turns in the following three chapters to states where some or all of the conditions for programmatic politics are absent. The politics of Ohio, Indiana, and Illinois remain fastened to the traditional job-oriented mold. The distinguishing characteristic of job-oriented politics is that most of the people who participate in politics on a day-to-day basis do so out of a desire for jobs or contracts rather than because of a concern for public policy. In political parlance, the result is election battles between the "ins" and the "outs." The "ins" are the people who have the jobs and the contracts and want to keep them. The "outs" are the lean and hungry individuals who want the jobs and contracts. The interest groups operate outside the parties, for they are concerned with issues rather than jobs. In the political campaigns, the job-oriented politicians use the issues as means of securing the support of interest groups and through them the votes to win the jobs and contracts.

In examining the politics of Ohio, Indiana, and Illinois, an effort will be made to assess the advantages and the disadvantages of job-oriented politics as well as the social and institutional factors responsible for the persistence of traditional political forms. Each chapter contains a description of the operation of the political system, an attempt to understand the social and economic forces shaping the political system, and an analysis of the impact of job-oriented parties on the performance of government and on the society at large.

Chapter 5

Issueless Politics
in Ohio

Ohio's politics cannot be understood without an appreciation of the generalized ignorance of and indifference to government and politics on the part of Ohio's citizenry in the 1960s. Louis Harris, the Kennedy pollster, noted in "A Study of Issues and Candidates in Ohio" in 1958 that there was "an almost complete lack of associating economic self-interest and the real problems in people's lives with their vote for state-wide offices in Ohio." As we shall see in our discussion of Ohio politics, there were several reasons for the failure of many of Ohio's voters to cast their ballots in terms of self-interest. However, the immediate cause was ignorance, ignorance born of indifference. And the indifference of Ohio's voters toward politics and government was a product of the history, culture, and power structure of the state.

Why were Ohioans indifferent to and ignorant of their state politics? In part, the answer resided in Republican State Chairman Ray Bliss's prescription for Republican victories in Ohio politics. The prescription read: "Keep issues out of campaigns." The other part of the answer resided in Democratic disorganization and consequent inability or unwillingness to insert issues into the campaigns.

Thus, the reason Ohioans were indifferent to state politics was that it was boring to them. The political races were often pointless contests of personalities, devoid of meaningful issues. Consequently, the reason Ohioans did not "associate the everyday problems in their lives" with their votes was that in fact there had rarely been any visible association between the two variables.

Now let us look, first, at the history of Ohio politics and then at the organization of the two parties, in an effort to determine how and why the Republican party kept issues out of elections and why the Democratic party was unable or unwilling to insert them into the elections. Then we shall look at the effect of issue-less politics on the voter and the welfare of the state.

Ohio's Political History

Ohioans were inclined to laugh when they read of the tradition-bound vote cast by residents of the South, for they took pride in their state's reputation for lively two-party competition wherein the "best" man won. However, analysis of the sources of strength for Ohio's political parties indicated that Ohioans, like lesser mortals in Kentucky and Mississippi, were influenced in casting their mid-twentieth-century vote by the battles of Bull Run and Gettysburg.[1] In addition, Woodrow Wilson's war with Germany and Franklin Roosevelt's Works Progress Administration (WPA), National Labor Relations Board (NLRB), and Agricultural Adjustment Administration (AAA) exerted an influence, albeit unconscious and invisible, on the Ohio voter's choice of candidates, as the following description of the sources of Republican and Democratic votes in the 1960s reveals (see Figures 5.1 and 5.2).

A very substantial proportion of the Republican vote, 1940–1960, was cast by residents of counties within the ancient and all-but-forgotten boundaries of the Virginia Military District, or the Ohio Company, Seven Ranges, and Western Reserve Areas.[2] Each of the areas was predominantly settled by Whig

---

[1] The study by Thomas A. Flinn, "The Outline of Ohio's Politics," *Western Political Quarterly*, vol. 13 (1960), p. 702, was very helpful in the following discussion of the origins of Ohio's two-party division.

[2] The Virginia Military District was located in the southwestern part of the state between the little Miami and Scioto Rivers and extended from the Ohio River on the south to Hardin and Marion Counties on the north. In all, twenty counties were included in whole or in part within the boundaries of the District and ten of them remained Republican strongholds in 1960. Virginia set aside the District to provide bounties for her Revolutionary soldiers. Consequently, many of the settlers entering the area originated from Kentucky and Virginia and approached the District along the Wilderness Road. They tended to be persons who had been displaced by slave labor and the planter and thus were "the poorer, more democratic, nonslaveholding class of the South. . . . Many of them were strongly opposed to slavery and all were interested in bettering their own economic condition." Further, the Southerners who entered the Virginia Military

partisans, and their sons and daughters, grandsons and granddaughters, great grandsons and great granddaughters tended to vote Republican thereafter. In sum, more than half of Ohio's regularly Republican counties (28 of 54 counties) in 1960 could trace their political ancestry back to the Civil War and beyond. The devotion of their citizens to Republican principles in 1960 was founded in their settlement by Whigs from Kentucky and New England. Most events in the intervening decades served to confirm their descendants in their inherited Whig and Republican predilections. These events ranged from Lincoln's successful war to save the Union through McKinley's crusade against

---

District largely emigrated from Whig areas in Kentucky. Thus, even though the area was settled by Southerners, it was a traditional Whig and Republican stronghold and remained in the 1960s one of the centers of Ohio Republican strength.

The second section which was Whig before 1856 and remained Republican thereafter is the area in southwestern Ohio purchased by the Ohio Land Company and which included within its boundaries, in whole or in part, Washington, Morgan, Athens, Meigs, and Gallia Counties. Four of the five counties remained bulwarks of the Republican party in 1960. The Republican bias of the people was rooted in the section's settlement by New Englanders who were Whig partisans on their arrival and were ardent abolitionists at the time of the Civil War. Nothing happened after 1856 to shake their political faith.

The third center of traditional Republican strength was in the "Seven Ranges," which was "the first land surveyed by Congress in the Northwest Territory . . . [and] was settled largely by Germans and Scotch-Irish from Pennsylvania and Virginia." The Seven Ranges comprised an area north of the Ohio Company purchase, including within its boundaries Jefferson, Carroll, Harrison, Guernsey, Noble, Belmont, and Monroe Counties. Four of the seven counties remained strongly Republican in 1960. However, the area was traditionally marginal politically because of the mixture of population elements and industrialization.

The fourth section of traditional Republican strength was the Western Reserve in northeastern Ohio. It included twelve counties within its borders, ranging along Lake Erie from Erie and Huron Counties on the west to the Pennsylvania border on the east. The area was settled by New Englanders and was the center of abolitionist agitation at the time of the Civil War. However, only three of the twelve Western Reserve counties could be classified as reliably Republican in 1960. The erosion of Republican dominance was caused by the widespread urbanization and accompanying industrialization of the section.

See George H. Porter, *Ohio Politics during the Civil War Period* ("Columbia University Studies in History, Economics, and Public Law," vol. 40 [New York: Columbia University Press, 1911]), pp. 15, 16; and Robert E. Chaddock, *Ohio before 1850* ("Columbia University Studies in History, Economics, and Public Law," vol. 31 [New York: Columbia University Press, 1908]), p. 33.

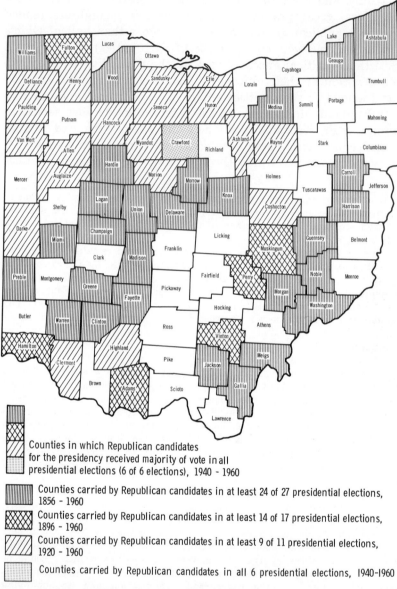

Counties in which Republican candidates
for the presidency received majority of vote in all
presidential elections (6 of 6 elections), 1940 - 1960

Counties carried by Republican candidates in at least 24 of 27 presidential elections,
1856 - 1960

Counties carried by Republican candidates in at least 14 of 17 presidential elections,
1896 - 1960

Counties carried by Republican candidates in at least 9 of 11 presidential elections,
1920 - 1960

Counties carried by Republican candidates in all 6 presidential elections, 1940-1960

FIGURE 5.1   OHIO'S REPUBLICAN COUNTIES in presidential elections,
1940–1960, by point in time at which majority of county's vote was committed to Republican candidates

Explanatory Note for Figures 5.1 and 5.2: The two maps are designed to
demonstrate the relationship between Republican voting strength in Ohio
and the reactions of the population to the Civil War, the effect on the

▦ Counties in which Republican gubernatorial candidate received a plurality of the vote in 1867

▨ Counties 20 percent or more rural farm, 1960 (excluding above)

▦ Counties in which 2200 or more people born in Germany resided in 1870 (excluding above)

FIGURE 5.2 OHIO'S REPUBLICAN VOTERS: Civil War Republicans, farmers, and Germans

farmers' vote and the vote of Americans of German ancestry of policies of Democratic Presidents after the Civil War.

Figure 5.1 shows that 54 of Ohio's 88 counties went Republican in every presidential election, 1940–1960, leaving only 34 counties in which a plurality of the vote went to the Democratic presidential candidate in at least one of the 6 elections. Perhaps the most interesting fact brought out by Figure 5.1 is that 28 of the 54 one-sidedly Republican counties, 1940–1960, have also been Republican strongholds since 1856. Comparison of Figures 5.1 and 5.2 reveals that every county but one that was Republican in presidential elections, 1856–1960, also was a Republican stronghold in the 1867 gubernatorial election. Comparison of the two maps also shows that the counties settled by Germans were also the counties that tended to move into the Republican camp in 1920 and thereafter. In fact, of the 8 non-metropolitan counties (1960) which had 2200 or more Germans in their population in 1870, 7 were Democratic before 1920. In 1920, 5 of them turned to the Republican party and a sixth made the leap in 1940.

The counties with large numbers of farmers were largely Republican strongholds, 1940–1960. In 21 of the 27 counties that were 20 percent or more rural farm in 1960, the majority of the voters cast their ballots for the Republican presidential candidate in every election, 1940–1960.

Bryan's silver heresy and Robert Taft's struggles against governmental controls emanating from Washington.

After the Civil War most of the state outside the Virginia Military District, Ohio Land Company section, the Seven Ranges, and the Western Reserve tended Democratic or was a political battleground "due to the large element of Scotch-Irish [from the South] and Germans."[3] However, beginning in 1896 and culminating in 1940, the traditional Democratic party strength in the state had diminished until by 1960 there was almost no county in the state that could be relied upon to go Democratic in good year or bad (from 1940 through 1960 only the people of Pike County cast a majority of their votes for the Democratic candidate in every presidential election).

The decline in Democratic fortunes in the state's traditionally Democratic counties was principally related to the policies of their presidential candidates. The damaging effects of Democratic presidential candidates' policies and associated events on the size of the Democratic vote were cumulative in the counties. William Jennings Bryan and his advocacy of "free and unlimited coinage of silver" cost the party its business support, which was substantial before 1896. Many businessmen regarded the Democratic party as the "safe and sane" political party prior to the 1896 election. For example, Mark Hanna, the Cleveland, Ohio, Republican political leader and political associate of William McKinley, very nearly failed in his amorous pursuit of his future wife because her father, Daniel P. Rhodes, an iron and steel magnate, disapproved of his Republican politics. He allegedly said to the young suitor, "I like you very well, Mark, but you are a damned screecher for freedom."[4] The allusion was to the abolitionist bias of Republican politics in the Western Reserve. After William Jennings Bryan, though, no businessman could regard the Democratic party as a safe repository for the destinies

[3] Chaddock, *Ohio before 1850*, p. 16.
[4] Herbert Croly, *Marcus Alonzo Hanna—His Life and Work* (New York: The Macmillan Co., 1919), p. 47.

of the nation. The second major element of Ohio's population alienated by a Democratic president was the Germans.[5] Ohio's German population was large and settled primarily in the northern and western parts of the state, and it was precisely these areas that turned Republican in 1920 and thereafter (see Figures 5.1 and 5.2).[6] Finally, Catholic candidates Al Smith and John Kennedy and the liberal Franklin Roosevelt alienated much of the remaining traditional rural Democratic vote which had been cast by Anglo-Saxons of Southern ancestry.

The rapid decrease of traditional Democratic strength in the rural-farm counties left Ohio with no counties 20 percent or more rural-farm that could be labelled as strongly Democratic in the 1960s.[7] The Republican proclivities of Ohio's farmers in 1960 may be explained, in part, by the fact that twelve of the state's twenty-seven rural-farm counties were among the traditionally Republican counties. The Republican bias of the people dated back to the Civil War and before, and neither war nor depression raised serious doubts in their minds concerning the wisdom of their forefathers' political choice. Another reason for the Republican vote of Ohio's rural areas was the large number of people of German ancestry residing in them. Ohio's Germans were Democratically inclined when they first cast their ballots and, indeed, remained Democratic until 1920. The tales told in German communities of bullying and outright repression by Democratic officials during World War I renders their change in political faith in the 1920 election and thereafter understandable. In some places, Democratic county chairmen bullied Germans into mortgaging their farms to purchase war bonds.

Perhaps the salient reason for the 1960 Republican voting

5 See V. O. Key, Jr., "Secular Realignment and the Party System," *Journal of Politics*, vol. 21 (1951), p. 198, for an interesting discussion of the process by which groups leave a party.

6 Of the eight nonmetropolitan counties (1960) which had 2200 or more Germans in their population in 1870, seven were Democratic before 1920. In 1920 five of them turned to the Republican party and a sixth made the leap in 1940 when Franklin Roosevelt was moving toward still another war with Germany.

7 The voters in twenty-one of the twenty-seven counties that were 20 percent or more rural-farm in 1960 cast a majority of their votes for the Republican presidential candidate in all six elections, 1940–1960. The remaining six rural-farm counties were more often on the Republican than the Democratic side over the same period. Before 1920 only twelve of the twenty-seven rural-farm counties could be labelled as one-sidedly Republican in political makeup. The remaining fifteen counties were either Democratic or political battlegrounds. Thus, it was only after World War I and the New Deal that rural Ohio could be regarded as a Republican stronghold.

habits of Ohio's farmers was that most of the state's rural-farm counties were in the corn belt, which included all of western Ohio with the exception of the counties bordering the Ohio River. The corn belt farmers were envied by the farmers in other areas of the nation. The 1954 level-of-living index for the corn belt farmer was 24 percent higher than the average for United States farmers. Corn belt farms were relatively pleasant places to live and work, for they were mechanized, had running water and electricity, made use of hired help, and, in general, had more of all of the amenities than farmers elsewhere.

Donald J. Bogue and Calvin L. Beale in *Economic Areas of the United States* summarized their observations concerning the corn belt as follows:

> The corn belt farmer tills some of the best land in the world, using the most modern farming equipment and the farm management practices which have been most recently recommended by scientists and research experts. More and more, he is becoming a technically trained and skilled specialist instead of a common laborer. His business of growing hogs and cattle, involving the messy chores of cleaning pens and hauling manure, may have its unappealing moments, but it is profitable.[8]

The 1960 Ohio farmer was, in large part, a successful businessman with a large capital investment in his enterprise and a payroll to meet, but was not, as yet, a land baron in the style of the South's black belt. He retained the democratic habits of dress, attitude, and freedom that were part of Ohio's frontier tradition. He was not looking for help from government or politicians or from anyone else. The banks loaned him money to purchase his equipment and he met the payments without too much difficulty. Thus, he was not unhappy with the banks. The prices he received for his farm produce were generally high, and when prices declined he vented his spleen on government controls rather than upon the traditional goat of more marginal farmers; that is, the railroads and the processors.[9]

[8] Donald J. Bogue and Calvin L. Beale, *Economic Areas of the United States* (New York: The Free Press of Glencoe, Inc., 1961), p. 143.
[9] The votes of farmers on U.S. Secretary of Agriculture Freeman's Supply-Management Plan, 1962, in the six Midwest states analyzed in this book are indicative of the anti-government attitudes of the corn belt farmers as opposed to the pro-government controls attitude of wheat farmers in Wisconsin and Minnesota. The vote, taken from the *Congressional Quarterly Almanac*, 1963, p. 796, was as follows: Ohio, 22.6 percent for; Indiana, 25.5 percent; Illinois, 30.3 percent; Michigan, 20.2 percent; Wisconsin, 55.7 percent; Minnesota, 65.7 percent.

In conversations with corn belt farmers, the dominant impression taken away was of great self-assurance accompanied by self-esteem and self-reliance. Much of it was blind and failed to take into account the extent to which their lives were interwoven into the fabric of the nation. It led them to vote against governmental price support and crop control programs and to identify restrictions on freedom exclusively with government. Government was the bane of their existence, for it taxed away a large part of their earnings and, as they saw it, provided little in return save restrictions and controls. The Ohio farmer's syndrome of taxes and controls was identified with the New Deal and the Democratic party.

Another explanation for the Republican vote cast in Ohio's corn belt in 1960 was the large number of Republican-inclined prosperous small towns, almost all of which were attracting industry and population. As Bogue and Beale put it:

. . . this area [western Ohio corn belt] is a case study in decentralized and deconcentrated industry. The major raw materials of industry (coal, ore, steel, chemicals, petroleum) can be delivered cheaply to many different points in this subregion, because of its proximity to the coal fields and to the Great Lakes ports. The many trunk line railroads and major national highways which pass through the area give each city quick access to materials and to each other. Plants located here sell their goods in the great markets along the southern shores of the Great Lakes, and still escape some of the costs of congestion which must be met in the great port metropolises. The well-educated labor force, drawn from stable middlewestern rural and urban families, is of high quality and is very productive. A great variety of manufacturing enterprises have found that this combination of factors offers a profitable place in which to build new plants or to expand existing facilities.[10]

The key words in the Bogue and Beale appraisal of corn belt towns for the purpose of political analysis are "decentralized and deconcentrated" and "well-educated labor force drawn from stable middlewestern rural and urban families." This indicates that most of the people drawn to the corn belt towns were from neighboring farms and communities, and consequently they tended to vote Republican by virtue of the established voting pattern of the area.[11] Few Democratically inclined foreign-born or Negro people entered the towns in search of employment. The

[10] *Ibid.*, p. 146.
[11] See Warren E. Miller, "One-Party Politics and the Voter," *American Political Science Review*, vol. 50 (1956), p. 707. Miller discusses the effect of party dominance on voting behavior.

percent of foreign-born (other than German) tended to be low in the western counties, even in large urban centers. For example, Hamilton County (Cincinnati) had a population containing only 11.4 percent foreign-born or natives of foreign or mixed parentage, and Franklin County (Columbus) had only 8.7 percent. By comparison, Cuyahoga County (Cleveland) had 33.5 percent foreign-born or children of foreign-born, and Mahoning County (Youngstown) had 30.1 percent. Cleveland and Youngstown, located in the northeastern part of the state, tended Democratic, whereas Cincinnati and Columbus, in the western portion of the state, tended Republican.

Students of politics would expect the Democratic vote in the corn belt cities and towns to increase with industrialization in spite of the Republican bias of the new population, whereas it declined. The failure of Democrats in western Ohio to capitalize on industrialization was due to industry's deconcentrated and decentralized character. There were two salient features of corn belt communities with deconcentrated industry which enhanced Republican fortunes. First, labor unions tended to be weak because they had few members. Therefore, the revenue from dues was not sufficient to employ a large union bureaucracy, and the unions were forced to concentrate on bread-and-butter issues rather than politics, because they had neither the time nor the money to influence government. Second, in the absence of strong unions the power structure in the small towns tended to be rather monolithic, with the business community holding sway. The Chamber of Commerce, Rotary Club, and other business organizations were virtually the only groups that met and discussed issues. Consequently, the point of view of the business community was virtually the only one that was systematically presented on a day-to-day basis. Further, the vice-president of the bank was not the faceless, bloated plutocrat to workers in the small corn belt town that he was in the big city. On the contrary, he drank his morning cup of coffee in the same restaurant and often at the same table as the shoe clerk and the mechanic. In these face-to-face situations he presented the business point of view concerning issues, and his word was accepted by the listeners as akin to law. After all, he was informed and articulate and a "good guy." Further, if a loan was needed, he was the person to whom it was necessary to go. Therefore, the business point of view was given more weight in the small towns than in the metropolises, and this almost invariably dictated a Republican vote in local, state, and national elections.

Republican candidates even received substantial votes in the great metropolises of the corn belt, such as Columbus and Cincinnati, because the cities were part of the corn belt culture. They had few foreign-born in their population and the native-born residents shared most of the cultural attitudes of the corn belt. The cities did have large Negro populations which tended to vote Democratic (14.4 percent in Cincinnati's Hamilton County and 11.9 percent in Columbus' Franklin County), but comparatively few Negroes were registered to vote.[12] In addition, numbers of Negroes voted the Republican ticket in Columbus and Cincinnati because the Democratic party was still associated, in the minds of older Negroes, with bitter opposition to emancipation of the slaves and post-Civil War Republican reconstruction policies.

In summary, the Republican party was geographically dominant in Ohio in 1960 with well over half the counties one-sidedly Republican. The people of the corn belt part of the state voted particularly one-sidedly Republican. There were thirty-seven counties included in the western Ohio corn belt, and in twenty-eight of the thirty-seven counties a majority of the votes were cast for the Republican candidate for President in six of six elections, 1940–1960. The principal components of the Republican vote were the descendants of the New England and Kentucky Whigs who settled much of Ohio, joined by Germans, farmers, and small-town Anglo-Saxon Protestants who objected to World Wars I and II, the Catholic Democratic candidates, or the New Deal's farm, civil rights, and spending policies. A very important feature of the Republican vote in the corn belt was that the people suffered less than most of the nation's citizenry during the Great Depression and were relatively more prosperous thereafter.

Turning now to sources of Democratic party strength, most of Ohio's strongly Democratic counties, 1932–1960, were located in the northern and northeastern portions of the state, which were also the most heavily industrialized and populated sections (see Figures 5.3 and 5.4). Toledo, Cleveland, Akron, Canton, and Youngstown were the largest cities in the section. The nine counties in northern and northeastern Ohio that voted Democratic in at least five of the eight presidential elections, 1932–1960, had a combined population of 3,479,153, which was 36

---

[12] According to Kenneth E. Gray, *A Report on Politics in Cincinnati* (Cambridge, Mass.: Joint Center for Urban Studies of MIT and Harvard, 1959), p. II–19, only 30 percent of the potential Negro vote was registered. Also, see Oscar Glantz, "The Negro Voter in Northern Industrial Cities," *Western Political Quarterly*, vol. 13 (1960), p. 999.

■ Counties carried by Democratic candidates in at least 5 of 8 presidential elections, 1932 – 1960

▨ Counties carried by Democratic candidates in at least 1 of 8 presidential elections, 1940 – 1960

FIGURE 5.3   OHIO'S DEMOCRATIC COUNTIES in presidential elections, 1932–1960

Explanatory Note to Figures 5.3 and 5.4: Figure 5.3 delineates the Democratic strongholds in Ohio. Figure 5.4 identifies the two variables which seem to be most closely related to Democratic voting strength in the state; that is, the Civil War Democratic vote and the foreign-born Democratic vote that was captured by the New Deal.

As Figure 5.3 illustrates, the Democratic party owned little consistent support in Ohio's counties, 1932–1960. Geographically, Ohio was overwhelmingly Republican in presidential elections. There were only 12 of 88 Ohio counties in which the majority of the votes went to the Democratic presidential candidate in over half the elections, 1932–1960. There was only

Population 14 percent or more foreign-born or mixed parentage

Counties in which Vallandigham (the pro-Southern Democrat) received a plurality of the vote in the 1863 gubernatorial election

FIGURE 5.4 THE DISINHERITED OF TWO GENERATIONS: Ohio's Democratic voters—the foreign-born and the Civil War Democrats

one county (Pike) where a majority of the votes went to the Democratic candidate for President in all 6 elections, 1932–1960. Eight of the 12 strongly Democratic counties (5 of 8 elections, 1932–1960) are also identified in Figure 5.4 as counties with large numbers of foreign-born in their population.

There were 21 other counties which went Democratic at least once in the presidential elections, 1940–1960. Comparison of Figures 5.3 and 5.4 shows that Vallandigham (the Copperhead Democrat) carried most of these counties in the 1863 election, and 12 of them remained among the 21 most Democratic counties outside northeastern Ohio, 1932–1960.

percent of the state's total 1960 population of 9,706,397. Therefore, the Democratic party's position in the state was not so
desperate as the geographic distribution of party strength
indicated.

The post-1932 switch of northern and northeastern Ohioans
to the Democratic party was caused by the movement into the
areas of a large foreign-born population which suffered greatly in
the Great Depression. These people were attracted mainly by
the steel and rubber industries. In the Great Depression the
industries were severely depressed and disproportionately large
numbers of the foreign-born population were unemployed. In
the 1937 steel strikes in Cleveland, Canton, and Youngstown,
the core of the union groups consisted of the foreign-born groups.
The picket lines were manned by Polish, Slovenian, and other
eastern European people. When the National Guard was dis-
patched to the cities to break the strike, it was their heads which
were cracked by rifle butts. Subsequently, when long lines of
cars containing "strikebreakers" were shepherded into the plants
by convoys of troops with bayonets fixed, it was the eastern
European people, living in ghettos adjacent to the plants, who
lined the streets by the thousands screaming epithets at the
"scabs." Some mothers gave pebbles to their children and in-
structed them to "throw rocks at the scabs, honey." Franklin
Roosevelt and his New Deal was the single friendly element during this tragic period for the northern Ohio immigrants. They
were given jobs and encouragement in their struggles with
management by Roosevelt and the national Democratic party.
Thereafter, they associated food, jobs, and dignity as human
beings with the national Democratic party.[13]

The industrial warfare of the 1930s was the wellspring of
most Democratic votes cast in 1960. The other large component
of the 1940–1960 Democratic vote in Ohio developed out of the
civil strife of the 1860s (see Figures 5.3 and 5.4). Outside the
industrial north and northeast, the Ohio counties in which
Democratic presidential candidates fared best, 1940–1960, were
in large part the same counties carried by the pro-Southern
Democratic candidate for governor in 1863, Clement L. Val-

---

[13] Statistics strikingly demonstrate the violence of the eastern European's
political reaction to the events of the depression. Eleven of the fifteen
Ohio counties which contained the largest percentage of foreign-born and
natives of foreign or mixed parentage, 1960, were among the counties which
the Democratic presidential candidate carried at least once, 1932–1960. Most
of the remaining twenty-two counties which went Democratic at least once
trace their Democratic affiliation back to the Civil War.

landigham.[14] Thus, much of the state's Democratic voting strength in 1960 was born of emotions and events surrounding the Civil War period.[15] The emotional foundations of this variety of Democratic strength can best be understood by examining the career of Vallandigham, the Copperhead Democratic candidate in the 1863 election.

Clement L. Vallandigham was born in Columbiana County, Ohio, and represented it in the state legislature for two terms. He subsequently moved to Dayton, Ohio, where he became an editor of a local newspaper and in 1858 was elected a U.S. representative. Thereafter, Vallandigham devoted his political life to a fight against the military actions taken against the South. It was a fight that provoked riots throughout the Midwest and led ultimately to his arrest and expulsion to the South. After his deportation to the South in 1862, he was nominated as the Democratic candidate for governor of Ohio and received 187,492 Democratic votes to 288,374 for Brough, the Unionist (Republican) candidate. Senator Sherman later wrote, "I have always regarded Brough's election [Vallandigham's defeat] in Ohio . . . as having an important influence in favor of the Union cause equal to that of any battle of the war."[16]

A good taste of Vallandigham's sentiments may be obtained from a speech made by him on January 14, 1863. In part, Vallandigham held that:

. . . not slavery but abolition was the cause of the war, he "blessed God that not the smell of so much as one drop of its blood" was upon his garments. The war for the union had been "a most bloody and costly failure." The President had confessed it in his Proclamation, and now it was to be changed to a war for the Negro. He denied the doctrine of an irrepressible conflict. The Union part slave and part free was one of the compromises of the Constitution. If the East continues until a separation be forced, "the day which divides the North from the South, that self-same day decrees eternal divorce between the East and the West." Asking if the war should continue, he answered: "No, not a day, not an hour. What then? Shall we separate? Again I answer, no. What then?" He would stop fighting and declare an armistice, reduce the armies to a peace footing, and when passion had cooled, settle the question on the basis of the

[14] In 1863 Vallandigham won eighteen Ohio counties, and twelve of the eighteen counties remained among the twenty-one most Democratic counties of the state outside northern and northeastern Ohio, 1940–1960.

[15] V. O. Key, Jr., discusses the persistence of Democratic strength in Copperhead counties in "Partisanship and County Office," *American Political Science Review*, vol. 47 (1953), p. 525.

[16] John Sherman, *Recollections*, vol. I (New York: The Werner Co., 1895), p. 328.

original Constitution, giving each section the power to protect itself within the Union. He would accept the offer of the French for friendly mediation, "as the speediest, easiest, most graceful mode of suspending hostilities."[17]

After 1932, then, Ohio's Democratic party was a curious mixture of urban liberals, east Europeans, Catholics and Negroes, joined by the descendants of Vallandigham's supporters. The sole adhesive which joined these elements of Ohio's society was that they were the disinherited of two generations. The forebears of the traditional Democratic party voters were branded as "promoters of sedition," as "traitors," and as "enemies to their country." The charges leveled against the labor unions in the 1930s had a similar ring even though the reasons for the charges were different. Thus, the disinherited of the Civil War and of the Great Depression joined ranks in the Democratic party.[18]

The rhetoric of the liberals in the 1930s rang almost as true to the traditional Democrat as to the New Deal Democrat. They, too, were exploited. It was not until the late 1930s and the 1940s, when the Democratic party was captured by its big city elements, that the traditional Democrats stopped identifying with the liberals' exploited groups.[19]

We now turn from Ohio's political history and the groups that associated themselves with the Democratic and Republican parties, to political organization. The following pages will show that the organization of a political party is largely determined by the character of the groups that belong to it.

[17] Porter, *Ohio Politics During the Civil War Period*, pp. 147–148.

[18] Evidence of the community of feeling among the disinherited of the two generations is provided by the cohesion of these two elements of the party in the Ohio legislature. See Malcolm Jewell, "Party Voting in American State Legislatures," *American Political Science Review*, vol. 49 (1955), p. 773.

[19] Statistical confirmation of the generalizations concerning party composition may be found in the simple and multiple correlations of political and demographic variables. The coefficients of correlation show that the percent vote by counties for Democrat Kennedy in 1960 and the percent foreign-born and children of foreign-born was .69, percent Catholic .57, percent urban .46, and percent non-white .51. On the other hand, the Kennedy vote related negatively to percent rural-farm $(-).54$. A multiple correlation of Kennedy's 1960 vote by counties with percent foreign-born and children of foreign-born plus percent Catholic resulted in an R of .73. In other words, the Democratic party in Ohio was largely composed of foreign-born and their sons and daughters, Catholics, and Negroes. The Republican party, on the other hand, obtained most of its votes from native white Americans from the less urban areas.

Republican Organization

The post-World War II Republican party in Ohio was exceedingly well organized. Ray Bliss, the long-time Republican state chairman who became national chairman in 1965, was a symbol of good organization. He was widely regarded as one of the best, if not the best, Republican state chairmen in the nation. He was Robert Taft's campaign manager in 1950, when Taft startled the nation with his overwhelming victory over Joseph T. Ferguson, the Democratic candidate for U.S. senator. He was given credit by many for Nixon's unexpected victory in Ohio in 1960.

However, Bliss was an effect of a well-knit party rather than a cause. True, he improved the Republican state organization while in office. But a badly split, factionalized party, such as Ohio's Democratic party, would never have chosen Ray Bliss for the job. In 1960, for example, Ray Bliss demanded that all Republican county chairmen clear statements with him before making them public, and enjoyed nearly perfect compliance with his demand. In the Democratic party, where county chairmen often regarded their organizations as totally independent entities with only a coincidental similarity of names to tie them with the state and national Democratic organizations, such a demand would have been ignored at best.

The foregoing would seem to say that the Republican party was well organized because it was well organized. More precisely, the Republican party was well organized because the people who identified with it were culturally and ideologically homogeneous and were acutely aware of a large number of interests that they had in common. They were also aware of the fact that they constituted a minority of the voting population of the state and thus were willing to submit to strong central direction of their party in order to achieve electoral victory over a disorganized majority.[20]

The people who identified with the Republican party in Ohio were mainly from the suburbs of the large cities and from the small towns. They were, in many cases, the grandsons and granddaughters of the people who arrived first in Ohio and settled

[20] According to Louis Harris' unpublished sample survey of "Issues and Candidates in Ohio," 1958, 42 percent of the electorate regarded themselves as Democrats, 31 percent Republicans, and 27 percent Independents. However, of the registered voters, 36 percent were Republicans, 35 percent Democrats, and 29 percent Independents.

and developed the land. They were, in other cases, the people who arrived later and developed small and large business enterprises that prospered. But the important thing they had in common was that they were "on top" and wanted to remain there. Consequently, they wanted a state government which was sympathetic to their aspirations. And in a democracy where each vote counts but once, the realization of this goal demanded strong political organization. Since the Republican "haves" were aware of the need for a strong central political organization, they contributed large sums of money to the Republican state headquarters. The possession of substantial financial resources is quite helpful in any kind of organization, but this is particularly true of a political organization.[21] By judicious use of campaign funds, the Republican state chairman was able to encourage able candidates to run on the Republican ticket and to discourage factional opposition to organization candidates in the Republican primaries. It required a brave if not foolhardy person to contend for the Republican nomination to an office when he knew that the organization candidate would enjoy the support of the state and county Republican organizations. Thus, there were seldom bitter Republican primary battles. In fact, from 1932 to 1962 there were only six contested Republican gubernatorial primaries out of fourteen primaries.

The geographic center of Republican organization strength was in Hamilton County (Cincinnati) and the remainder of western Ohio. An illuminating statistic that supports this observation is that the counties that most consistently supported the winning candidate in Republican gubernatorial primaries, 1932–1962, were Hamilton and Lawrence Counties, and most of the counties that ranked second in ability to pick the winner in the Republican gubernatorial primaries radiated like spokes from Hamilton County (see Figure 5.5). Republican organization strength in Cincinnati was based on the patronage and campaign contributions available to it. No other local Republican organization had comparable job and money resources.

According to observers of Cincinnati politics, the Republican party controlled about 2500 county and courthouse jobs from which it obtained about $200,000 yearly in the form of a 2.5 percent "voluntary contribution."[22] In addition, the Republican

[21] See Alexander Heard, *The Costs of Democracy* (Chapel Hill, N.C.: University of North Carolina Press, 1960).
[22] See Kenneth E. Gray, *A Report on Politics in Cincinnati* (Cambridge, Mass.: Joint Center for Urban Studies of MIT and Harvard University, 1959), pp. II–28–29.

Plurality of county's vote cast for winning candidate in every primary, 1932 - 1962

Plurality of county's vote cast for winning candidate in all but one primary, 1932 - 1962

FIGURE 5.5 OHIO'S REPUBLICAN ORGANIZATION STRENGTH in Republican gubernatorial primaries, 1932–1962

Explanatory Note: The map is designed to provide visual confirmation of the statement in the text that the Cincinnati (Hamilton County) Republican machine is dominant in state politics. As shown by the map, Hamilton County was on the winning side in every primary, 1932–1962, and the other counties that almost invariably landed on the winning side radiate like spokes from Hamilton County.

Cincinnati machine had close ties with the business community. The business affiliations, reportedly, extended outside Cincinnati, for due to its dominant role in Ohio state politics the Republican machine was also important nationally. Important business leaders, such as Ben Tate, served as chairmen of the executive committee and raised funds for the party when needed.

Therefore, the Cincinnati Republican party had job and money resources, and it also commanded jobs and money at the state and national levels because of its ability to affect the results of Republican primaries. Political power, such as that in Hamilton County, tends to grow geometrically. Because of its resources, the Hamilton County organization was able to help friendly Republican county chairmen when they required campaign funds or jobs for the faithful. Because of propinquity, most of the friendly ties tended to be with Republican chairmen in neighboring counties, which helps explain the voting behavior in Republican primaries shown in Figure 5.5.

Because of the vote-producing power of the Hamilton County organization, there were seldom any Republican primary contests in either Hamilton County or in the state gubernatorial primaries. In 1958 not one of the twenty-one Republican county nominations was contested in Hamilton County. And there were only six contested Republican gubernatorial primaries out of fourteen contests from 1932 to 1962.

Therefore, the Republican party was well organized in Ohio for two main reasons. First, it was well organized out of necessity. The rural and small-town Republicans knew that party cohesion was vital for statewide victory, and the plums of the victories tasted very sweet to them because of the lack of local job and money resources. Secondly, it was well organized because of the concentration of Republican vote, job, and money resources in only one large city (Cincinnati). The Republicans were relatively powerless in most of the major cities and, consequently, the Cincinnati Republican leaders enjoyed power which was unchallenged elsewhere in the state.[23]

The Republican position in Ohio in 1960 may be described as follows. First, the Republicans were dominant in most of the rural counties. Secondly, they controlled Hamilton County (Cincinnati) and also received a large vote in the corn belt cities and towns. Third, the Republicans were handsomely financed by the Ohio business community. In elections, then, the objective of the Republican leadership was to maximize its vote in the rural areas, Cincinnati, and the smaller cities, and at the same time minimize the Democratic vote in the metropolitan areas

---

[23] See Robert H. Salisbury, "St. Louis Politics: Relationship among Interests, Parties, and Government Structure," *Western Political Quarterly*, vol. 13 (1960), p. 498. Salisbury reports much the same findings in St. Louis.

of northeastern Ohio. The way for it to accomplish these objectives was through excellent organization in its strongholds, thus "getting out" the Republican vote, and by keeping issues such as right-to-work (which aroused dormant underdog attitudes on the part of the urban "have nots"), out of the campaigns, thus keeping down the Democratic vote. The formula did not enjoy invariable success, but it kept Ohio a dominantly Republican state while sister states drifted toward the Democratic party. We have seen some of the reasons for the Republican party's excellent organization. Now we shall search for the causative agents behind the poor organization and lack of success of the Democratic party in Ohio.

Democratic Political Organization

Organizationally, Ohio's Democratic party in the 1960s, was more akin to the loosely knit parties of the deep South than to the well-organized political machines in most industrial states. There was, in fact, no statewide Democratic party in Ohio. The state's Democratic party was an aggregation of city machines which had little or no interest in statewide elections unless the candidate was from their city. Ray Miller, the Cuyahoga County (Cleveland) Democratic boss, explicitly maintained that his organization was an independent entity with neither legal nor moral ties with a state Democratic party.

The principal elements responsible for Democratic disorganization and failure were: (1) the large number of medium-sized cities, in each of which there was a Democratic organization whose leader shared Ray Miller's attitude of independence toward the state Democratic party; (2) the weakness of the Cuyahoga County Democratic organization; (3) the aloofness or impotence of the state's labor organization with respect to state and local politics; and (4) the existence of a conservative rural element in the party.[24]

[24] Statistical evidence of the organizational weakness of Ohio's Democratic party is provided by the coefficients of correlation (r) between the votes of several of the party's candidates. The closest relationship is between Kennedy's 1960 vote and DiSalle's 1962 vote (.92). However, Lausche's 1962 vote was related only at the .64 level with DiSalle's 1962 vote and at the .72 level with Kennedy's vote. This is the weakest relationship between the votes of Democratic candidates in any of the states studied. In Indiana, Illinois, Wisconsin, Minnesota, and Michigan, the relationship of the votes of the candidates was always at or above the .90 level. One reason for the failure of Lausche's vote to relate at a higher level with the votes received by Kennedy and DiSalle is also shown by the coefficients of correlation. Ac-

The first requirement, then, is to explore the "how" and the "why" of the city-based factionalism of Ohio's Democratic party. The 1958 Democratic gubernatorial primary provides a good example of this city-based factionalism. It brings to mind for the student of politics a Mississippi Democratic primary. In the 1958 primary there were seven candidates for the Democratic gubernatorial nomination, including the mayors of Youngstown, Cleveland, Columbus, a former mayor of Toledo, a Cincinnati attorney, the Cuyahoga County (Cleveland) engineer, and a Columbus woman whose platform featured a demand for sterilization of the feebleminded.

Mike DiSalle, former mayor of Toledo, one-time head of the Office of Price Administration (OPA) and unsuccessful candidate for governor in 1956, was the only Democratic candidate with a statewide following (due largely to his OPA incumbency), and consequently he won the nomination with 226,580 votes, or 39 percent of the vote. However, each of the mayors received large votes and each carried his home county. In addition, Celebrezze (mayor of Cleveland) won four neighboring counties and Sensenbrenner (mayor of Columbus) won two neighboring counties. Jackson, mayor of Youngstown, won only his home county, Mahoning, but ran a close second in neighboring counties. Gorman, the Cincinnati attorney, carried his home county of Hamilton and two nearby counties. Porter, the Cuyahoga County engineer, was the candidate of the Cuyahoga County (Cleveland) Democratic organization. Porter did not carry a single county, but he ran a close second to Celebrezze in Cuyahoga County (34,079 votes for Celebrezze to 29,114 votes for Porter) and in adjoining counties, thereby robbing Celebrezze of decisive-enough margins to seriously threaten DiSalle's nomination. Thus, the state's vote was fragmented by the cities, and the vote of the state's largest city was fragmented by the candidacy of the mayor and the organization-backed county engineer.

Reasons for Democratic Disorganization

The significance of the 1958 primary rests in the fact that there was no authority within the party that was able to give a single candidate for the nomination the money and potential

---

cording to the data, the percentage-point difference of Lausche's vote over DiSalle's in 1962 was most closely related to percent rural-farm and was negatively related to most of the variables associated with the Democratic party. Thus, Lausche's vote appeal transcended normal party lines and attracted into the party people with strongly Republican voting tendencies.

votes to frighten away other candidates. In 1958 and in most Democratic primaries, anyone from a large city with a local base of support had at least an outside chance of victory. Consequently, the party was plagued by bitter primaries, the wounds from which were rarely healed by election time.

The Democratic political disorganization observed in the 1958 primary was partially a product of the large number of medium-sized cities with Democratic mayors, which made it impossible for any single city organization to dominate the nomination process. Therefore, each city leader preferred the role of prince of his own province to that of satrap in an effective state organization. Cuyahoga County (Cleveland) was the only metropolitan area potentially large enough to dominate state Democratic politics. However, Ray Miller's Democratic political machine in the county was singularly weak and ineffective. In 1962 he was unable to secure the nomination of his mayoralty candidate on the Democratic ticket. In fact, independent Democrats controlled City Hall in Cleveland after 1935, when Harold H. Burton won election. The Cuyahoga County Democratic organization was impotent because of poor leadership. Ray Miller, the long-time Democratic boss, never attempted to develop a political organization transcending ethnic lines in the city. He never used labor or liberal leadership to develop programs designed to provide Slovenians or Italians or Polish people reasons to vote for a candidate transcending nationality lines. Therefore, Lausche and Celebrezze and other independent Democrats won elections by "playing on the nationalities like a guitar."[25]

Similarly, the labor unions in Ohio were seldom united as a statewide labor movement. There were scores of small and large unions in the state and no single union was able to dominate the labor movement on a statewide basis. Therefore, each labor leader preferred negotiating his own political arrangements with candidates. Moreover, most of Ohio's labor leaders were "bread-and-butter" oriented rather than issue-oriented because no union had the financial resources to extend its efforts far beyond the narrow objectives of improving the wages, hours, and working conditions of its members. They could not afford the staff and other expenditures involved in attempts to influence broad public policy.

Another reason for the weakness of labor unions in Ohio compared with some other states, such as Michigan, Minnesota, and Wisconsin, was the deprived cultural and educational back-

[25] Martha Derthick, *Cleveland* (Cambridge, Mass.: Joint Center for Urban Studies of MIT and Harvard University, 1963), p. 19.

grounds of many of the Ohio workers. Beginning with Henry Ford and the five-dollar day for auto workers, the auto industry attracted the aristocracy of labor. By contrast, the steel industry traditionally was regarded as one of the least attractive sources of employment and tended to attract workers who were unable to find jobs elsewhere. The leadership of the Ohio unions reflected the rather narrow intellectual horizons of their members.

In the absence of a wealthy labor union with a large hierarchy, there was little institutional support for liberalism in Ohio. By way of contrast, in Michigan the liberals found a home in the United Auto Workers bureaucracy. Their liberalism, in many cases, first found expression during the New Deal period through the National Youth Administration (NYA), the Civilian Conservation Corps (CCC), or picket-line activity. After World War II, some attended college and then sought employment that would fit in with their political views, such as in the United Auto Workers. Quite naturally, they also tended to be active in organizations such as Americans for Democratic Action, where they came in contact with other liberals from the academic world and the professions. As a product of the institutional support for liberalism and the continuing interaction of people from the UAW with other liberals, there was born the liberal-labor coalition which dominated Michigan politics.

In Ohio there was no large core of active liberals in the labor movement or anywhere else. Many of the labor leaders in Ohio were of the hard-bitten old school who looked with suspicion on liberals and had little in common with them. Consequently, there was little interaction between the two groups, and the liberals lacked institutional support and the labor movement was without backing beyond the confines of its membership. Thus, Democratic politics was left to the professional politicians in Ohio, and the professional Democratic politicians were a diverse and divided lot, having little in common except the name Democrat and a desire for the spoils of public office.

A final feature of Ohio's Democratic party which accounted, in part, for its factionalism was the existence of a rural Democratic vote in the state. The rural Democratic vote dated from the Civil War and before and was cast largely by people whose forebears entered Ohio from the South. In many ways, this rural Democratic vote was similar to the rural conservative Democratic vote cast in the Border States.[26] But most important,

---

[26] See Fenton, *Politics in the Border States.*

the traditional rural Democratic vote kept Ohio a two-party state after the Civil War. The sections settled by Southerners were Copperhead strongholds during the Civil War and were unswervingly Democratic thereafter. Therefore, the Democratic party was a continuing threat to the Republican party both in the legislature and in statewide elections. Consequently, Ohio's Democratic party was not an empty shell. This distinguished Ohio from states, such as Michigan, Minnesota, and Wisconsin, where the pre-Great Depression Democratic party represented no serious threat to the Republicans. In these three states it was relatively easy for urban liberal-labor elements to wrest control of the party from the traditional job-oriented Democratic politician. In Ohio, seizure of the Democratic party by a liberal-labor coalition was a much more formidable task. Ohio had entrenched urban political machines, such as Ray Miller's Cuyahoga County organization, as well as the rural Democratic strongholds.

By way of summary, the causative factors behind Democratic disorganization and Republican unity in Ohio include the following:

(1) Ideological and ethnic homogeneity of the people in the Republican party versus the heterogeneity of the groups identifying with the Democratic party. Rural and urban Republicans tended to be conservative, the "haves," and Yankees. The Democrats, on the other hand, included under their generous tent rural conservatives, urban low-income folk, labor unions, liberals, many ethnic groups such as Cleveland's Slovenians, Negroes, and urban political organizations.

(2) Democratic electoral strength centered in a number of medium-sized cities, while Republican votes came largely from the suburbs and rural areas. As a consequence, urban Democratic leaders enjoyed substantial patronage from city and county governments and were relatively unconcerned with the fate of the party on a statewide basis. No Democratic leader possessed enough electoral strength to dominate the party statewide. Lacking such strength, each preferred being a city Caesar to a role as a statewide lieutenant. Therefore, each jealously guarded his own authority and resisted the development of a strong central Democratic organization. This resulted in factionalism and a "friends and neighbors" vote in Democratic primaries which was more akin to Mississippi and Alabama than to most northern states. The Republican party, on the other hand, lacked the patronage of city governments and thus was

more concerned than Democratic leaders were with controlling the state government. As a consequence, they consciously sought a strong central Republican organization in order to win state offices.

(3) The power structure of the state. Ohio's labor unions were relatively weak and did not seriously contest control of state government with the business community. Ohio's labor organizations were primarily "bread-and-butter" oriented and concentrated their energies on the relatively narrow objectives of higher wages, shorter hours, and improved working conditions. The unions had neither the requisite resources nor the skills to seek a major hand in the conduct of state government.

The business community, on the other hand, used its financial and propaganda resources very skillfully in Ohio. It contributed generously to the Republican state organization and to certain Republican candidates. Consequently, the state Republican headquarters had the necessary resources to command the respect of local Republican organizations. In addition, the business community, primarily through the newspapers, successfully sought and often secured the nomination of conservatives on the Democratic ticket. Democrats, such as conservative Frank Lausche, enjoyed a uniformly good press in Ohio, and, in the absence of effective counter-propaganda on the part of labor organizations, received the vote of low-income Democrats in the cities as well as the vote of suburban and rural conservatives. The net result was conservative dominance in the state.

Political Change in Ohio

The preceding pages dealt with the history of Ohio politics, political organization, and the areas of Democratic and Republican voting strength. Attention now turns to the changes in Democratic and Republican voting strength produced by personalities and events over the 1920–1960 period. Pronounced plus-Democratic change in presidential elections (plus 15 percentage points or more) over the 1920–1960 period was confined to northeastern Ohio. Furthermore, thirteen of the fifteen counties in which marked plus-Democratic change occurred, 1920–1960, were also among the fifteen counties with the largest proportion of foreign-born and natives of foreign or mixed parentage.[27]

[27] The measure of change used is a product of all the presidential elections over the 1920–1960 period, and not just the first and last elections. The

There is no need to relist the reasons already given for plus-Democratic change in northeastern Ohio. Suffice it to say that it was the principal center of industry in the state in 1960 and that the foreign-born and Negro population provided the unskilled labor for the industries.[28] In the 1930s the depression caused great hardship in the section, and the working people identified the Republican party with the poverty and the Democratic party with recovery. The surprising feature of the vote in northeastern Ohio is that, in spite of the marked plus-Democratic change in the area, some of the counties remained Republican strongholds in 1960 and others were political battlegrounds. The primary explanation for the failure of Democrats to capture control of all the northeastern Ohio counties is that the native population was traditionally Republican, dating from the settlement of the Western Reserve by New Englanders, and remained devoted to that party. Other reasons include the foreign flavor of the Democratic party in the northeastern Ohio cities, a thing that repelled natives. Further, the unions in the area took no consistent interest in local or state politics and, consequently, provided little help to the Democratic party.

Moderate plus-Democratic change, 1920–1960, (plus 5–14 percentage points) occurred in the metropolitan areas of southern Ohio (Cincinnati, Dayton, Springfield). The most visible feature that distinguished the southern from the northeastern industrial counties that witnessed more dramatic plus-Democratic change, 1920–1960, was the relatively smaller proportion of foreign-born and children of foreign-born in these corn belt cities.[29]

---

technique used was to compute a line of regression for each county, which is a line showing the secular trend of the county. The measure of political change is the percentage-point difference between the beginning and the end of the line.

[28] See Ben A. Arneson and William H. Ellis, "Voting Behavior in 1948 as Compared with 1924 in a Typical Ohio Community," *American Political Science Review*, vol. 44 (1950), p. 432. They found that the greatest plus-Democratic change occurred among foreign-born.

[29] The importance of the Negro and foreign vote to the Democratic party is given emphasis when the characteristics of Cincinnati's Democratic wards are noted. According to knowledgeable politicians, in 1962 there were eleven Cincinnati wards dependably Democratic. Two wards in the city were overwhelmingly Catholic (Wards 20 and 25) and both of them were among the eleven Democratic wards. Four Cincinnati wards were "Negro" wards (Wards, 9, 16, 17, 18) and all four were among the eleven Democratic wards. One ward contained a large number of both Jewish and Negro people (Ward 13) and it was also among the eleven Democratic wards. Of

There was little pronounced plus-Republican change in southern Ohio generally. This section, ranging from Monroe County on the east to Hamilton County on the west, is part of the Central and Eastern Upland Region. The economy and culture in 1960 were similar to bordering areas in Kentucky and West Virginia. Farming was generally marginal and there had been a substantial amount of coal mining in the area. The Republican party failed to gain votes in the area because of the pro-Democratic bias of the miners after the events of the Great Depression and the New Deal. Significantly, the people of southern Ohio generally cast overwhelming votes against right-to-work in 1958, even where coal mining had declined as an economic force.

In summary, the Democratic vote increased in both northern and southern Ohio (along Lake Erie in the north and the Ohio River in the south), 1920–1960. The reasons for plus-Democratic change were similar in both regions: industrialization and the events of the Great Depression. Let us now turn to the locations and reasons behind plus-Republican change in the presidential elections, 1920–1960.

The overwhelming majority of the counties in which pronounced plus-Republican change occurred, 1920–1960 (plus 5 percentage points or more), are located in the corn belt of western Ohio (twenty-eight of the thirty-seven counties in which pronounced plus-Republican change occurred are in the corn belt). The increasing preference for Republican candidates by the people of the corn belt is explainable (as was discussed above) by the large German population of the section, the relative prosperity of the farm population as well as the townspeople, and the fact that the depression weighed relatively lightly on their shoulders. The corn belt industries were diversified and not too sensitive to fluctuations in the demand for automobiles and other hard goods. Further, the corn belt farms were twice as productive as the average farm in the United States,[30] and thus the farmers could make a profit or at least survive economically when other farmers faced bankruptcy. The political by-product of the relative prosperity of corn belt residents in good times or

---

the remaining four Democratic wards, two (Wards 6 and 10) were downtown wards with a polyglot low-income floater population, and the remaining two Democratic wards (Wards 11 and 21) had large Negro populations. The data concerning Cincinnati were derived from interviews and from Kenneth E. Gray, *A Report on Politics in Cincinnati*, pp. II–30 through II–35.

[30] See Bogue and Beale, *Economic Areas of the United States*, p. 142.

bad was that 88 percent of the nonmetropolitan corn belt counties (twenty-eight of thirty-two counties) were among the counties which registered pronounced plus-Republican change, 1920–1960, compared to only 25 percent of the nonmetropolitan counties (nine of forty counties) in the remainder of the state.

Holmes County is typical of the counties in north-central Ohio where pronounced plus-Republican change also occurred. Holmes County was traditionally Democratic before the New Deal. It was one of the eighteen counties carried by the Copperhead Democratic gubernatorial candidate in 1863. Until 1940 it was one of the most faithfully Democratic counties in the state. However, the spending, farm, and civil rights policies of the New Deal alienated the conservative Democrats of the county, and its plus-Republican change, 1920–1960, was the most pronounced in the state. In 1960 it was primarily a farm county and was one of the few counties in the state in which right-to-work received a majority of the vote in 1958.

In summary, the political change in Ohio, 1920–1960, was largely a product of the entry into the Democratic party of large numbers of foreign-born and Negroes, followed by the movement into the Republican party of traditional Democrats.[31] The Republican party also gained votes in the prosperous corn belt counties. As the following discussion indicates, the net result of the shifts in party loyalties was to leave Ohio fairly securely Republican but within a two-party framework.

Ohio's Two-party Division

In 1960 Ohio was justifiably regarded as a Republican-inclined state. In that year Richard Nixon defeated Kennedy in Ohio by 167,652 votes. In 1962 Democratic Governor Mike DiSalle lost a bid for reelection to James Rhodes, his Republican opponent, by 555,911 ballots. In the same 1962 election, every Republican candidate for lesser state office won election, as did a majority of Republicans in both houses of the state legislature. In addi-

---

[31] The coefficients of correlation of political change with other variables, 1920–1960, also confirm these observations. The multiple correlation (R) of the percent Democratic change, 1920–1960, by county with percent foreign-born and children of foreign-born, 1960, plus the percent Democratic vote in 1860 is .82. This rather conclusively demonstrates that the political change which occurred in Ohio, 1920–1960, had to do in very large part with the entry into the Democratic party of the foreign-born and their children, followed by the escape from the party to the Republicans of many of the formerly Democratic native whites.

tion, eighteen Republicans won election to the U.S. House of Representatives as opposed to only six Democrats. However, in the same 1962 election Democratic Senator Frank Lausche won reelection by 692,521 votes. And in 1958 the Democrats won both houses of the state legislature as well as the governorship, every minor state office save one, and a U.S. Senate seat when Stephen Young defeated John Bricker.

Therefore, Ohio was a two-party state in the 1960s, though definitely inclined in a Republican direction. After 1856, when the Republican party was born, and through 1964, the Republican party candidates for President won Ohio in twenty-one elections, leaving only seven victories for the Democrats. Between 1932 and 1964, however, the Republicans and Democrats divided the spoils of victory on a four-to-five basis in favor of the Democrats. The first Republican candidate for governor of Ohio appeared on the ballot in 1855. After 1855 and through 1962, the Democrats won twenty-three gubernatorial elections and the Republicans thirty. In the post-World War II years, 1946–1962, Democratic candidates won five gubernatorial elections and Republican candidates only three. It should be noted, however, that Democratic governors were frequently more conservative than their Republican opponents.

The records of the general elections for secretary of state and of the presidential elections are, perhaps, the best indices of relative party strength. Republican candidates won the secretary of state elections in forty-three of fifty-four contests, 1855–1962, and in eleven of sixteen contests, 1930–1962. In the state legislature, too, the Republican party was dominant. From 1941 to 1963 the Republicans controlled both houses of the state legislature on seven occasions and the Democrats won control only twice (1948 and 1958).

If trends are a useful guide, the Democratic party would seem to face an unhappy political future (see Figure 5.6). Though Ohio's support for the two major parties underwent startling changes after 1868, the more it changed the more it remained the same through 1960. Before 1932 the principal sources of Republican pluralities were the northern Ohio cities. After 1932 the same cities were the Democratic party's principal vote resource. However, the more rural counties, and particularly the corn belt counties, provided large enough Republican pluralities to tip the balance against the Democratic margins of victory in the cities in every presidential election, 1944–1960, except in 1948, when Truman won by 7107 votes. In 1964 Lyndon Johnson

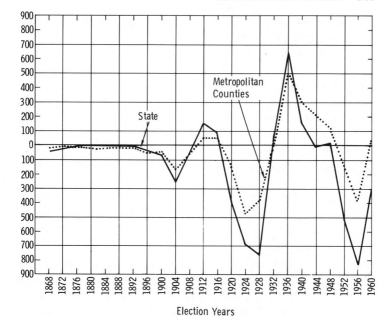

FIGURE 5.6 OHIO'S VOTE PLURALITIES by state and metropolitan areas in presidential elèctions, 1868–1960

Explanatory Note: The purpose of Figure 5.6 is to show the relative narrowness of the vote differences (or margins) between the two parties over much of the state's political history. The line through the middle of the graph designates a 50–50 split of the vote; for example, if the Republican presidential candidate received 500,000 votes and the Democrat also received 500,000 votes, the result would be a zero plurality. Above the 50–50 line are Democratic margins or pluralities and below the line are Republican pluralities. The graph shows that Republican candidates have won the state more often than not, but that the margin has generally been narrow. The graph also shows the pronounced and growing tendency for the state's metropolitan counties to be more Democratic than the remainder of the state.

won Ohio by a landslide margin over Republican Goldwater. The 1964 vote reflected the basic conservatism of Ohioans. Goldwater, like right-to-work in 1958, represented radical change of a right-wing character and Ohioans rejected the radical conservative as emphatically as they shunned radical left-wing nostrums in other elections.

Ohio's Governmental Expenditures

The majority of Ohio's voters were inclined in a Republican direction throughout most of the state's history. But it was not the Republican bias of the voters that produced conservative government in Ohio. Minnesota and Wisconsin were dominantly Republican states before the Great Depression, but the governments were not notably conservative. The conservatism of Ohio's elected officials and government emerged out of the issueless character of the state's politics wherein the parties failed to provide the voters with meaningful policy alternatives in elections.

Frank Lausche, Ohio's popular governor from 1944 to 1946 and 1948 to 1956, was a Democrat, but the policies he pursued were as conservative as those advocated by any of his Republican opponents. Public servants in fields such as education, welfare, and finance, as well as working newspapermen, claimed that Lausche was one of the poorest governors in the history of the state. As evidence, they pointed out that he did not have the political courage to ask the state legislature for tax increases to pay for the increased costs of state government, and balanced income and outgo through extensive debt financing. (From 1948 to 1956, while Lausche was governor, Ohio's per-capita total general revenue increased 45 percent, compared with 60 percent for the all-state average, and the per-capita total debt increased 5403 percent, compared with an all-state average increase of 221 percent.)

Lausche's critics in state government also attacked his policy of minimizing expenditures on education and welfare and the investment of substantial sums in highways. When Lausche was elected governor in 1948, Ohio's per-capita expenditures for education, welfare, and highways were about the same as the average for all states. In 1956, when he left for the U.S. Senate, Ohio's per-capita state expenditures for education were $22.48, compared with the all-state average of $34.75; $13.85 for welfare, compared with the all-state average of $16.35; and $42.16 for highways, compared with the all-state average of $32.74.

It was claimed by the people in finance, as well as in education and welfare, that a major share of the direct burden of Lausche's policies fell on children, especially those who attended public schools, received aid (aid to dependent children was 80 percent of "established need," compared to 100 percent for old age assistance, aid to the needy blind, and general assistance), and resided in public institutions. For example, in 1956, at the close of Lausche's period in office, some 1000 boys were in residence at the Boys' Industrial School, which admitted to a rated capacity of about 600. In the sleeping quarters of the school there were as many as seventy beds jammed one against the other so that the only access to beds beyond the outer row was to step from bed to bed. According to Lausche's critics, the reason for spending so little on children's services was that they did not vote. Lausche invested substantial sums in a highway program because, first, it was needed and, second, because money spent on highways provided the biggest political payoff in terms of jobs, campaign contributions from contractors, and visible evidence of achievement.

Lausche's successful political career as a conservative Democrat illustrates why the state's government was conservative. Lausche attracted votes from conservative Republicans. These votes, when superimposed on the Democratic votes cast by ill-informed lower-income voters in the cities, provided him with comfortable majorities in the general elections. Other successful Ohio politicians followed a similar strategy. Robert Taft and John Bricker won elections by conducting generally bland campaigns designed to keep divisive issues to a minimum, and once in office pursued conservative policies.

The "payoff" was a state government that spent very little, whether considered in terms of comparative total expenditures or comparative "effort." Looking, first, at comparative total expenditures, Ohio spent $16.27 less per capita than the average for "all states" in 1951 and $22.12 less in 1960.[32] It ranked fortieth in 1951 and forty-second in 1960 in per-capita expenditures among the forty-eight states. Thus, Ohio's citizens, in dollar terms, were farther behind most other states in their state government expenditures in 1960 than in 1951. Secondly, when comparative "effort" is the measuring stick, Ohio was once again behind most other states. Ohio's proportionate relationship between per-capita state expenditures and personal income was 5.4 percent in 1960, compared with 6.7 percent for the "all states" average, placing Ohio among the very last states in an "effort" ranking.

Ohio's expenditures, though small in general, were even more markedly below the national norm in the fields of education and welfare. In 1961, education represented 27.3 percent of Ohio's total general expenditures, about the same as most other states; but in 1960 education represented only 23.6 percent of total general expenditures. The average for "all states" showed an increase in the proportion education represented of total general expenditures from 28.6 percent in 1951 to 32.8 percent in 1960. Thus, the slice of the total-state-expenditures pie allocated to

[32] In every instance, "all states" figures refer to forty-eight states, excluding Alaska and Hawaii.

education declined proportionately in Ohio, whereas nationally the tendency was to provide a larger "slice" to education. When Ohio's state and local expenditures were compared with those of other states, the finding in 1959 was that Ohio spent $87.99 per capita, compared with $99.75 for the "all states" average. In the field of welfare, Ohio ranked thirtieth in the nation in average payments for aid to dependent children in December 1960, behind virtually every industrial state and behind many states with much lower per-capita income, and was comparably low in its relative expenditures for old age assistance, aid to the needy blind, and general welfare.

Summary and Conclusions

The primary question raised by the foregoing data on the expenditures of Ohio's government is the "why" of it. Why did upper-income people in Ohio seemingly vote in terms of their economic self-interest, while low-income people failed to associate their economic problems with their votes? Part of the "why" is that in Ohio the businessman, both large and small, was systematically fed information by the Ohio Chamber of Commerce, the Ohio Retail Merchants Association, the Ohio Association of Manufacturers, and other business organizations. The Ohio businessman found it exceedingly difficult to avoid knowing that Lausche, Bricker, and Robert Taft were alive to and sympathetic with the problems and aspirations of the business community. Further, this information was supported by specific data concerning policies and votes with respect to taxation, governmental regulation, and problems peculiar to the trade of the individual businessman. Consequently, almost all Ohio businessmen (and through them, their wives, friends, and close associates) found it relatively simple to identify the candidates for public office who would maximize their profit and minimize their costs.

The workingman in Ohio seldom had sources of information comparable to those enjoyed by the businessman. One explanation for the political naïveté of Ohio's less well-to-do voters and the relative political sophistication of high-income voters is that many working-class voters were socially isolated, whereas high-income voters were part of a close-knit community.[33] A large

[33] There are many studies which have reported similar findings; see, for example, Bernard R. Berelson, Paul F. Lazarsfeld, and William N. McPhee, *Voting* (Chicago: University of Chicago Press, 1954), pp. 54–75, 88–100, and 114–115.

proportion of Ohio's working-class voters were socially isolated because of their occupational diffusion in a large number of medium-sized cities. According to the 1960 census, Ohio had more cities (five) with a population of 150,000 to 500,000 than any other state.

The effect of a diffusion of the working population, as opposed to their concentration, on attitudes and voting behavior was profound. In mining communities or large cities where workers tended to live in working-class ghettos, every aspect of the environment reinforced a working-class psychology and identification. People in such environments identified with the working class and judged political candidates on the basis of their support of or opposition to measures which promoted the interests of the working class. Because of the high level of cohesion in such laboring-group communities and the possession of common attitudes vis-a-vis the outer community, the residents tended to be rather well informed concerning the identity of conservative and liberal candidates. They were well informed because of their intense interest in politics, a concern emerging out of strong in-group feelings that produced sentiments of loyalty to the working class and hostility to the business community. Consequently, labor organizations and political parties which furnished them with information concerning candidates and issues found a receptive audience.

The parallel between the cohesion of people in working-class ghettos and those in upper-middle-class ghettos is impressive. The residents of upper-middle-class neighborhoods were isolated from working-class people and arguments, possessed a common frame of reference, strong in-group attitudes, and emotions of loyalty to the business community and hostility to the "out-groups." These well-to-do folk were eager to secure information identifying their political friends and enemies, and thus were an excellent market for information provided by such agencies as the Chamber of Commerce, the National Association of Manufacturers, and, in some areas, the John Birch Society.

Contrast the working-class ghettos in Chicago and New York City and the upper-middle-class ghettos in every urban area with the residential and group membership patterns of a large proportion of the working class in the medium-sized cities in Ohio. The following statement concerning lower-middle-income neighborhoods in Ohio is, admittedly, largely impressionistic, but it is based upon long acquaintance with such Ohio neighborhoods and upon friendships and interviews with people from several similar sections of Ohio cities.

In 1960, many of Ohio's workingmen lived in lower-middle-income neighborhoods. The most striking feature of such neighborhoods was the infrequency with which people interacted with one another. In some cases, next-door neighbors were well acquainted. However, even in these instances the interaction was largely of the casual "over-the-fence" variety. The social isolation of the families was remarkable in view of their physical proximity and length of residence. The homes were divided by either a plot of grass or a driveway not more than ten to fifteen yards wide. The garages were generally parallel, so that the ordinary passing to and from the house to drive or wash the car inevitably entailed frequent physical confrontation of neighbor with neighbor. Nevertheless, in most instances, the neighbors remained virtual strangers with few common ties.

In many ways the resident of the lower-middle-income Ohio neighborhood was kith and kin of the suspicious, isolated French peasant. He was almost totally absorbed in his one-half acre, his family, and his television set. In fact, in some respects the French peasant seemed like a cosmopolitan sophisticate in comparison to his Ohio counterpart, for at least the French peasant had forty acres and some cows and chickens in addition to his family.

The reason for the social isolation of families in the lower-middle-income neighborhoods was that they had little in common. The postman did not talk the same language as his accountant neighbor, and the accountant was in a different world from the skilled workman at Timken Roller Bearing who lived across the street. Thus, conversation between them usually took the form of monosyllabic grunts about the weather or the future of the Cleveland Indians (almost invariably grunts of despair where the Indians were concerned).

What, then, was the result of this pattern of group associations on the political behavior of the less well-to-do people in Ohio? The result was that they failed to identify with a working class or with a neighborhood or with any group much larger than their families. Consequently, the unions to which they belonged were politically weak and the Democratic party to which they gave nominal allegiance was divided into many factions and was virtually nonexistent as a statewide entity. The disunity of unions and the Democratic party in Ohio was a faithful reflection of the social disorganization of their members.

Consequently, neither the Democratic party nor the labor unions provided a cohesive cement for the atomized, less well-to-do voters of Ohio. They were unable or unwilling to provide the low-income voters with the information which would have enabled them to relate their self-interest with their vote.

Given this frame of reference or state of mind of the low-income electorate in Ohio, how did they discriminate between candidates for political office? The first mental screen through which candidates were passed by Ohioans was the "middle class" myth. Ohio has been called "the great middle class state." The middle class myth was a blend of Horatio Alger and the rugged individualist attitudes associated with the frontier. It found concrete expression in a dedication to the homely virtues of honesty, thrift, steadiness, caution, and a distrust of government. Freedom was prized, and restraints tended to be associated almost exclusively with government.

Not entirely coincidentally, there was a nice correspondence between the narrow economic self-interest of upper-income people and the middle-class political myth. Low-income people, on the other hand, were rarely aware of cross-pressures between the myth and their economic self-interest when they cast their votes. They were unaware of cross-pressures because, first, there was rarely any discernible difference between the candidates in terms of their devotion to the middle-class myth; and, second, where a difference did exist, the low-income voters, more often than not, were not informed of it.

In the absence of a class or community basis for voting, the response to candidates was in terms, first, of personalities, and, second, of problems, real or imagined, that impinged directly on the family. Thus, the candidate who was honest, pleasant, and genial, a good family man, capable, and was in favor of the full lunch pail and capital punishment, and was opposed to higher taxes, gambling, prostitution, and other forms of organized crime, attracted their vote. Failing a personality or a home-and-hearth issue on which to peg a vote, then the decision was often in terms of religious or ethnic group memberships. For example, Lausche received a substantial vote from fellow Catholics and Slovenians. The fact that Lausche was a Catholic was not of compelling importance to the Catholics who voted for him. However, in the absence of any other reason to vote for or against a candidate, religious or ethnic identification (the two were usually intertwined) was a convenient peg on which to hang a vote.

As C. Wright Mills put it in *The Sociological Imagination*:

Is it any wonder that ordinary men feel they cannot cope with the larger worlds with which they are so suddenly confronted? That they cannot understand the meaning of their epoch for their own lives?

That in defense of selfhood they become morally insensible, trying to remain altogether private men?[34]

The lower-middle-income and working-class vote in Ohio was a statistical expression of the retreat from reality of the ordinary men of the society. The "larger world" baffled them, partly because of its complexity but primarily because of the failure of anyone to explain it to them in terms that related it to their lives.

Ohio was not different in kind from other industrial states but was different in degree. All states had isolated voters. Almost all voters in all states were opposed to Communism and racketeers and corrupt political bosses. Few voters liked taxes. Most subscribed at least in part to the middle-class myth. But in most industrial states there were labor or political groups which introduced other factors into the voting equation, such as the narrow economic self-interest of the low-income voter. The justification for intruding the narrow economic self-interest of voters into elections is that when there is well-regulated, democratic class conflict, there sometimes emerge out of it, through political compromise, public policies which take into account the interests of the whole community. But where, as in Ohio, a minority is intensely class-conscious, whereas the majority is atomized, the result is imposition by the minority on the majority of its narrow class-oriented objectives.

[34] C. Wright Mills, *The Sociological Imagination* (New York: Grove Press, 1959), pp. 4–5.

Chapter 6

Corruption and Competition
in Indiana

Indiana, more than other Midwest states, was a "border state" in the 1960s. The intensely partisan flavor of its politics, the speech and attitudes of its people were more akin to Kentucky and West Virginia than to Ohio and Illinois. And, in truth, more of its people, past and present, were born in Kentucky and other southern or border states than was true of other Midwest states.

In 1850, more than 39 percent of Indiana's population were people from the southern United States, compared to 21 percent in Ohio and 27 percent in Illinois. Perhaps as important for Indiana's culture was the comparatively small number of New Englanders who settled there (11,000), compared to the much larger number of Yankees who made their homes in Ohio (66,000) and Illinois (37,000) by 1850. The reason for the failure of easterners to settle in Indiana was the swampy land in northern Indiana, which seemed unsuited for agriculture but which later proved to be extremely rich farm land. The early settlers from the east traveled the Erie Canal to the Great Lakes, boarded boats which took them to northern Ohio, southern Michigan, and, later, Illinois and Wisconsin, but which tended to bypass Indiana.

The land which appeared best suited to agriculture and which was first "opened" to settlement was in the southern part of the state. Most of the early waves of immigrants to Indiana reached the lands from the Wilderness Road through Kentucky. Many also followed the National Road (presently Route 40) to Wheeling, West Virginia, thence via waterway down the Ohio River to Vincennes (the earliest Indiana settlement) or another of the Ohio River towns. The settlers found their way to the interior of the state along rivers, such as the Wabash and Whitewater River valleys.

Later the National Road was extended to Indiana, entering the state on the east at Richmond and running through Indianapolis to Terre Haute on the west (see Figure 6.1 for the National Road or Route 40). The road, in the minds of its people, bisects the state culturally and politically. The people in the area south of the National Road have long been regarded as predominantly southern and Democratic, and the people north of the road as largely northern and Republican.

Thomas Marshall observed:

> The Commonwealth was and is, yet, indeed, two states. The old National Road that ran from Wheeling to St. Louis . . . is really the dividing line between these two states. South of that line the vast majority of the people who came in were from Virginia, the Carolinas, and Kentucky. . . . The northern part of the state was very largely settled by New Englanders, New Yorkers, Pennsylvanians, people from Ohio, to which were added after the Revolution of 1848, vast numbers of liberty-loving Germans, who came with Carl Schurz to this country.[1]

Marshall, it may be noted, carefully and correctly distinguished between the southern immigrants who represented the "vast majority" of the people in southern Indiana and the northern immigrants who only "very largely settled" the area north of the National Road. For, in truth, the Indianans from the South were an important part of the population in every section of the state.

It was the early settlement pattern of the state in combination with the Civil War which formed the basis for the electoral division between the Republican and Democratic parties (see Figures 6.1 and 6.2).[2] A tabulation of the counties that were strongly Republican, 1932–1960 (six of eight presidential elections), reveals that fifty-three of Indiana's ninety-two counties were dominantly Republican and forty-four of the fifty-three dominantly Republican counties, 1932–1960, were Republican in the Civil War presidential election of 1860.

Further computations reveal that there were thirty-two Indiana counties in which the people either split even or voted

---

[1] Thomas Marshall, *Recollections of Thomas R. Marshall: Vice-President and Hoosier Philosopher* (Indianapolis: The Bobbs-Merrill Co., 1925), p. 56.
[2] Similar findings are contained in Key and Munger, "Social Determinism and Electoral Decision: The Case of Indiana," in *American Voting Behavior*, Burdick and Brodbeck, eds. (New York: The Free Press of Glencoe, 1959), pp. 284–286.

Democratic more often than Republican in the presidential elections, 1932–1960. Once again, comparison of the figures shows that twenty-one of the thirty-two more Democratic Indiana counties were also Democratic at the time of the Civil War in the 1860 election and that many of the remaining ones were metropolitan counties, 1960.[3]

There is an apparent contradiction between the statement that Indiana was settled mainly by Southerners and the dominantly Republican cast, geographically, of the state indicated by Figure 6.1. There are two explanations for the contradiction. In the first place, Indiana was never so one-sidedly Republican as the figure would imply. In the years after the Civil War, from 1868 to 1892, the Democrats won the state in three of seven presidential contests and emerged victorious in four of seven gubernatorial elections. Many of the counties that voted Republican in 1860 were narrowly divided between the two parties after the Civil War, leaving Indiana a two-party state in which either party could win through a shift of only a few votes. It was only after 1896 that the state moved in a Republican direction, although it remained a political battleground.[4] After 1932, the Republican party was dominant geographically, but the Democrats balanced the electoral scales with a large urban vote. The second part of the explanation for the Republican bias of the state in spite of its dominantly southern settlement pattern may be found by looking at Kentucky, from which so much of its population originated.

Kentucky was Henry Clay's home. The central Bluegrass (Lexington and surrounding country) and the eastern Kentucky mountains were largely Whig before the Civil War. When the sons of the Kentucky Whigs moved to Ohio, Indiana, and Illinois, they voted Whig. During and after the Civil War the eastern Kentucky people and, to a lesser extent, the voters of the central Bluegrass, supported the Union and voted Republican, leaving Kentucky narrowly and rigidly divided between the two parties, but leaning in a Democratic direction.

---

[3] Additional statistical confirmation of these observations is provided by the simple coefficient of correlation between the percent two-party vote for the Democratic candidate for governor in 1960 (Matthew Welsh) and the percent two-party Democratic vote in the 1860 presidential election which resulted in an r of .48.

[4] See Key, "A Theory of Critical Elections," *Journal of Politics*, vol. 17 (1959), pp. 3–18, for an interesting discussion of the effect of the 1896 election.

FIGURE 6.1 INDIANA'S DEMOCRATIC AND REPUBLICAN COUNTIES in the presidential elections, 1932–1960

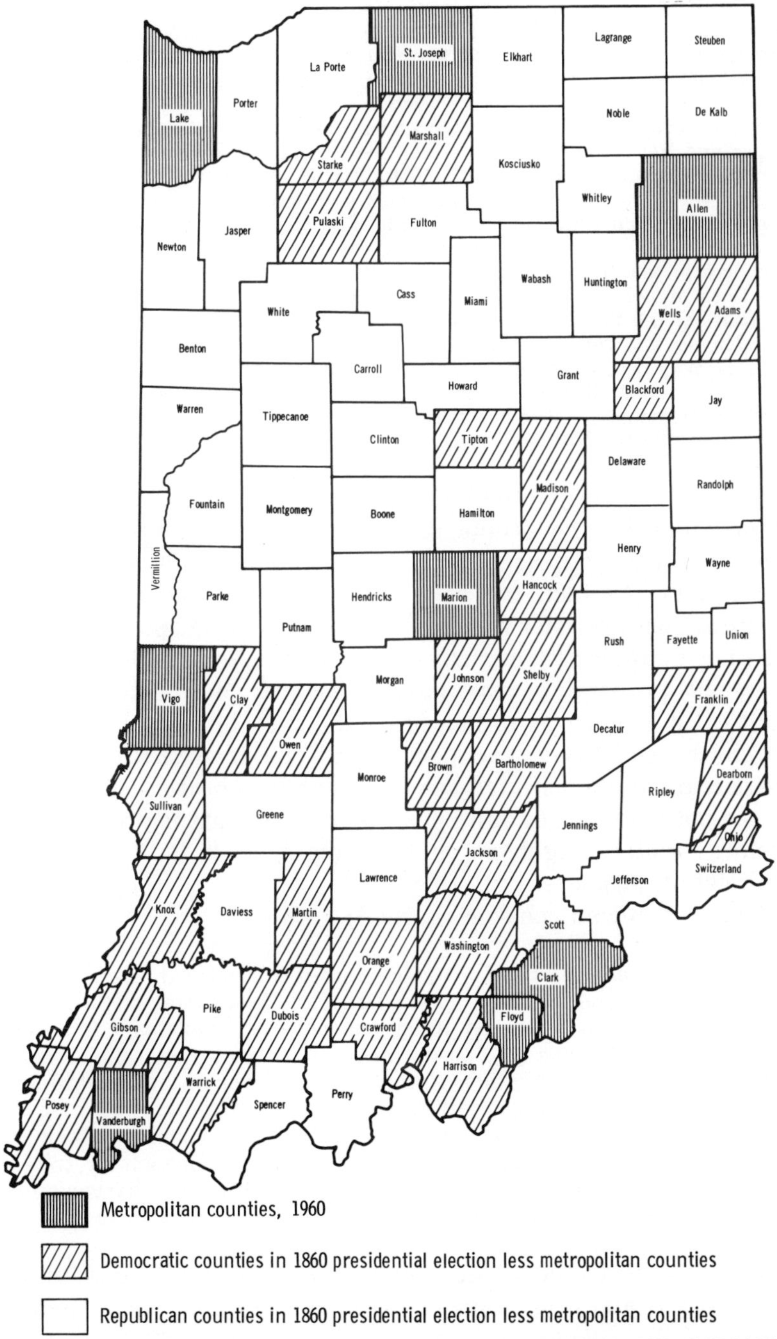

Metropolitan counties, 1960

Democratic counties in 1860 presidential election less metropolitan counties

Republican counties in 1860 presidential election less metropolitan counties

FIGURE 6.2 THE BASIS FOR POLITICAL DIVISIONS IN INDIANA
The metropolitan counties and the counties won by the Republican and
Democratic candidates in 1860

Explanatory Note for Figures 6.1 and 6.2: The two figures are designed to provide visual confirmation of the statement in the text that it was the early settlement pattern of the state in combination with the Civil War which formed the basis for the electoral division between the Republican and Democratic parties. Figure 6.1 identifies the counties in which Democratic and Republican candidates for the Presidency won a majority of the vote more often than not, 1932–1960. Figure 6.2 shows (1) the counties which were carried by the Democratic and Republican candidates in the Civil War presidential election of 1860, and (2) the metropolitan counties, 1960. Visual comparison of the two figures indicates (1) that the lines of Democratic and Republican electoral success, 1932–1960, tended to follow the lines of political division at the time of the Civil War. The only important change that has taken place to disrupt the ancient Civil War political cleavages is the tendency of voters in the great metropolitan areas to vote Democratic, a change that was produced by the Great Depression and Franklin D. Roosevelt's New Deal, and (2) that the 1860 and 1960 political cleavages tend to cut along the north-south division of the state as marked out by the National Road.

Further, as was pointed out in an earlier chapter dealing with Ohio, many of the people moving into the Midwest from the South had been displaced by the slave economy and were strongly antislavery. In fact, the only surprise occasioned by Indiana's political position after the Civil War is that the Republican party was not more dominant than the election returns indicate.

In all probability, the narrowness of the post-Civil War political division was produced by the very bitter political campaigns of the Civil War period and the identification of the Democratic party with treason by Republican orators. The nature of the political battles quite possibly aroused latent pro-Southern feelings which might never have emerged in a less charged political atmosphere.

One Republican speaker charged:

> Every unregenerate rebel . . . calls himself a Democrat. Every bounty jumper, every deserter, every sneak who runs away from the draft . . . every man . . . who murdered union prisoners . . . every wolf in sheep's clothing . . . every one who shoots negroes in the streets, burns negro schoolhouses and meetinghouses, and murders women and children by the light of their flaming dwellings, calls himself a Democrat. . . . In short, the Democratic party may be described as a common sewer and loathsome receptacle, into which is emptied every element of treason North and South and every element of inhumanity and barbarianism which has dishonored the age.[5]

In retrospect, the speech may appear extreme. But to the Republicans and pro-Unionists of the period there was abundant

[5] Frank James Munger, "Two-Party Politics in the State of Indiana" (unpublished dissertation, Harvard University, 1955), p. 43.

evidence to support the charges. The Southern sympathizers in Indiana organized the Knights of the Golden Circle and enlisted tens of thousands of members (mostly Democrats) in Indiana. Democrats received Vallandigham (the pro-Southern Democrat from Ohio) with cheers. Thus, many Democrats did oppose the war and most pro-Southern traitors were Democrats (although not all Democrats were pro-Southern traitors—an important distinction).

In the meantime, the Republican party, which was in political charge of the state, prosecuted the war with more vigor than in other northern states. Governor Oliver Morton, who was elected in 1860, was a radical Republican and, more than anyone else, was responsible for Indiana's deep involvement in the Civil War. He helped send 196,363 Hoosiers to war, representing 74.3 percent of Indiana's population capable of bearing arms. Of these 196,363 men, 13 percent or 25,000 died.[6]

It was out of this background that draft riots broke out in Democratic areas where support of the war was lukewarm from the beginning. The riots and the accompanying pro-Southern sentiments expressed by Democrats were followed by severe repression. Republican Governor Morton claimed that the Knights of the Golden Circle planned to murder him. Thereafter he established a military dictatorship, the writ of habeas corpus was suspended, and leaders of the Knights were arrested (the U.S. Supreme Court upset one conviction in ex parte Milligan, a landmark Supreme Court decision). Out of these events, Indiana soldiers and their families found good reason to identify the Democratic party with treason. Bereaved families of soldiers killed in action saw the Democratic party as the political expression of the rebel devil that had snuffed out the lives of their sons.

On the other hand, Democrats who were not anti-Union at the beginning of the war but retained some ties of sentiment with the South found fresh reason for hatred of Republicans during the war. Their sons were drafted into an unwanted war, and when they expressed opposition to the draft, their leaders were clapped in prison.

The Civil War, then, during which Indianans enlisted more soldiers, proportionately, than any other northern state, forms the bedrock of Indiana politics in the mid-twentieth century. The emotions induced by that conflict probably had as much to

[6] John Button Martin, *Indiana: An Interpretation* (New York: Alfred A. Knopf, Inc., 1947), p. 63.

do with the votes cast in the 1952 or the 1960 presidential elections as Catholicism, Communism, or Korea.

Between the Civil War and 1896, few Hoosiers deviated from the political convictions induced by civil strife. In the seven gubernatorial elections, 1868–1892, the Democratic percent of the two-party vote was never less than 49.2 percent (1880) and never more than 50.8 percent (1884). The two-party division could hardly have been narrower or more rigid.

After 1896, however, the Democratic party slowly lost adherents. The silver heresy of 1896 cost it much of its business support in the cities, and because businessmen often affected or controlled the votes of their workers, the Democrats also lost the support of workingmen. More importantly, the Democratic machines in the cities no longer received financial support from businessmen. The 1904 gold deviation of the Democrats when they nominated Parker for the Presidency robbed the Democrats of much of the rural support that accrued to them through Bryan's nomination. Then in World Wars I and II the Democratic party lost a part of its German vote.

Thousands of Germans settled in Indiana after the 1848 revolution and were followed by thousands more in the latter part of the nineteenth century. The Germans (and especially the Catholic Germans) tended to vote Democratic. The cause of their Democratic bias was the nativism of the Whigs and Republicans, which was given political expression by the Know-nothing groups in the mid-nineteenth century. Although the Democratic party was not free of antiforeign, anti-Catholic sentiment, politically it was concentrated in the Republican party. Consequently, the Germans tended to gravitate into the Democratic party.

However, when the Germans were persecuted during Woodrow Wilson's administration with almost the same venom as the Republicans persecuted Copperheads during the Civil War, there were defections of Germans to the Republican party. During the 1920s, the Ku Klux Klan emerged as a potent political force in Indiana. It was powerful in both parties, but its main center of strength was in the Republican party. In 1924, a Ku Klux Klan-backed candidate for governor was nominated on the Republican ticket and subsequently elected. The identification of the KKK with the Republicans, plus the nomination of Al Smith, a Catholic, for the Presidency in 1928, pulled German Catholics back into the Democratic party, although there remained a net loss to the Democrats. Subsequently, the economic policies of Franklin Roosevelt which offended the conservative Germans (only partially redeemed among beer-loving Germans by repeal under Roosevelt), plus another Democratic-sponsored war against Germany in the 1940s, cost the Democratic party much of its remaining German voting strength.

Dubois County is regarded by all Indianans as the most German county in the state. The county was 70 percent or more Democratic in every election, 1892–1912. In 1916, the Democratic percent of the vote dropped slightly to 68 percent; in 1920 it fell precipitously to 52 percent, rose again in 1924 with Ku Klux Klan activity, increased again in 1928 and 1932 with Al Smith and the Great Depression, but fell in 1936 in response to the New Deal and declined secularly thereafter, and was lost by the Democrats for the first time since 1840 (when it went Whig) in 1952 and 1956, when Eisenhower carried the county. In 1960 Kennedy received 61 percent of Dubois County's vote, but this probably represented a temporary recapture of a part of the German Catholic vote.

The Democratic party also lost much of its traditional Civil War vote over the 1932–1960 period. In the presidential elections, 1932–1960, only four of the traditionally Democratic counties remained strongly in favor of the Democratic ticket (6 of 8 elections). Thus, in a geographic sense, the Democratic party lost a great deal of voting strength in Indiana from the Civil War to 1960. Only nine of the state's ninety-two counties were strongly Democratic in the presidential elections, 1932–1960, whereas fifty-three counties were strongly Republican over the same period. However, as we shall see in the following discussions of political organization and political change, the Democrats gained votes in the state's cities that compensated for the loss of traditional adherents to the Republicans.

Political Organization

Hoosiers love both basketball and politics. According to legend, every Hoosier baby is born with a ballot in his hand—and, it might be added, is teethed on a basketball hoop. And according to many observers, both sports have been equally meaningful— or meaningless.

But meaningful or not, Indiana unquestionably enjoyed a virile two-party system in the 1960s, for both parties were well organized and in elections either one of them had an excellent chance of emerging victorious. In sharp contrast to Ohio, where the Democratic party was found to be virtually nonexistent on the state level, the Democratic party in Indiana was probably the better organized of the two parties in the early 1960s. The reason for the excellent state of Democratic political organization was that it controlled the Statehouse through the person of Democratic Governor Matthew Welsh. And in Indiana, control of the Statehouse provided a party with ample financial resources. For example, in the 1962 campaign for U.S. senator between Birch Bayh and Homer Capehart, the Democrats spent $514,174.18 on direct campaign expenses, July 15–November 15, 1962. In addition, the Democratic State Committee expended $399,897.42, May 15–November 15, 1962, for operating expenses. The balance left in the coffers of the Democratic State Committee after the 1962 campaign was $211,968.60.

Indiana is the only state studied where the governor and other important state officials described quite frankly and in detail the sources of the campaign funds. They were disarmingly frank because they saw nothing wrong in the techniques employed to raise funds, and neither did the opposing political party nor the press nor, presumably, the citizenry.

According to Democrats, they raised more than $800,000 in 1962, mainly through a 2 percent levy on the annual salaries of approximately 8000 state employees who were outside civil service. The amount realized through this 2 percent club was about $275,000 in 1962. A second source of funds was four cents received by the Democratic State Committee for each state license plate sold in the state, amounting to a total of about $75,000. The procedure followed with respect to the sale of auto licenses was to let the franchises for the sale of the plates to the county Democratic organization. There was a fifty-cent fee for the sale of each plate, and the county organization pocketed four cents of the amount and an additional four cents went to the Democratic State Central Committee.

A third source of funds for the Democratic State Committee was $260,000 which was obtained from the county Democratic organization through an assessment based upon $100 for each delegate to the Democratic State Convention. The county Democratic organizations usually paid their assessments, for failure to pay often involved the loss of state patronage. For example, in 1962 the Marion County (Indianapolis) Democratic organization failed to pay $34,000 owed to the Democratic State Committee. Therefore, the State Committee withdrew the franchise for the sale of license plates from the Marion County organization and sold them directly, thus avoiding the middleman.

Another reason the county organizations generally paid their assessments is that insurance commissions for the sale of insurance to the state were distributed by the Democratic State Committee to the county organizations. In 1961, $36,000 in commissions was distributed this way. The formula followed was to give each county $9 in commissions for each delegate to the Democratic State Convention.

A final source of funds for Democrats in 1962 (and for Republicans when they were in office) was about $200,000 in individual contributions. Economy and efficiency experts would approve of the procedures followed in seeking contributions. Automatic computers were used to compile a listing of every vendor from whom the state purchased goods and services, including the total amount of the purchases. Subsequently, the vendors were informed of the degree to which they were dependent upon state business and were asked to contribute to the Democratic party.

Such practices were not unique to Indiana. And, of course, they were not confined to the Democratic party, for the Republicans followed the same time-hallowed means of raising funds when they were in office, which explains why Republicans did not criticize Democratic practices when they (the Republicans) were out of office. The unique quality of Indiana politics was the extent to which "corrupt practices" were institutionalized and accepted as a normal part of the political game by the press and citizenry of the state. One result of such a free and easy political morality was an endless succession of scandals. The most recent were the road scandals during the Craig administration and the Lake County (Gary) scandals.

The highway exposés involving Governor George Craig's administration, 1952–1956, astonished even Hoosiers and were partly responsible for Democratic victories in 1958, 1960, and 1962. According to the Grand Jury report, carried in the *Indianapolis Star*, June 28, 1957, Virgil W. Smith, Craig's chairman of the State Highway Commission, was guilty of collusive land profiteering and soliciting and taking bribes. According to the report, Virgil Smith, Highway Department head, "did in several instances furnish friends and business associates of his from Milan, Indiana, with specific information that enabled them to purchase lands which they knew the State Highway Department would therefore purchase in turn from them. Mr. Smith then approved the purchase grants and ordered the payment of excessive prices for these realty parcels from his friends at State expense." In addition, they found evidence of bribes and kickbacks received by Smith from A. J. Mogilner Distributors, Inc. The Grand Jury report said: "The evidence shows that out of the large commissions earned by his said corporation from such sales to the State Highway Commission, Mr. Mogilner made nine (9) payments to Mr. Virgil W. Smith aggregating $41,498.66."

An example of the way in which Indiana's taxpayers were robbed by Smith and his friends was the time in June 1955 when the state purchased 148 (55-gallon) barrels of a gasoline additive. In bidding on the purchase, Mogilner submitted a bid in the amount of $8 per gallon for an additive called "Glo." Another firm submitted a bid in the amount of $3.78 for another additive called "Miracle Power." Tests indicated there was no substantial difference between the two products. Nevertheless, the bid was accepted from Mogilner at $8 per gallon.

Again quoting from the Grand Jury report:

When the large 148-barrel order arrived, Mr. Mogilner had substituted Miracle Power. No protest was ever made by anyone at the Highway Department, although they had been led to believe they were to receive Glo (for which they were willing to pay $5 more per gallon on the basis of driving tests).

On November 2, 1957, Virgil Smith was convicted in criminal court of conspiring to embezzle public funds, sentenced to two to fourteen years, and fined $5000. On November 25, 1958, he was convicted in criminal court of solicitation and accepting of bribes, sentenced to two to fourteen years, and fined $20,000 on this charge. Also, convicted of corrupt practices were William E. Sayer, an administrative assistant to Governor Craig; Elmer W. (Doc) Henwood, adviser and friend of Governor Craig; the state purchasing director and highway right-of-way director under Craig, as well as eight other men.

The Lake County scandals in 1962 surprised few Hoosiers, for the county had long suffered from a reputation for political corruption. The only surprise expressed was that the guilty parties were caught and prosecuted. In 1962, Mayor George Chacharis of Gary, Indiana; Peter Mandich, the Sheriff of Lake County; and four other persons were indicted and stood trial for failing to pay federal income taxes on some $226,686 received through kickbacks and bribes from companies doing business in and with Lake County. According to testimony in the trial, Chacharis and Mandich established four dummy corporations through which companies purchased nonexisting services for the privilege of doing business in Lake County. An example of the method of operation of Lake County politicians is provided by the following account of testimony in the trial:

> Gary Mayor George Chacharis received more than $100,000 in under-the-table payments to pave the way for construction of the Indiana toll road across Lake County, an Ohio businessman testified.
>
> The testimony came from Robert Altreuter, Columbus, project manager for Union Building and Construction Corporation of Passaic, New Jersey, who said the alleged kickbacks gave his firm clearance for toll road construction work. . . . Altreuter said Chacharis himself picked up the checks, some made out to various individuals and firms for "service rendered." The government contends three of the companies were set up as dummy outfits to channel the alleged kickbacks to Chacharis.
>
> The witness said Chacharis and Harold A. Zweig, Gary City Engineer, told him in September, 1955, it would cost 5 cents a cubic yard to obtain permits to bring in sand for highway fills.
>
> "I said to Chacharis that we were talking about an awful lot of money," Altreuter said. "Chacharis said it was not a holdup. He was going to have companies and individuals bill us for services."
>
> Altreuter identified 20 checks which he said were given to Chacharis in the alleged deal during 1955 and 1956, when Chacharis was Gary city comptroller. They totaled $100,300.
>
> Included were checks made out to Richton Survey, Braeburn Engineering, and Construction Survey, alleged dummy corporations.
>
> Altreuter also testified that no actual work was done by any of the individuals or firms which received the checks.[7]

Subsequently, Chacharis was convicted of evading the payment of $107,974 in income taxes on the kickback money and received a three-year prison term. Sheriff Peter Mandich was freed because he was wise enough to pay taxes on the money he received.

Numerous additional examples of political corruption could be cited, such as the jailing of Governor McCray in the 1920s. But repetition would only dull the sense already conveyed of rather widespread political corruption in Indiana. The existence of widespread corruption in a state with vital two-party competition is puzzling, for one theoretical function of two-party competition is to keep a check upon just such malpractices. A partial explanation for the corrupt flavor of Indiana politics was the dominance in both parties of job-oriented professional politicians to whom issues were unimportant save as they served as means by which to secure the jobs. Consequently, it is essential

---

[7] *Indianapolis News*, November 17, 1962, p. 11. I am grateful to the *Indianapolis Star* and *News* for the help provided me in obtaining data on political corruption in Indiana. The people in the papers' library were especially kind.

to an understanding of Indiana politics to examine the formal organization and the personalities in the Republican and Democratic parties.

Republican Party Organization

In 1962 formal party organization was more important in Indiana than in many states because the incumbent governor generally worked within the party organization. In some states, such as Kentucky, the governor established an informal political organization consisting of administration men in each county who handled patronage and provided the governor with political support within the counties.

Within the formal organization of Indiana's Republican party, the only party officials elected directly by the voters were the precinct committeemen, one for each of the precincts in the state. The elections occurred in the primary election held the first Tuesday after the first Monday in May in even-numbered years. After election, the precinct committeeman appointed a vice-committeeman of the opposite sex—often the person's wife or husband.

Subsequently, the precinct committeemen and vice-committeemen of each county met and elected a county chairman, vice-chairman (of the opposite sex), secretary, and treasurer. The county chairmen and vice-chairmen of each congressional district then met as district committees and elected a district chairman and district vice-chairman (of the opposite sex). The district chairmen and vice-chairmen met as the state central committee and selected a state chairman. The state chairman and district chairmen were powerful figures within their parties, especially when their party controlled the governorship, for most patronage was distributed through them.

Another reason for the importance of formal party organization in Indiana was that statewide elective candidates were selected in party conventions rather than through the popular primary.[8] Indiana experimented briefly with the popular primary for statewide elective offices in the 1920s, but returned to the convention system.

[8] See V. O. Key, Jr., *American State Politics* (New York: Alfred A. Knopf, Inc., 1956), pp. 169 ff, where Key points out that nomination by convention prevents the atrophy of political organization at the local level. Also see V. O. Key, "The Direct Primary and Party Structure: A Study of State Legislative Nominations," *American Political Science Review*, vol. 48 (1954), pp. 1–26.

Delegates to the parties' state conventions were selected at the same May elections in which the precinct committeemen were elected. Delegates to the conventions were apportioned on the basis of one delegate for each 400 votes cast by that party for secretary of state in the previous general election and were parceled out to the counties and districts on that basis. Generally, the county organizations entered slates at the elections and in most cases the slates won election. The state party conventions, in addition to nominating candidates, selected delegates to the national conventions in presidential election years.

Thus, the formal political organizations in Indiana were important, and the people who held party posts at the state, district, county, and precinct level were powerful personages by virtue of their political positions. They gave jobs and contracts and insurance commissions to their friends and supporters and denied them to their enemies. They also played a part, however minor, in selecting party nominees for President, governor, U.S. senator, and other statewide elective offices, by virtue of their control over the slating of candidates for election as convention delegates.

For most Indiana·politicians, then, politics was a central part of their lives, not an avocation. They were professionals as opposed to the amateur part-time politicians often found in states where reforms, such as the popular primary and civil service, have robbed the political party of the nominating and patronage functions.

The professional character of Indiana politics helps explain much that is enigmatic and paradoxical in the state's politics. Outside Indiana, the state's Republican party was regarded as extremely conservative, based largely upon the records of Senators William Jenner and Homer Capehart. Senator Jenner secured a certain notoriety by referring to General George Marshall as "a living lie."

There was more than a little truth to the conservative brand when applied to Indiana Republicanism. Most of the party's voting strength was located in the less urban portions of the state, and the people of nonmetropolitan Indiana tended to be quite conservative. Therefore, the Republican party leaders were alive to the demands of the state's conservative strongholds. However, the party professionals were also aware of the fact that about half of the state's population resided in the ten metropolitan counties and that the party was doomed to defeat if it ignored the needs of the urban residents.

The Republican party professionals, as a group, were not

very concerned with ideology. Their main interest was in winning elections in order to control the emoluments of power. Much of the professionals' time was spent in placating and soothing the injured feelings of the party's conservatives while attempting to secure the nomination of candidates palatable to urban Indiana. In 1958, 1960, 1962, and 1964 they were unsuccessful in three U.S. Senate and two gubernatorial elections. The central reason for their election failures was the division within the party between the professionals and the ideologists.

The Republican party's schism was called Craig versus Jenner-Capehart from 1952 to 1956. After 1956 it took the form of pro-Jenner and anti-Jenner factions. Some said that the factions simply represented disagreements between personalities within the party and did not represent fundamental differences dividing Republicans on issues. However, Republican party leaders in their inner councils and in frank conversations recognized that the continuing intraparty conflicts transcended personalities. In private conversations, most Republican leaders stated that the party's schism was identified with personalities but basically involved issues. The party split took many forms: north Indiana versus south Indiana, the "ins" versus the "outs," Jenner and anti-Jenner. But the one constant thread running through all the party disputes was the party's right wing versus the moderates and professionals.

North-South Republican Factionalism

The north Indiana versus south Indiana division within the party was often manifested in the vote cast in Republican state conventions for candidates for nomination to office and in the Republican State Central Committee on issues and the election of the state chairman. Examples of north-south division of the Republican party are provided by the vote in the 1952 Republican State Convention for the gubernatorial nominee and by the 1954 Republican primary when Republican precinct committeemen were elected.[9]

[9] Frank James Munger, "Two-Party Politics in Indiana" (unpublished Ph.D. dissertation, Harvard University, 1955). Professor Munger's dissertation is, with little doubt, the most widely read unpublished dissertation in the United States. The data concerning the 1952 convention and 1954 primary were taken from Professor Munger's dissertation, and I have drawn heavily upon the dissertation in this analysis of the politics of the state. Also see Frank Munger, "The Struggle for Republican Leadership in Indiana, 1954," Eagleton Institute Cases in Practical Politics, 1960.

In 1952 the Republican party was out of power in the state and, consequently, there was no strong party organization which could control large numbers of votes in the convention. Therefore, the vote of the convention delegates tended to break along sectional lines, because one of the major contenders for the nomination, Craig, hailed from southern Indiana, and his opponent was from northern Indiana. The vote was largely based on "friends and neighbors" ties, emerging out of hope for party preferment based upon propinquity in the event of party victory. On the third and last ballot of the convention, Craig received more than 65 percent of the delegate vote in all but eight counties in southern Indiana and received less than 65 percent of the vote in most of the northern counties. Another issue in the convention, however, was a liberal versus conservative fight revolving around the conflicting claims of Eisenhower and Taft for convention delegates pledged to them. Craig was for Eisenhower, as was H. Dale Brown, the Republican leader from Indianapolis. H. Dale Brown helped obtain votes for Craig from Marion County and adjacent counties, in part because of his moderate views. Thus, the vote received by Craig in 1952 was for both sectional and ideological reasons, with the sectional factor dominant.

During Craig's administration he was involved in a continuing battle with Senators Jenner and Capehart over control of the state party machinery. The 1954 primary, when Republican precinct committeemen were elected, was a battle between the Craig forces and the Jenner-Capehart forces for control of the party. In the 1954 primary, Craig once again obtained the support of southern Indiana Republicans and lost much of northern Indiana.

The reasons for the 1954 victories of Craig-backed precinct committeemen in south Indiana, however, were largely different from those for his 1952 convention support. In 1954 he was governor with control over the distribution of jobs and contracts and other perquisites of political power. His opponents, Jenner and Capehart, had relatively few federal jobs available to them through which to attract support. And in much of southern Indiana a job with the highway department was more important than in relatively wealthy north Indiana. Southern Indiana was culturally and economically a part of the western Kentucky hills. The land was poor, the families large, and a contract or a job loomed large in anyone's scale of values. Consequently, an incumbent governor of either party could usually rely upon the vote of southern Indiana in a convention or in the State Central Committee. (As will be shown later, Governor Welsh, a Democrat, enjoyed similar success in securing the votes of southern Indiana delegates to the 1962 Democratic State Convention for his candidate for U.S. senator).[10]

In 1954, however, as in 1952, the Republican division also had ideological overtones. Jenner and Capehart accused Craig of liberal heresy and secured substantial support from Republicans who were not overly dependent on state patronage for ideological reasons.

The 1956 Republican State Convention provided yet another illustration of the effectiveness of the governor's patronage power in securing votes from southern Indiana. Indiana law did not permit the incumbent governor to succeed himself. However, Governor Craig supported Millis in the 1956 convention and Millis received almost all his convention votes from the southern Indiana low-income counties' delegates. Seventeen of the thirty-one counties carried in the convention by Millis, Craig's candidate, were also among the thirty-three lowest income counties in the state. On the other hand, the political leaders in wealthier counties provided the votes to nominate Handley over Millis. The Indiana findings correspond with those for Kentucky, where the governor had similar patronage powers. In Kentucky the governor could usually rely upon the low-income counties for political support, whereas wealthier counties were less predictable in their political behavior.[11]

Conservative-Moderate Republican Factionalism

In 1960, Matthew Welsh, a Democrat, was elected governor and, consequently, in the 1962 Republican State Convention there was no Republican administration that could demand support for its candidate from job-hungry southern Indiana. Therefore, in the 1962 convention another pattern of Indiana factionalism emerged.

The most important vote in the 1962 Republican State Convention was the nomination for state treasurer. Hughes, a Jenner man, was the incumbent and enjoyed Jenner's support.

[10] See V. O. Key, Jr., *Southern Politics* (New York: Alfred A. Knopf, Inc., 1950), pp. 65–69 and Fenton, *Politics in the Border States*, pp. 27–38, for discussions of the support received by organization candidates from low-income counties, and particularly low-income counties controlled by the other party.
[11] See Fenton, *Politics in the Border States*, pp. 30–38.

Hughes was opposed by the moderate or more professional element of the party, and mainly by H. Dale Brown, the Marion County and Eleventh Congressional District chairman; and by Charles Halleck, U.S. representative from Indiana's Second Congressional District. The fight between Jenner and Halleck dated back to the Eisenhower administration when right-wing Indiana Republicans attempted to read Halleck out of the party because he "played footsie" with the "left-wing" Eisenhower Republicans. Hughes won the nomination overwhelmingly, carrying all but twenty-one of the state's counties. However, he lost the majority of the counties (six of eleven) in Halleck's Second Congressional District as well as Marion County, Brown's bailiwick. The other counties lost by Hughes were in districts where Brown or Halleck had influence, mainly the Sixth, Eighth, and Eleventh Congressional Districts.

Thus, Republican factionalism broke along regional lines, along economic lines, along friends-and-neighbors lines, along congressional district lines, and along ideological lines. Important Republican leaders, such as H. Dale Brown, identified former Senator William Jenner as the principal culprit responsible for the party's ideological divisions. According to their accounts, Republican leaders devoted considerable energy and ingenuity in efforts to keep Jenner out of Indiana. Their feeling was that he could do less harm as one of ninety-six senators in Washington than as governor of the state of Indiana.

According to people in Republican State Headquarters, they "got rid" of Jenner in 1946 when he was nominated and elected to the U.S. Senate. Jenner wanted the nomination for governor, but responsible Republicans, such as Governor Gates, hated and feared him. After election to the U.S. Senate, Jenner frequently called people in Republican State Headquarters and pleaded with them to help him "get back to America—to get away from this crazy Communist joint." Republicans, such as Dale Brown and Charles Halleck, feared that if he campaigned for the nomination for governor that he might win. Therefore, in an attempt to preserve the political sanity of their beloved state, they telephoned Herbert Hoover and persuaded him to call Jenner and put pressure on him to run for U.S. senator.

The next day Jenner called Republican State Headquarters (1952) and said, "The President called me." The person to whom he was talking could only say, "Huh?" thinking that the president was Harry Truman. "Yes," said Jenner, "President Hoover called me and said it was my patriotic duty to run for reelection to the U.S. Senate."

Thereby, Indiana Republicanism was preserved for six more years from the direct impact of Jenner, although during the Craig administration he sought to wrest control of the party organization from Governor Craig. In 1958, though, Jenner had had his fill of "that crazy Communist joint" and returned to "America."

People in Republican State Headquarters testified that after Jenner's return, his faction within the Republican party had been "like the OAS in Algeria." According to Dale Brown and others, "these people feel that if you are not for Goldwater and Jenner that you are thereby a Communist by definition."

Democratic Party Organization

The formal organization of Indiana's Democratic party was identical to the Republican party's, as both were established by law. However, the Democratic party's factionalism and informal organization were somewhat different.

As in the Republican party, Democratic factionalism was commonly identified with personalities, but behind the personalities were more important economic and social divisions. The broad divisions within the party may be described as the labor or AFL-CIO group; the big city machines; that is, Lake County (Gary, East Chicago, Hammond), Terre Haute, Evansville, Fort Wayne, Muncie-Richmond-Anderson, and South Bend; the liberals; and the traditional Democrats from less urban areas.

In the 1950s the more important personalities identified with each of the factions were Frank McKinney and Frank McHale, who represented the traditional Democrats or more conservative wing of the party; Paul Butler, former Democratic national chairman, who died in 1958, who led the state's liberals; Dallas Sells, president of the Indiana State AFL-CIO and leader of the labor group; and Mayor George Chacharis of Gary, Indiana, who was sentenced to a three-year prison term in 1961 for tax evasion on money received through bribes and kickbacks from people doing business with the city and state and who was a leader of the big-city Democrats.

According to legend, the two most powerful personalities in Indiana's Democratic politics were Frank McKinney and Frank McHale, both aging veterans of state politics. Perhaps the best approach to understanding Democratic party organization is to first meet these men and then observe the extent and nature of their influence within the Democratic party.

In 1962 Frank McHale was a successful attorney with offices in Indianapolis. Like many Indiana Democrats, he became prominent in state politics during the Paul V. McNutt administration in the 1930s, when he was a prominent adviser of the governor. Later he served as Democratic national committeeman from Indiana. He was also active in the American Legion as were many prominent Democratic and Republican politicians after World War I.

In an interview in 1962, Frank McHale described himself as a conservative who represented big business within the Democratic party. McHale said, "I have often been accused of bossing the Democratic party in Indiana, but in reality all I do is represent big business in the state." McHale took pride in the fact that his firm had represented such firms as Cummins Engine Company, Tropical Fruit Corporation of Cuba, Indiana Brewers Association, National Liquor Corporation, General Tire and Rubber Company, the Union Carbide Corporation, the Nickel Plate Railroad, Chesapeake and Ohio Railroad, and the Pennsylvania Railroad. He also took pride in his close friendships with important conservatives in both political parties.

Frank McKinney, Democratic national chairman during a portion of Truman's administration, was board chairman of the American Fletcher National Bank in Indianapolis in 1962. He was also president of the Fidelity Trust Company of Indianapolis, treasurer of the Universal Broadcasting Company, and a director of the Indiana Bell Telephone Company.

McKinney's political and business careers were inextricably intertwined. In the 1930s he was an obscure Irish Democratic politician. However, he managed to win election as tax collector in Indianapolis at a time when people with taxes in arrears were earning enough money to pay their tax obligations. As tax collector, McKinney was paid a proportion of the taxes collected and, due to the rush of payments, his earnings approached $100,000. He invested the money in a local bank, which was in financial difficulty because of the depression, and, using this as a base, became one of the state's leading bankers.

Democratic state treasurers deposited the state's funds in McKinney's bank. For example, when Jack Haymaker was state treasurer, 1957–1961, the entire Indianapolis checking account, fluctuating between $20 million and $105 million, was deposited in the American Fletcher National Bank. However, reportedly because of McKinney's and McHale's close relations with Republican Bill Jenner, even after a Republican, Hughes, was elected state treasurer, about one-third of the account was left in the American Fletcher National Bank.

Thus, both McHale and McKinney were a part of the Indiana and national big business and financial community. To them, politics was simply an extension of their business activities. The question that remains is the process by which they combined these two activities. The following account of the means by which McKinney and McHale exerted influence in Indiana politics is largely taken from an interview with Frank McHale.

According to McHale, the organizational key to Democratic politics in Indiana was the convention system of nominating candidates and the close and friendly relations existing between Democratic leaders, Republican leaders, and the business community. McHale said that Republican leaders consulted him in selecting candidates and that he accorded them the same courtesy.

In selecting candidates, both groups (Republican and Democratic) were primarily concerned with nominating people "who are the backbone of the party and the state—financial and other leaders." And, according to McHale, it was these people who usually dominated the conventions. The testing ground for leadership in both parties was the American Legion. McHale, McNutt, and Craig, among others, were American Legion officers. McHale shook his head sadly over Craig's performance as a Republican governor and remarked that the reason Craig failed was "that he was brought up too fast. He was National Commander of the Legion, but never the State Commander. Consequently, he didn't know the feelings of the people of the state."

McHale saw nothing sinister in these relationships. On the contrary, he regarded it as a healthy means by which Indiana avoided a Huey Long or a Walter Reuther. According to McHale, "so long as Indiana retains the convention system of nominating candidates, neither party will nominate a radical." As McHale saw it, "it makes impossible the domination of the party by labor or minority groups. Rather, it means that the responsible financial and business leadership of the state maintains firm control."

The dynamics by which this process worked is made apparent by the 1956 and 1960 Democratic conventions, when the party nominated Ralph Tucker for governor in 1956 and Matthew Welsh for governor in 1960. The 1956 convention is particularly interesting for what it reveals concerning Democratic factionalism.

The 1956 and 1960 Democratic Conventions

There were four candidates for the gubernatorial nomination in the 1956 convention. Each represented one of the major factions of the party. Branigan was the McHale candidate; Welsh the McKinney candidate; Tucker the labor and big-city candidate; and Dillin was Butler's or the liberal candidate. In the early balloting, Tucker (labor and big city) and Dillin (Butler and liberal) divided the vote of the more urban centers of the state. Butler's candidate carried South Bend, Muncie, and the Ohio River counties, whereas Tucker won the East Chicago-Hammond-Gary area, Terre Haute, Anderson, and neighboring urbanized counties. The McKinney and McHale candidates divided the less urban remainder of the state. Indianapolis was the only major city which was won by Welsh, and Branigan carried the Fort Wayne delegation. Under these circumstances, with the conservatives dividing the less urban vote, and labor-liberal-big city people dividing their vote, it was impossible for any candidate to win a majority of the vote.

After the fifth ballot, the convention chairman announced: "Attention, delegates to the convention. Mr. McHale and Mr. McKinney are having a meeting and they want a thirty-minute recess, whereupon we will continue the balloting." Reportedly, this bold assertion of the political primacy of McHale and McKinney "brought the delegates storming out of their seats with boos and hoots," thus costing Welsh votes in the ninth and final balloting. According to McHale, the principal reason for the final labor-liberal-big city victory was that his candidate (Branigan) refused to withdraw in favor of Welsh. McHale claimed that he wanted to throw his support to Welsh, but had to protect his reputation for political steadfastness and honesty by staying with Branigan.

However, Butler did swing his liberal forces behind Tucker and on the ninth ballot the labor-liberal-big city machine candidate emerged victorious. With the exception of three, Tucker carried every county in the convention that contained a city of any consequence; that is, Gary–Hammond–East Chicago, South Bend, Terre Haute, Muncie-Anderson, and the Louisville area on the Ohio River. Indianapolis, Fort Wayne and Evansville were the cities won by the conservative candidate.

The vote of the Indianapolis delegates for the conservative candidate was not surprising to observers. In spite of its size (697,567 in metropolitan area, 1960), it was a long-time center of political conservatism. In the 1950s it elected Democratic mayors (such as Phil Bayt) who opposed federal school lunch programs, federal flood control aid, and federal urban renewal aid as a matter of principle. The conservative Democrats received the combined support of McKinney-McHale, much of the business community, and the ultra-conservative *Indianapolis Star*. Under the circumstances, the citizens of Indianapolis might be forgiven some confusion concerning the policies of their parties. Many Republicans as well as Democrats testified that the refusal of federal aid programs was a "phoney." According to them, the city took help for programs that favorably affected the business community, such as highway and hospital aid. However, where the aid was "only" for the poor, such as school lunch or slum removal programs, they nobly refused the "tainted" federal money.

The McHale-McKinney axis was defeated in the 1956 convention by the labor–big city combination. However, in the subsequent campaign McKinney refused to serve as finance chairman and both he and McHale "sat out" the election. As a result, the Jenner-backed Republican candidate, Harold Handley, was elected by a large margin and the state was left secure against "radical government." It is true that 1956 was a Republican year, but 1960 was also a Republican year in Indiana and the Democratic candidate won with the combined support of McKinney, McHale, labor and liberals.

In the 1960 convention, the labor and liberal Democrats approached McHale and McKinney in a chastened frame of mind. According to McHale, "they are a bunch of prostitutes. All they are interested in is being on the winning side." Whatever the reason, labor and the liberals supported conservative Matthew Welsh in company with McKinney and McHale. Welsh won easily in the convention. In the following campaign, McKinney served as finance chairman and, with a well-financed, unified party in back of a conservative candidate, the Democrats won the governorship in the face of a landslide victory for Richard Nixon.

After 1960 Welsh was the most important figure in the Democratic party. In an interview, he vigorously and no doubt truthfully denied that McKinney or McHale or any other figure dictated his party or governmental policies. He was boss of the party because of his control over patronage. However, McKinney and McHale were happy because they had a governor whose policies generally corresponded with their preferences, and more especially they were left with power where it touched their pocketbooks, such as in the office of treasurer and various commissions.

Thus, Indiana's Democratic party was a well-organized and essentially conservative party. It was conservative because of the presence within the party of a minority of traditional Democrats, who would cost the party victory in any election where a liberal-labor Democrat headed the ticket. The liberal-labor elements in the party were too divided to retaliate in kind when conservatives were nominated.

Another conservative influence on the Indiana Democratic party was the bipartisan arrangements between the parties concerning patronage and other spoils. A Lake County Democrat, Eugene Bainbridge, proposed a reform to Governor Welsh while he was head of the Department of Administration, which contained the politically sensitive purchasing division. He proposed to Welsh that instead of granting contracts on the basis of friendships and *quid pro quo* arrangements between Republicans and Democrats, they be granted on an entirely political basis; that is, to good Democrats. Mr. Bainbridge lost his job.

Most Democrats and Republicans despaired of eliminating the bipartisan split of the spoils that they said weakened the policy positions of their parties. The bipartisan split of spoils had been institutionalized in many ways; for example, beer wholesalerships were owned jointly by Democrats and Republicans, companies employed teams of Democratic and Republican salesmen, law firms were divided between Republican and Democratic members. The consequence of these arrangements, according to scores of Democrats, Republicans, and people from the League of Women Voters, was a state government virtually paralyzed policywise and parties that did not provide meaningful alternatives to the voters.

Political organization may affect the results of closely contested elections, but it seldom, if ever, induces enduring political change. In the following section we will examine the impact of events and the reactions of parties and office holders to the events on the political loyalties of the voters.

Political Change in Indiana

Significant plus-Democratic change in presidential elections (5 percentage points or more) took place, 1920–1960, in eleven of Indiana's ninety-two counties.[12] Another fifteen counties, or a total of twenty-six counties, recorded some plus-Democratic change over the period.

The localities in which plus-Democratic change tended to occur in Indiana, 1920–1960, were those which were highly urbanized or with a great many foreign-born or where coal was produced in quantities. Sixteen of the twenty most urban counties (54 percent or more urban, 1960) were among the twenty-six counties in which plus-Democratic change occurred, 1920–1960. Also, six of the counties in which 14 percent or more of the population was foreign-born or of foreign parentage, 1960, were among the plus-Democratic counties. Finally, three of the five counties which were important coal-producing centers, 1954, were included among the plus-Democratic counties.

The three categories of urbanism, foreign ancestry, and coal production accounted for twenty-one of the twenty-six counties in which plus-Democratic change occurred.[13] Four of the remaining five counties in which plus-Democratic change occurred were part of or bordered on urban complexes (Randolph and Henry Counties were within the Richmond-Marion-Kokomo urban and industrial area, and Warren and Parke Counties bordered on the Terre Haute standard metropolitan area). Switzerland was the lone county remote from industry or mining in which plus-Democratic change occurred.

The reasons for the plus-Democratic change in industrial areas and in places where there were large concentrations of immigrants were explored in the earlier chapter dealing with Ohio. However, in addition to the New Deal's economic and labor policies, which had such a profound impact on urban working-men, another important reason in Indiana for the affiliation of immigrant workers with the Democratic party was the relationship of the Ku Klux Klan with the Republican party in the 1920s.

Indiana was a peculiarly fertile ground for the Klan. In 1924 it claimed approximately a half million members, more than

[12] The measure of change is a product of all the presidential elections over the 1920–1960 period, rather than simply the first and last elections of the time series. The method employed to measure change was a line of regression for each county. The increase or decrease in the Democratic percent of the total vote along the line of regression is the measure of change used.
[13] The totals of plus-Democratic change in the several categories of counties is more than twenty-one because some counties were in more than one category.

one-tenth of Indiana's total population. One writer explained the growth of the Klan in Indiana as follows:

The war's background favored its growth, but so did the conditions. There was the boredom of the small towns. There was the old tradition of intolerance—before the 1914–18 war you could hear whispers that every Catholic church was fortified and built on a hilltop to command its town with firepower, and you could see roadside signs at village outskirts: "Nigger, Don't Let The Sun Set On You Here." Although thousands of Europeans had come to work in the steel mills and coal fields, Catholics, Jews, and foreigners were oddities in central Indiana. The old stiff-backed yeomanry, the farmers and the small-town merchants, were set in their ways, resentful of outsiders. . . . And now in 1920 the postwar scramble for jobs was on, with foreigners and Negroes competing with returning veterans. Hoosiers were sick of world problems, they were hell-bent for normalcy. And any organization sworn to uphold hearth and fireside and womanly virtue, "Americanism" and law and order, was assured of welcome. The Klan waged righteous war on Bolsheviks, Catholics, Jews, Negroes, bootleggers, pacifists, evolutionists, foreigners, and all persons whom it considered immoral.[14]

The Klan was nonpartisan and worked within both political parties. However, it won power largely through the Republican party, when in 1924 it nominated and elected a Klan-backed candidate for governor on the Republican ticket. Unhappily for the KKK and the Indiana Republican party, there were many "immoral" people in Indiana, as well as Catholics and Jews and believers in evolution. The result was to raise a permanent doubt in the minds of "immoral" people concerning the wisdom of voting the Republican ticket.

There were two large metropolitan centers which failed to record a plus-Democratic trend over the 1920–1960 period: Marion County (Indianapolis) and Allen County (Fort Wayne). The Indianapolis Standard Metropolitan Area had a 1960 population of 697,567 persons, the most populous metropolitan area in the state. The reasons for the failure of Indianapolis to record a plus-Democratic change, 1920–1960, were very nearly identical to those given for Columbus, Ohio's deviation from the urban plus-Democratic political pattern. It was the capital of Indiana and had a large white-collar population. Also, like Columbus, it never attracted many foreign-born people. Most of its new citizens were of native stock from surrounding corn-belt rural areas. In 1960 only 6.5 percent of its people were foreign-born or of foreign parentage. Again, like Columbus, it did have a comparatively large Negro population (14.4 percent). However,

[14] Martin, *Indiana: An Interpretation*, pp. 189–190.

many of the Negroes voted Republican because of an absence of Negro leadership and a plethora of good Republican leadership in the county and city.

Perhaps one of the more important variables accounting for Republican strength in Indianapolis was the *Indianapolis Star*, the major newspaper in central Indiana. The *Star* was extremely conservative and invariably supported Republican and Democratic conservatives for local and state offices.

Another reason for Democratic weakness in Indianapolis was a chronic liberal-conservative schism within the party, with the conservatives triumphant more often than not. Democratic mayors in Indianapolis earned the plaudits of the conservative *Indianapolis Star* by rejecting federal school lunch programs, flood control programs, and urban renewal, because of ideological objections to them. Needless to say, a conservative Democratic party was not an attractive alternative for underdog Negro and worker elements in Indianapolis. The failure of the Democratic party to prosper in Fort Wayne was largely due to the defection of its sizable German population from the Democratic party because of World Wars I and II.

Turning now to the localities in which the Republican party gained votes, we find that there were forty-six, or exactly half of Indiana's ninety-two counties, in which the voters shifted markedly in a plus-Republican direction in presidential elections from 1920 to 1960. Almost all of the counties where plus-Republican change occurred were either in the corn belt or were traditionally Democratic counties. More precisely, thirty-five of the forty-nine least urban and most rural-farm corn belt counties registered marked plus-Republican change and ten of the thirteen most Democratic counties, 1856–1928, were also among the forty-six counties in which the Republican party prospered.

These findings are quite similar to those already noted for Ohio, and the reasons are similar. The Democratic party alienated the good yeoman farmers and shopkeepers of the corn belt by its economic policies and by virtue of its identification with underdog groups in the population. The corn belt farmer could be accused of many failings, but an underdog role was not among them. In most cases, he was white, Anglo-Saxon, Protestant or German Protestant, and had prospered. The corn belt farms were among the wealthiest in the nation. The farmer's forebears killed Indians for their land,[15] and worked hard to make it fertile. One headstone in the corn belt is inscribed:

[15] As late as 1814, the Indiana legislature offered a bounty for Indian scalps.

> Thirteen years I was a virgin,
> Two years I was a wife,
> One year I was a mother,
> The next year took my life.[16]

The descendants of the people who shed the blood and did the work which had produced a prosperous state were "on top" as a consequence of their labor or good fortune, and they intended to remain there. Perhaps they feared that the immigrants were modern-day pioneers and that, if they did not fight to remain on top, they might suffer the same fate as the Indians. The Democratic party became even more closely identified than in the past with the threatening alien groups during the New Deal period, and subsequent events confirmed the fears of some native white Hoosiers that the party of Franklin Roosevelt was an advance agent for a plundering horde of foreigners led by the Pope.

The increased Republican vote in traditionally Democratic counties had at its roots the same psychology as in the corn belt. The traditionally Democratic counties were largely rural and they reacted to the New Deal and the nomination of Catholic candidates for the Presidency with fear and loathing. Their forebears hated Republicans because they were "damn screechers for freedom." Now the Democratic party screeched for freedom for Catholics and Jews and foreigners, as well as Negroes.

In summary, the Democratic party lost a large part of its traditional vote, 1932–1960. On the other hand, it attracted a substantial urban vote from those of foreign ancestry, Negroes, and the disinherited. The Republican party maintained its hold over the vote of its traditional partisans and enjoyed an increased vote among native Americans and Germans who were once Democratic partisans. In the following section we will look at the Indiana vote in both metropolitan and rural areas, as well as the state at large in an effort to assess the net impact of the political changes on the vote cast.[17]

---

[16] Martin, *Indiana: An Interpretation*, p. 34.

[17] There are several multiple correlations of demographic data with election returns that provide support for the observations concerning the causative factors behind political change in Indiana. When the percentage-point Democratic change in presidential elections, 1920–1960, by counties was related to percent urban plus percent foreign-born and children of foreign-born, the result was an R of .51, and when Democratic change by counties was related to percent rural-farm plus percent Democratic vote in 1860 (the traditional vote) the outcome was an R of (−).49.

Two-party Divisions in Indiana

The preceding pages have dealt with the geographic distribution of Democratic and Republican strength, political organization, and location of political change in Indiana. Attention now turns to the end result in terms of victory or defeat for candidates of the two parties.

Indiana, like Ohio, was a two-party state from its admission to the Union through 1960. In presidential elections, 1836–1852, the majority of the state's voters cast their lot with the Whigs twice and with Democrats on three occasions. From 1856 through 1892, the Republicans won in six presidential elections and the Democrats in five; from 1896 to 1928 the state's voters turned to the Republican party with eight victories for Republican candidates for President to only one for the Democrats; and they remained dominantly Republican, 1932–1964, when there were six Republican and three Democratic victories.

Turning to Figure 6.3, we see that Indiana was very narrowly and rigidly divided between the parties following the Civil War and until 1896, with shifts of only a few thousand votes accounting for party victories or defeats. The votes of the towns which later became cities did not differ markedly from the more rural portion of the state during the 1864–1896 period. As in Ohio, the legacy of the Civil War determined voting lines.

In 1896 the Democratic party experimented with Populism in the person of William Jennings Bryan and the results were disastrous for the Democrats in Indiana. With the exception of 1912, when the Republican party split its vote between Teddy Roosevelt and William Howard Taft, the Democrats rarely came close to carrying the state again until the Great Depression and the 1932 election. The decline in Democratic strength after 1920 was in large part due to the defection of German voters.

In 1932 and 1936 the Democratic party swept Indiana with pluralities of 185,000 and 243,000 votes. But after 1936 the massive defection from the Democratic party of voters from the less urban portions of the state carried the political day for Republican presidential candidates in every election, 1940–1960. The Democratic party also lost ground in the metropolitan counties after 1936, but remained the majority party until 1952, when even the people of the metropolitan counties cast a plurality of their votes for Dwight Eisenhower. However, in spite of some urban disaffection, the main source of Democratic despair after 1936 was rural and small town Indiana's reaction to the New Deal. In the Indiana corn belt, as in Ohio's corn belt,

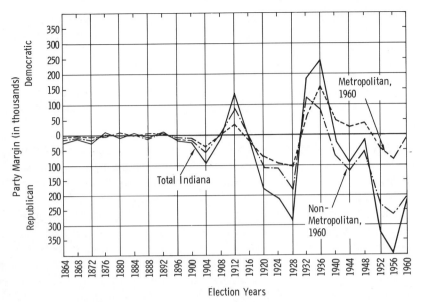

Election Years

FIGURE 6.3   THE WAY INDIANANS DIVIDED THEIR VOTES, 1864–
1960, by state and sections in presidential elections

Explanatory Note: The lines on the chart trace the two-party vote margins
by which Republican and Democratic presidential candidates won Indiana
(the solid line), the metropolitan counties as defined in 1960 (the broken
line), and the nonmetropolitan or more rural counties (the line with
alternating dashes and dots). In 1960, Richard Nixon carried the metropolitan counties by more than 10,000 votes, the nonmetropolitan counties by
about 210,000 votes, and the state by approximately 220,000 votes over John
F. Kennedy. The line dividing the chart in two marks an even division between the two parties. The fact that the state's vote has tended to hover
around the zero division is indicative of the state's two-party competitive
character. After 1896, the state's vote fluctuated more widely than during
the immediate post-Civil War period. After 1932, the votes of the metropolitan and nonmetropolitan areas went their separate ways, with the
metropolitan areas on the Democratic side of the line in most elections and
the nonmetropolitan areas casting steadily larger pluralities for the Republican candidates.

the depression did not produce either as much unemployment
or as much suffering among farmers as in less favored regions
of the nation. A good example of the difference in attitudes in
the corn belt as opposed to other areas is provided by a survey
conducted by Lou Harris in 1958. When he asked Hoosiers
whether they felt a lot more should have been done to attract
new industry to Indiana, he obtained the following results:[18]

[18] Louis Harris and Associates, "A Survey of Issues and Candidates in
the 1958 Indiana Election (First of Two Surveys)," September 1958
(unpublished), p. 10.

AREA	PERCENT AFFIRMATIVE
Whole state	40
Gary–South Bend	53
Indianapolis area (Corn Belt city)	20
Southern tier of counties	53
Middle and north counties (Corn Belt)	35

Thus, where Democratic strength was greatest in Indiana (Gary–South Bend and the southern part of the state), the voters were concerned about jobs, whereas in Indianapolis and the center of the corn belt ("middle and north"), there was much less concern with employment opportunities.

In the corn belt, both country and city, the "economic bite" was primarily felt in the area of expenditures. Jobs were not too scarce and people were worried about where their money was going. In the other areas of the state, however, many voters were either without jobs or were fearful of losing their jobs. Consequently, their attention was turned to the income side of the family's economy.

The people concerned with jobs were largely Democratic voters and the people whose attention was turned toward expenditures tended to vote Republican. The Democratic party, particularly after Franklin Roosevelt, was associated in voters' minds with positive programs to alleviate unemployment. Positive programs cost money which helped the disinherited in Gary, but the taxes to pay the costs were paid by the employed in the corn belt and elsewhere. Therefore, the relatively prosperous person in Indianapolis and the corn belt voted Republican, whereas the less secure resident of Gary or South Bend tended to vote Democratic.

Indiana was not nearly so one-sidedly Republican in elections for governor and other statewide elective offices as in presidential elections, 1932–1960. The Democrats won six and lost only three gubernatorial elections, 1932–1964; and Democratic candidates for U.S. senator emerged victorious in six elections and the Republicans in seven elections, 1932–1964. In 1962 and 1964 Indiana's Democratic party enjoyed political prosperity unparalleled since the days of the Great Depression when they held the governorship and both U.S. Senate seats. In the state legislature, the Republicans controlled both houses nine times, 1932–1964; the Democrats controlled both houses four times; and control was split on four occasions. In the vote for U.S. representatives, 1932–1964, the Democrats elected eighty-five and the Republicans 107 U.S. representatives.

Thus, by almost every measure except in the elections for President, Indiana was a marginal two-party state, 1932–1964, though it was inclined just a bit in a Republican direction. However, in the 1958, 1960, 1962, and 1964 state elections the Democratic party shook the Republicans when two Democratic governors and two Democratic U.S. senators were elected.

Further, in the state's mayoralty elections in 1955 and 1959, the Democrats captured approximately 70 percent of the mayoralty posts settled by a partisan ballot, compared to only 30 percent in 1951. In 1963 the Democrats lost some ground in the mayoralty elections, winning in but forty-nine of the 111 cities in the state. The question that concerned Indiana politicians was whether the resurgence of Democratic strength in Indiana was a deviation from established voting patterns or the beginning of a new trend. Figure 6.4 represents an attempt to isolate the locations of plus-Democratic change, 1958–1962. As the figure shows, the most pronounced plus-Democratic change occurred in the northern tier of counties and in the northeastern corner of the state.

The explanation for increased Democratic strength in the northern tier of counties has two sides, both on the same economic coin. First, the northern counties were most affected by the growth of heavy industry in cities, such as Gary and South Bend, and consequently there was population growth in all the counties which in one way or another was associated with the industries. The most important industries in the north of the state were steel in Gary and, until 1964, automobiles in South Bend. Unemployment was a chronic concern in both industries, which induced pronounced feelings of economic insecurity.

The increased Democratic vote cast out of the section was a result of (1) the 1958 recession and the rebirth of half-forgotten memories of 1932, (2) the nomination by the Democrats of a Catholic candidate for President, who was popular in Catholic South Bend (home of Notre Dame) and Lake County, (3) the increased population of the area that was mainly Democratically inclined, (4) strong Democratic political organizations in Lake County and South Bend, and (5) scandals involving Republican Governor George Craig.

In the northwestern Indiana counties, that is, Allen (Fort Wayne) and surrounding counties, where the Democrats enjoyed a pronounced recrudescence of voting strength, 1958–1962, there was a large German Lutheran population. The Germans tended Democratic before 1920, but thereafter voted Republican in increasingly large numbers. One reason for their switch to

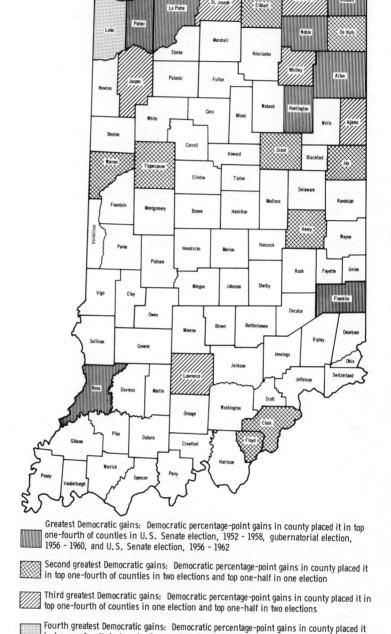

Greatest Democratic gains: Democratic percentage-point gains in county placed it in top one-fourth of counties in U.S. Senate election, 1952 - 1958, gubernatorial election, 1956 - 1960, and U.S. Senate election, 1956 - 1962

Second greatest Democratic gains: Democratic percentage-point gains in county placed it in top one-fourth of counties in two elections and top one-half in one election

Third greatest Democratic gains: Democratic percentage-point gains in county placed it in top one-fourth of counties in one election and top one-half in two elections

Fourth greatest Democratic gains: Democratic percentage-point gains in county placed it in top one-fourth in two elections and top three-fourths in one election

FIGURE 6.4 **WHERE INDIANA'S DEMOCRATS GAINED VOTES IN 1958, 1960, AND 1962 VICTORIES** in 1958 election for U.S. senator, 1960 election for governor, and 1962 election for U.S. senator

Explanatory Note: The primary purpose behind the construction of Figure 6.4 was a search for clues to the causative agents behind the stunning Democratic electoral victories in 1958, 1960, and 1962. The resultant clustering of counties with the most pronounced plus Democratic change along the northern and eastern borders of the state justified the informed "guess" in the text that industrialization and the reaction of the Americans of German ancestry to Lutheran candidates were two of the more important causes of plus Democratic change.

Democratic ranks in 1958, 1960, and 1962 was that Vance Hartke, the 1958 and 1964 Democratic candidate for U.S. senator, Matthew E. Welsh, the 1960 Democratic candidate for governor, and Birch Bayh, the 1962 Democratic candidate for U.S. senator, were all German Lutherans and the Democrats made every effort to acquaint the good burghers of northeastern Indiana with this fact.

Lou Harris, the pollster employed by the Democrats to sample Indiana opinion in 1958, made the following observation:

Hartke should be able to make real inroads among Germans and he has indeed shown a marked increase in strength among them. Again, once he is better known [among Protestant groups] as a Lutheran, it will help.[19]

Democratic successes in Indiana, 1958–1962 then, were, in part, a product of secular increases in Democratic voting strength in the industrial north of the state and, in part, a result of the reaction of Germans to the Democratic candidates in 1958, 1960, and 1962, as well as to some negative reactions in the state-at-large to the Republican candidates and to the road scandal involving Republican Governor Craig. Let us turn now to the effect of Indiana's two-party competition on the measurable performance of state government.

State Government Performance—The Product of Party Competition

Indiana's political parties were found to be somewhat better organized and more competitive than Ohio's. It would be expected, then, that if there is a relationship between political party competition and state government programs that Indiana would spend more than Ohio for programs designed to reallocate goods and opportunities.

[19] Louis Harris and Associates, "A Survey of Issues and Candidates in the 1958 Indiana Elections (Last of Two Surveys)" October 1958 (unpublished), p. 21.

This proves to be the case. Indiana ranked eighteenth nationally in terms of the competition of its parties, 1946–1958, compared to a ranking of twenty-first for Ohio.[20] On an effort scale, which ranked states according to the percentage that their per-capita state and local tax revenue from own sources were of per-capita income, Indiana ranked thirty-third, compared to forty-second for Ohio.

In general, Indiana's ranking with respect to expenditures corresponded with its competitive ranking. Among the states, Indiana ranked fifteenth in its per-pupil expenditures and ninth in salaries of its teachers. Its welfare programs, however, were underfinanced. For example, the state ranked twenty-ninth in per-recipient payments for aid to dependent children, twenty-third in aid to the blind, and twenty-eighth in old-age assistance.

The evidence indicates that one important distinguishing feature between traditional two-party states and issue-oriented-party states was the support for welfare programs and especially for aid to dependent children. There were few votes to be obtained from aid to dependent children. The dependent children did not vote, and their mothers were not politically conscious. Consequently, a non-issue-oriented politician gave the program short shrift. In education, however, there were many votes. The Indiana State Teachers' Association was one of the state's most effective pressure groups. The teachers in small communities often "ran the polls" and were important opinion leaders. Therefore, education fared relatively well and welfare did poorly.

Summary and Conclusions

The geographic location of party strength in Indiana and the political trends, both long- and short-run, show marked similarities to those observed in Ohio. The sections of the state settled by Southerners historically leaned toward the Democratic party. The Democratic preferences of most Hoosiers in southern Indiana were based, in the main, upon the Civil War. After the New Deal, traditional Democrats gravitated toward the Republican party. However, in contrast to Ohio, a substantial part of the traditional vote remained attached to the Democratic party.

The principal component of Democratic voting strength, 1932–

---

[20] The measure of competition is a product of the divisions in the state between the two major parties in gubernatorial elections and in the state legislature, 1946–1958.

1962, in Indiana was in urban sections and particularly where there were large concentrations of immigrants and their children, mainly from eastern Europe. The reasons for their affiliation with the Democratic party were many. However, the central causative factors were economic. As the most recent immigrants, the eastern Europeans were assigned some of the least attractive jobs in the nation. This was the reason for their concentration in steel cities, such as Gary, Indiana, where the work was unpleasant and the likelihood of periodic unemployment great. The eastern Europeans, along with Negroes, tended to be the first to be laid off and the last to be rehired in periods of economic distress. Therefore, their economic concern was with jobs rather than taxes or inflation, a factor that made them turn to the Democratic party, which emphasized services from government.

Republican voting strength was great throughout the state, but was centered in the less urban and more rural-farm portions of the corn belt. The Republican party also fared well in some corn belt cities, such as Fort Wayne and Indianapolis. The reasons for Republican success in the corn belt revolved around economics, but also involved the reaction of Germans to World Wars I and II. The corn belt people, both in the city and country, generally did not suffer the same economic privation in periods of depression and recession as the residents of steel cities or more marginal farm lands. Consequently, they did not benefit to the same degree from New Deal depression measures as did unemployed steel workers in Gary. They did not recall the New Deal with gratitude as an administration which rescued them from economic despair. Rather, they remembered it as an administration which gave their money to foreigners and Negroes through increased taxes and also reduced their relative income and political influence by increasing the power of labor unions.

The result in terms of vote shifts, statewide, was very nearly a standoff, over the 1920–1960 period. The shift of workers in Gary and South Bend from the Republican to the Democratic party was matched by the movement of traditional Democrats and Germans from the Democratic to the Republican party. It may well be, as V. O. Key has pointed out, that there is a tendency toward an equilibrium between political parties that automatically produces such compensating shifts between parties whenever the equilibrium is disturbed. In Indiana, the influx of immigrants and Negroes into the Democratic party frightened native whites out of the party.

There is conflicting evidence with respect to whether the new equilibrium between the parties was more or less advantageous to the Democrats. Certainly, it left the Democrats as the minority party in the state. However, it also identified the Democratic party with the more urban and populous portion of the state's population. Table 6.1 shows the degree to which the Democratic party was Indiana's political representative of urban interest, 1932–1960. As the table shows, the proportion of the total Democratic and Republican votes from the metropolitan counties was about equal in 1932 in the gubernatorial election. However, after 1932 and through 1960 the Democrats consistently relied more on the metropolitan vote than did the Republicans for the support necessary for election victory.

Similarly, in the state legislature prior to 1932 the Democratic party drew most of its strength from southern Indiana. By 1960

Table 6.1

PERCENT THAT DEMOCRATIC AND REPUBLICAN METRO-
POLITAN VOTE REPRESENTED OF TOTAL DEMOCRATIC AND
REPUBLICAN VOTE IN GUBERNATORIAL ELECTIONS, 1932–1960

	1932	1936	1940	1944	1948	1952	1956	1960
Democratic Metropolitan	38.2	42.1	43.5	46.2	44.1	46.7	45.9	48.3
Republican Metropolitan	39.1	34.7	37.8	38.8	38.6	42.7	43.3	42.6

most Democratic legislators hailed from the more urban portions of the state. Ominously for the Republican party, the metropolitan counties were growing rapidly, 1930–1960. In 1930 the metropolitan counties represented 41.9 percent of the state's total population, and in 1960 the ten metropolitan counties represented 48.1 percent of the total population. If the Republicans remained a primarily nonmetropolitan party representing nonurban interests at the expense of the residents of metropolitan areas, the long-term prospects of the party were not bright.

On the other hand, the Democratic party had lost much of its traditional vote. Consequently, there were many more people in Indiana who thought of themselves as Republicans than regarded themselves as loyal Democrats. For example, in Louis Harris' 1958 study of the Indiana voters, he remarked:

. . . the work of a Democratic candidate today is cut out for him—he must bring many voters with established Republican voting histories behind them over into his column. All the Republican needs do is to concentrate on keeping in his column those people who have voted for him in the past, or who consider themselves "normal Republicans"![21]

American political parties have ordinarily required a core vote of unswervingly loyal supporters to survive. Areas where a party lacks such support tend to degenerate into one-party areas.

Thus, the future of the parties in Indiana is obscure. The 1958, 1960, 1962 and 1964 Democratic successes demonstrated that party's strength and weaknesses. The victories required three elements: (1) large Democratic pluralities from the cities; (2) relatively unattractive Republican candidates and Republican scandals; and (3) the deliberate cultivation of the German Lutheran vote. This formula for political success rested on exceedingly shaky ground because, first, the Democrats could not be certain that the Republicans would invariably oblige them by nominating unattractive candidates. Second, the continued cultivation of the German Lutheran vote would almost certainly alienate eastern European elements within the party.

The long-run Democratic and Republican prospects depended in part upon economic conditions and upon the actions of the parties' officeholders in the executive branch and the state legislature. If the Republican party's rural legislators ignored the interests of metropolitan residents, they ran the risk of producing an ever-swelling Democratic vote out of the large cities, which would have disastrous long-run implications for the Republican party. On the other hand, if the Republican leadership remained in relatively sophisticated and urban-oriented hands, such as Lieutenant Governor Richard Ristine or Dale Brown, Republican boss in Marion County and Indianapolis, the long-run prospects of the Republican party in Indiana were bright.

We turn now to Illinois, the last of the traditional two-party states discussed. Ohio's politics was featured by a strong Republican organization and a weak Democratic party. Indiana, on the other hand, had two well-organized and competitive political parties, albeit diluted by a bipartisan concern with the spoils of government. As we shall see, the dominant feature of Illinois' politics was the existence of an unusually strong Democratic organization in Chicago which dominated the state's Democratic party and had some impact on Republican party organization.

[21] Louis Harris and Associates, "A Survey of Issues and Candidates in the 1958 Indiana Election (First of Two Surveys)," p. 4.

Chapter 7

Political "Clout"
in Illinois

The visitor's initial reaction to Illinois and Illinois politics is a half-hidden yawn. The cornfields engulf the landscape and the occasional towns blend in all too easily. The state conforms so closely to the comedians' and social critics' stereotyped parody of American political life that it is impossible to either giggle or glare. The inclination is to look away out of boredom. But the political "clout" found in Chicago erases ennui. More political "clout" is contained in Chicago than in any other American city. "Clout" is a term meaning "raw power" and it is no accident that the descriptive adjective was invented there.

But before examining Chicago and Illinois politics, it is necessary to pass quickly through the cornfields. In Illinois, as in Ohio and Indiana, the Democratic party claimed the affection of the disinherited of two generations over the 1932–1960 period (post-Civil War Copperheads and post-1929 unemployed), and the remainder of the population tended to vote Republican. In Illinois, once again as in both Ohio and Indiana, the native white disinherited of the Civil War generation were dead and their sons and daughters were deserting the Democratic party because the alien foreign and Negro elements in the cities who were formerly helpful sources of votes were now in control of the party.

Illinois was a two-party state before the New Deal when Franklin Roosevelt turned the political world upside down. The pre-1932 division between the two parties was sectional in nature and, like Ohio and Indiana, was a product of the differing flows of people into the state. Before 1860 the state was dominantly Democratic with most of the Democratic vote cast by the people who had emigrated from the South and the Republican or Whig vote cast by people emigrating from the northern and eastern states. After the Civil War the sectional lines between the two parties hardened. Every county in the northern portion of the state was Republican, 1860–1892, while the southern part of the state was almost equally Democratic. The north-south political division of the state had its roots in pre-Civil War political differences, but after the Civil War the Democratic proclivities of the people in southern Illinois were intensified, and the Republican tendencies of the people in north Illinois were likewise strengthened.[1]

Over the 1896–1928 period, Democratic strength declined throughout the state, but the nature of the political divisions remained substantially unchanged, with south Illinois a Democratic stronghold and north Illinois the center of Republican electoral strength. The most serious losses of Democratic votes, 1896–1928, occurred in the urbanized areas of Peoria, Springfield, and East St. Louis, where Bryan's silver policies were perceived as a threat to the foundations of the nation.[2]

The net impact of the events and personalities that affected the lives of Illinois' citizens for good or ill, 1860–1928, was to make it a dominantly Republican state, although within a two-party framework. In the presidential elections, 1860–1928, the Republican candidate carried Illinois sixteen times to only two Democratic victories (1892 and 1912). In the gubernatorial elections the Democratic candidates likewise won only two elections, 1860–1928.

After 1932, Illinois was transformed from a relatively safe Republican stronghold to a marginal state politically. In the presidential elections, 1932–1964, Democrats won seven and the Republicans only two contests; and in gubernatorial elections the division of victories was five to four in favor of the Democrats. It was in the cities of Illinois that the Democrats won the votes that enabled them to challenge Republican hegemony. Only two counties in north Illinois turned consistently Democratic after 1932, but they were the heavily populated metropolitan centers located in Cook County (Chicago) with a population of

[1] Chapters 5 and 6, dealing with Ohio and Indiana political history, relate in detail the reasons for the tendency of settlers from the South to vote Democratic.

[2] See Duncan MacRae, Jr., and James A. Meldrum, "Critical Elections in Illinois: 1888–1958," *American Political Science Review*, vol. 54 (1960), p. 669.

5,129,725 people, and Rock Island County (Moline and Rock Island) with 150,441 people, which together contained well over half of the 1960 total population of the state (10,081,158). In southern Illinois, too, the principal Democratic strongholds tended to be in the industrial centers rather than in the rural areas after 1932, mainly the St. Louis metropolitan area in Madison County (97,904 people) and St. Clair County (67,367 people). Nevertheless, the Democratic party managed to retain the loyalty of some of the traditional Democrats. Many of the Democratic strongholds in southern Illinois, 1932–1960, remained traditional centers of Democratic strength, dating from the Civil War or before, but their Democratic loyalties were much diluted except where urbanism or coal production served to reinforce traditional Democratic voting tendencies (see Figure 7.1).

In sum, after 1932 Democratic strength in Illinois tended to be concentrated in the most metropolitan centers with the highest proportion of foreign-born (mostly eastern European and Catholic) and Negroes, and in the traditionally Democratic Little Egypt section of southern Illinois, where most of the residents were white Anglo-Saxon Protestants.[3]

It is worth a few words to describe the dynamics by which the disinherited of two generations were kept within the Democratic fold, despite their divergent social, ethnic, religious, and economic interests.[4] Conversations with Democratic and Re-

[3] Simple coefficients of correlation of the 1960 percent Democratic in the presidential and gubernatorial elections by counties with percent urbanism (.16 and .27), percent foreign-born and children of foreign-born [(−).07 and (_).08], percent Negro (.35 and .22), percent Catholic (.35 and .23), and percent of farmers [(−).24 and (−).27] reveals that the 1960 percent Democratic vote by counties was not very closely related to any of the variables. The most significant relationship of the 1960 vote was with the traditional Civil War component as measured by the two-party political division in 1860 (.37 and .27), followed by the non-white and Catholic variables. The explanation for the low degree of relationship between the Illinois Democratic vote and the variables listed is that the traditional component of the Democratic vote was rural and native white Protestant, while the more recent immigrant Democrats tended to be Catholic, foreign, urban, and non-white. The result was that the statistical relationship of the Democratic vote by counties with any of the variables was "flattened out." The level of cohesion of the Illinois Democratic party was markedly affected by the widely different social characteristics of the two main elements of the party. The coefficient of correlation of the 1960 presidential vote with the 1960 gubernatorial vote by counties was .89, the smallest found in any Midwest state save Ohio.

[4] The degree to which the Illinois Democratic party was a coalition of the

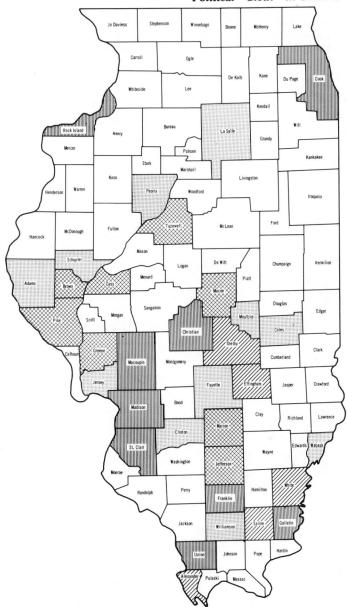

Strong Democratic: Democratic in 6 or more of 8 elections
Weak Democratic: Democratic in 5 of 8 elections
Marginal: Evenly divided in 8 elections
Weak Republican: Republican in 5 of 8 elections
Strong Republican: Republican in 6 or more of 8 elections

FIGURE 7.1   ILLINOIS' DEMOCRATIC AND REPUBLICAN COUNTIES
in the presidential elections, 1932–1960

Explanatory Note: Fig. 7.1 is designed to acquaint the reader with the political geography of the state and especially the north-south division of party strength that persisted into the 1932–1960 period. Note that the only Democratic counties in northern Illinois are Cook and Rock Island, which are both metropolitan centers.

publican small businessmen in rural and small-town Illinois were revealing. Studies of public opinion indicate that most small businessmen tend to vote Republican. They vote Republican partially because of tradition but also because they associate high taxes with the Democratic party by virtue of the spending policies of the New Deal. The small businessman reacts violently to taxes because he undergoes more psychological suffering from the payment of taxes than other persons in the United States. Most employed persons never see the money that goes to Washington in the form of income taxes. The money is taken from their paycheck relatively painlessly and sent to the Internal Revenue Bureau by their employer. The small businessman, however, actually fingers the money he sends to Washington. He sees it, touches it, and almost tastes it. If only he could keep the money, the year would be a prosperous one. He could build an addition to his store or garage or send his son to Harvard rather than the state college.

In point of fact, the small businessman benefits financially from computing his taxes. He is often able to pocket a portion of his income without reporting it. Garage owners often "forget" to enter payments for wrecker services provided at night. But in spite of the financial benefits that accrue to the small businessman from fingering the money (some "sticks") before paying it, the pain suffered from the payment is greater than for the workingman whose payments are made for him.

Selective Perceptions of Party Adherents

But in spite of the psychic pain from paying taxes, many small businessmen in southern Illinois remained Democratically inclined in the 1960s. Conversations with Democratically inclined small businessmen revealed that their perception of the political

---

disinherited of two generations is most dramatically revealed through multiple correlations of the 1960 percent Democratic vote for Kennedy with the traditional plus the Catholic components of the vote. The multiple coefficient of correlation (R) of Kennedy's percent vote by counties with the 1860 percent two-party Democratic vote in the presidential election plus the 1957 percent Catholic population by counties is .59.

environment was extraordinarily selective. In discussions of politics they tended to avoid topics such as taxes and civil rights. Rather, they emphasized the danger of depression under the Republicans. And instead of blaming taxes for their marginal economic position, they tended to fasten on big business or "do-nothing" Republicans as the causative agents behind their economic difficulties.[5] The Democratic automobile dealer in, say, Pike or Brown County blamed the policies of General Motors or Ford or Chrysler for their small profit margins. They pointed to "arbitrary" requirements of the manufacturers concerning the purchase of parts or new automobiles as a cause of their difficulties. To them, the Democratic party was the party of the common man, whereas the Republican party was identified with the "big business devils" in Detroit who tortured them with unreasonable demands.

The political testimony of Republican auto dealers was strikingly different from that of the Democratic auto dealers. As the Republicans saw it, the Democratic party wasted money on welfare programs and foreign aid and it was this waste that was responsible for the high taxes which meant the difference between affluence and near-bankruptcy for them. They also blamed the high cost of labor on Democratic-sponsored pro-labor laws. In addition, they tended to fix responsibility on the Democratic party for the high cost of automobiles, the "blame line" going back to the increased cost of labor. The Republican small businessmen, on the other hand, avoided discussing depression or the policies of big business. If forced to enter into a discussion of the depression, they often claimed that their economic position was better then than now. They concentrated on the fact that the items they purchased then were much less expensive than in the 1960s. In addition, they felt that their relative economic position had deteriorated, which caused more psychic pain than an absolute loss of dollars. They felt that the mechanic, the bricklayer, the plumber made more money than they, and with less effort and risk. They complained that they were not adequately recompensed for their investment and for the hours of additional work and worry associated with owning a business.

The laments of the Republican small businessman were more cogent than those of the Democratic small businessman, and the former seemed surer of his ground. The Democratic small busi-

---

[5] A good discussion of the dynamics of selective perception of parties and candidates is contained in Angus Campbell, *et al., The American Voter* (New York: John Wiley & Sons, Inc., 1960), pp. 59–60.

nessman was beset by increasing doubts concerning the rationality of his political preferences, and the results were reflected in the political changes occurring in Illinois and throughout the Midwest.

The selective perceptions of the big-city adherents of the Democratic party were less befogged by cross-pressures, and also better served their immediate economic self-interest. The foreignborn or Negro Democrat was almost invariably a workingman who worried about unemployment rather than taxes, and expensive governmental programs were advantageous to him. Therefore, it required few perceptive illusions for him to see the Democratic party as serving his self-interest, because the objective political environment largely supported this perception.

The net result of the reactions of traditional and big-city Democrats to the post-1932 policies and candidates of the parties was a Democratic party increasingly composed of the disinherited of the twentieth century and a Republican party which represented a growing proportion of the native white residents of both the suburbs and the less urban portions of the state. Therefore, the broad outlines of Illinois politics had a classic simplicity about them by the 1960s. Chicago was one-sidedly Democratic and, on the balance, the less urban remainder of the state was Republican by political preference. In statewide general elections, the question posed to Illinois' political leaders was whether the Chicago Democrats could muster large enough pluralities for their candidates to outweigh the pluralities posted by downstate Republicans for their candidates.

Political Organization in Illinois

In Republican and Democratic internal politics, the political equation was almost as simple as the broad outlines of Illinois politics. In the statewide primaries of both parties, the Chicago Democratic and, to a lesser degree, the Chicago Republican leaders were able to produce one-sided pluralities for the candidates of their choice. The political theme that ran throughout internal politics in Illinois was downstate resentment at attempts by Chicago leaders to dominate their parties. The hope of antiChicago candidates in party primaries was for large enough downstate pluralities to outweigh the Chicago vote, a hope rarely realized in the Democratic party. Therefore, the requisite first step in understanding Illinois politics is an examination of Chicago politics, for Illinois' political "clout" was concentrated there.

As was mentioned above, "clout" is a term that originated in Chicago and refers to power, and, as the term implies, it means power that is raw and brutal in nature.

In 1963 the boss of the Chicago Democratic machine was Mayor Richard Daley. He was the latest in a long succession of strong, able, and successful Democratic political leaders including Brennan, Cermak, Nash, Kelly, and Colonel Jacob Arvey. The Chicago Democratic machine was unique in American politics for its unwavering unity and continued success in dominating Chicago and Cook County politics.

Democratic and Republican big-city machines in cities such as New York, Philadelphia, Cleveland, St. Louis, and Kansas City waned in power after the 1930s. Some students attributed the decline in the power of big-city political machines to the introduction of social services for low-income people by the New Deal, services which were formerly provided by the political machines. Other students of politics pointed to a more sophisticated electorate as the explanation for the decline of the political machine. Whatever the reason or reasons for this decline, it is true that in most cities in the early 1960s the city machines had degenerated into squabbling congeries of ward bosses who were little kings of ward empires that rarely combined into a citywide political machine.

The Chicago Democratic political machine remained an exception to the nationwide decline of big-city machines in 1962. Jake Arvey attributed the success of the Democratic machine to high morale. According to Arvey, the Chicago Democratic leaders felt themselves a part of a going concern. They were proud of the vote they obtained from their wards and felt themselves an integral and important part of the city machine. Because of the high morale and able leadership, there developed a habit on the part of ward leaders of accepting the decisions of the Cook County Democratic Central Committee with respect to candidates and other questions of political organization. In addition to habit as a factor in political machine cohesion, there was the undeniable fact that the ward leaders benefited from their cohesion. By virtue of the large pluralities produced by Chicago for organization candidates in Democratic primaries and for Democratic candidates in the general elections, Mayor Richard Daley and the Cook County Democratic machine monopolized patronage in Chicago and Cook County and received at least their share of state and federal patronage. The incumbent Democratic governor elected in 1960 was nominated and elected by virtue of Daley's support, and Democratic President Kennedy's election hinged in large part on the staggering Democratic vote he received in Chicago.[6]

Another reason for the Chicago Democratic organization's success was its ability to secure the support of both the business community and the city's seamier element. Big-city political leaders have often attempted the same perilous balancing act, but have more often than not alienated the business community by virtue of their insatiable greed for graft (Pendergast of Kansas City is an example) and consequent failures in the business of managing the affairs of the city. Mayor Richard Daley, though, was the darling of Chicago's business community in 1962. In the mayoralty election of that year a committee of leading conservative businessmen was formed to support Daley. The comments of the businessmen concerning Daley are reminiscent of those made by businessmen in Memphis, Tennessee, concerning long-time Democratic boss Ed Crump. Like the Tennessee people, they averted their eyes from the vote base of Daley's strength and concentrated instead upon his performance in office. And they professed to be eminently well-satisfied by Daley's job performance. They pointed to the highly visible road-building program that made State Street as easily available to shoppers as suburban shopping centers. They applauded the urban renewal, street lighting, and other building programs that made the Chicago Loop a model which other metropolitan centers sought to emulate. The pride they took in the accomplishments of their city under Mayor Daley affected the political attitudes of all Chicagoans.

By virtue of such positive programs and accomplishments, Mayor Daley pulled the teeth of budding reform movements by providing what businessmen called "good government." There was no effort by business leaders to organize a good government league to produce anti-organization voters in middle-income wards. Therefore, the stunning vote margins received by Daley-

---

[6] See Edward C. Banfield and James Q. Wilson, *City Politics* (Cambridge, Mass.: Harvard University Press and MIT Press, 1963), pp. 123–124, for a good statement of the reasons for the survival of the Chicago Democratic machine. Banfield and Wilson believe that the reasons include the "accident" of able leaders of the machine who recognized that "reform" was necessary in order to carry suburban Cook County. Consequently, Mayor Daley inaugurated civic projects that would suit the good government voter without costing very much; for example, street cleaning, street lighting, road building, a new airport, and a convention hall. Most importantly, they were highly visible, noncontroversial, and pulled the teeth of any reform movement.

backed candidates in organization wards remained unchallenged by a well-organized, anti-machine vote. Thus, one foot of Daley's power was securely anchored in the approval of the business community. The other foot was equally well anchored in the low-income and vice-ridden organization wards. Typical of the organization wards was the famous "first," the home of such colorful characters in American political history as "Bathhouse" John Coughlin and "Hinky Dink" Kenna and infamous scoundrels such as Al Capone and Frank ("the Enforcer") Nitte. The careers of the colorful political characters and the infamous scoundrels were inextricably intertwined because the success of the scoundrels was dependent upon the tolerance of the politicians.

In 1962 the ward remained the home of the poor, the immigrants in search of a job, the derelicts, as well as the place of business for the powerful. Within the ward were banks, City Hall, the Loop, the Museum of Natural History, the Planetarium, Grant Park, theaters, and luxury hotels, as well as "the valley," Maxwell Street, and Chinatown. According to estimates by politicians, its 1962 population included 30,000 Italians, 15,000 Negroes, 14,000 Mexicans and Puerto Ricans, 10,000 Bohemians and Poles, 3,000 Jews, 2,000 Irish, 3,000 Chinese, and 200 to 250 Greeks. It was a point at which the American melting pot continued to boil.[7]

Politically, the first ward was a mainstay of the voting support which kept Daley and the Chicago Democratic organization in power. In the 1960 Democratic gubernatorial primary, Otto Kerner, the organization's choice for governor, received 11,452 votes in the first ward to only 970 for Joseph Lohman and 268 for Stephen Mitchell, his opponents. In the 1960 general election, John F. Kennedy received 16,984 votes to 4,182 for Richard Nixon in the first ward; and Otto Kerner, the Democratic gubernatorial candidate, obtained 16,916 votes to only 3,948 for William G. Stratton, his Republican opponent.

Racketeers in Chicago Politics

According to the U.S. Department of Justice, there was a "main line" connection between the first ward Democratic organization and Chicago racketeer elements in 1962. Specifically, the

[7] The account of Chicago's first ward is taken from interviews and accounts which appeared in the *Chicago Sun-Times* and *Daily News*. I am grateful to the *Chicago Sun-Times* and *Daily News* for the use of their library.

Federal Bureau of Investigation found that Sam (Mooney) Giancano, Chicago's best-known racketeer, bossed the first ward Democratic organization. Giancano received national attention because of his romance with Phyllis McGuire, one of the singing sisters, and because of his complaint that he was followed by hordes of FBI men, especially on a golf course he frequented. One judge enjoined the FBI from detailing too many G-men to follow Giancano.

Giancano's criminal record dated back to 1926 when he was accused of murdering a cigar-store owner. Fortunately for Giancano, the state's star witness against him was murdered in the doorway of his home. Subsequently, Giancano was sent to prison for burglary, auto larceny, and bootlegging. Most Chicagoans believed that he engineered a $100,000 kidnapping involving a fellow racketeer. While Giancano was in prison he met members of the so-called "syndicate." After his release he became a member of the syndicate and in 1962 was the chief figure in Chicago's gambling, numbers racket, and prostitution.

In 1961 the alderman and political leader of the first ward was John D'Arco. According to newspaper accounts, D'Arco offended Giancano when he shook hands with an FBI man while they were enjoying dinner together at a Chicago restaurant. Presumably, the social *faux pas* upset Giancano's digestion. As D'Arco and Giancano left the restaurant, D'Arco reportedly muttered to the FBI man, "Thanks to you, I'm through." The next day D'Arco entered a hospital and announced that he would not seek re-election as alderman because of ill health. Subsequently, racketeer Giancano informed the first ward Democratic organization of his choice for alderman to succeed D'Arco. According to the FBI, Giancano's political orders were issued through Pat Marcy, secretary of the first ward Democratic organization. His choice for the post was Anthony J. DeTolve, a member of the Illinois State Senate from the first ward. DeTolve had won renown, if not distinction, in Springfield for proficiency at the piccolo at parties and for his steadfast opposition to legislation that discriminated against criminals. For example, he was the lone member of a twenty-eight-man legislative committee to oppose a bill outlawing the manufacture of slot-machines.

Giancano thought such political courage should be rewarded. Undoubtedly, too, the fact that DeTolve was a cousin by marriage to Giancano operated in DeTolve's favor. In any event, DeTolve filed for election on the nonpartisan Alderman's ticket with the support of the regular first ward Democratic organization. When questioned, Mayor Daley pretended that DeTolve's candidacy was none of his business—that this was entirely a matter for the voters of the first ward to decide, and that he could not be held responsible for the endorsements of the first ward Democratic organization.

Cousin Anthony DeTolve's candidacy proved embarrassing to Giancano, the first ward Democratic organization, and to Mayor Daley. Events indicated that a "clown" could be sent to the Senate in Springfield without provoking comment from the press or public, but that the press and public maintained somewhat higher standards in assessing candidates for the Board of Aldermen of the City of Chicago. In the first seven weeks of the campaign, DeTolve made no speeches, had no meetings with the ward workers, never appeared on radio or television, and held no press conferences. When reporters approached his office, they found that it looked like an old speakeasy. The door was made of iron bars, was padlocked, and was equipped with a peephole. When reporters asked for an interview, his invariable reply was, "I am busy, all the time busy." As a consequence, he earned the nickname Anthony "Busy-Busy" DeTolve.

Anthony DeTolve's campaign lasted only ten weeks, after which both Giancano and Mayor Daley tired of his buffoonery. Reportedly, Daley feared that DeTolve would jeopardize his own election. Finally, at a meeting of first ward precinct captains, DeTolve announced his withdrawal from the race. He said, "I don't want to embarrass anyone . . . [and] my voice will be more useful to the party in Springfield than in the City Council." The first ward Democrats were left without a candidate on the very eve of the election, since it was DeTolve's name that was on the ballot. After days of indecision, the first ward Democrats were told that their candidate would be Michael Fio Rito. Allegedly, the order once again came from Giancano through Pat Marcy, the secretary of the regular Democratic organization.

The announcement of the name of the new candidate was made on Thursday, February 21, 1963, only five days before the election on February 26. The first ward Democratic precinct captains faced a challenge virtually unprecedented in American politics. They had to organize a write-in campaign for an unknown candidate in a period of about four days in a ward where many of the citizens did not know how to read or write or even speak English. The staggering dimensions of the job that faced the first ward organization may be appreciated from the fact that fifty-five of the sixty precincts had voting machines and the voter was forbidden to use stickers or stamps with Fio Rito's name on them. Consequently, to write in his name on the machine, the voter had to push back the slide above the aldermanic candidate. On the paper ballots in the other five wards, the voter had to write Fio Rito's name and address on the aldermanic ballot and place a box with an "X" on it before the name. DeTolve's name remained on the ballot, which compounded the problem for the voter. In addition, a Republican hopeful's name was on the ballot. The Democratic organization was given help by the election board when it ruled that if the write-in name sounded like that of any candidate, it was acceptable, no matter how it was spelled, and this included even Chinese spelling of the name.

The challenge posed by the write-in campaign exhilarated rather than depressed the Democratic precinct leaders. Fio Rito, the new candidate, issued a statement that his campaign platform would be, "Make the first ward Chicago's No. 1 ward in civic, social and cultural improvement." One veteran precinct captain jubilantly told a reporter that the regular Democratic organization never had been able to bring out any Democratic voters from among the high-rise hotels on Michigan Avenue. "But now it's different," he said. "With the cultural platform, he suits these people, too. And you don't have to teach them how to write."

The organization and its friends leaped excitedly into the write-in campaign. In Chinatown, its so-called "mayor," Jim Wong, restaurant owner and president of the On Leong Association, mustered write-in votes for Fio Rito from about 1000 Chinese. The collusion of Republicans with Democrats in the ward was made unusually visible when State Senator Peter Granata, GOP first ward chairman, together with another legislator who fought bills discriminating against racketeers, issued a statement in which he said: I don't know much about Fio Rito [the Democratic write-in candidate], but I've met him and he is a high-class fellow!" Granata was typical of the "tame" Republican leaders in Chicago's Democratic organization wards. The Republican as well as the Democratic legislators from the ward were generally members of the "West Side Bloc," which consisted of legislators who protected the interests of racketeer elements. Further, the first ward Republicans received patronage crumbs from Daley and the Democrats and rarely provided the Democrats with more than token opposition. In return, they were allowed to provide Republican organization candidates for nomination to statewide office with one-sided pluralities.

Pedagogues should study the education program instituted by the first ward Democrats. Judging by the results, adoption of their methods by educators would enable them to wipe out illiteracy in a few days. Fio Rito won by a margin of 8-1, receiving 9304 write-in votes to 1320 for Michael J. Curran, the Republican candidate, 1062 for Mrs. Scala, and 390 for DeTolve. In a first ward victory celebration after the election, attended by Mayor Daley, the first ward precinct captains were told that they had passed the acid test. "You were given a write-in candidate only fifty-five hours before the election and I'm sure you edified the entire city by your fine work in seeing that he was elected."

Unhappily for the first ward Democrats, however, their work was for naught. After the election, investigation by the sheriff and other law enforcement officials indicated that Fio Rito's candidacy was fraudulent and he was forced to resign from the board of aldermen. More precisely, investigation showed that Fio Rito's claim that he had been a resident of the city for one year and of the ward for thirty days was false. At the time of his entry into Chicago politics, he lived in a suburban community, Wilmette, outside the Chicago city limits.

Statewide Politics

We now turn to Illinois state politics. It is impossible to understand Illinois politics without some "feel" for Chicago politics, for the two are intertwined, particularly in the Democratic party. It is Chicago politics that gives the state its sharply competitive two-party character as well as its malodorous reputation. Chicago's organization wards help elect presidents and nominate and elect governors. They play a key part in the operation of American democracy and the government of the nation.

State politics in Illinois closely resembled Chicago politics in 1962, for patronage was an important element and every county leader wanted his share of the spoils. For example, in July of 1961 Dr. Martin S. Sloane, superintendent of East Moline State Hospital, received a letter telling him that he would have to fire twenty-two employees. "This is ridiculous," he said. "Twelve of them are trained steam and stationary engineers who operate our power plant." Dr. Sloane was informed that the twenty-two were to be fired because they had failed to kick back $4 per month to the Blackhawk Club, which was part of the Rock County Democratic organization. Coincidentally, the county chairman of the Rock County Democrats was also the assistant state public welfare director. Dr. Sloane finally capitulated, saying, "As much as I don't want politics involved in the staffing of a hospital, I guess that we just have to learn to live with the system."

Contracts were as important as jobs in state politics. Following are two examples of the way in which friendly members of the business community received state money. During Governor Stratton's (Republican) administration, when out-of-state insurance companies applied to do business in the state there were endless delays. They soon learned that if they retained George F. Barrett to handle their applications, approval was quickly granted. Barrett was a prominent Republican and a close friend of Justice T. McCarthy, director of insurance for the State of Illinois. Again in 1956, State Superintendent of Public Instruction Vernon L. Nickell had control of the distribution of surplus foods and had the power to grant contracts for distribution without competitive bids. He used this privilege to give an exclusive contract to an old Republican friend, James W. Dunbar, who headed Dunbar and Company, Truckers. Dunbar profited extravagantly from the contract and Nickell relied upon Dunbar for generous campaign contributions.

One result of this extravagant use of patronage and contracts both in Chicago and the state was a great deal of bipartisan collusion, as Democrats bought off Republicans in their strongholds and Republicans reciprocated where Democrats were strong. The election of the Speaker of the Illinois House of Representatives in 1961 is one example of the way in which bipartisanship operated. In 1961, the Republicans had eighty-nine seats in the Illinois House to eighty-eight for the Democrats. Therefore, the Republicans expected to elect the Speaker and organize the House. However, when it came time to elect the Speaker, three "tame" Chicago Republicans were absent. The three absent Republicans held jobs with the Chicago Sanitary District, controlled by the Democrats. The Republicans thereupon left the House and the Democrats were unable to continue the session because they lacked a quorum. The next day two of the Chicago Republicans recovered from their illness and helped elect Powell, a Democrat, Speaker of the House. Similarly, in 1958 the Democrats won a majority of the seats in the Illinois House of Representatives, and the minority Republicans joined with rebel downstate Democrats to elect Powell Speaker.

There were many reasons for bipartisan collusion in Illinois, including the traditional one of job hunger on the part of Republicans in Democratic Chicago and of Democrats in Republican downstate counties. However, Illinois' "cumulative voting" method of electing members of its House of Representatives was an additional factor encouraging bipartisan collusion which was unique to Illinois. Under the cumulative voting system, Illinois had three-member districts for election to its House of Representatives. The voters in each district cast their three ballots in any of four ways: (1) all three votes for one candidate; (2) two votes for one candidate and one vote for another candidate; (3) one and one-half votes for each of two candidates; and (4) one vote for each of three candidates.[8]

The intent of the framers of the Illinois Constitution was to insure minority representation in the legislature. They succeeded. Between 1930 and 1961, the minority representation in Illinois' House of Representatives never dropped below 42.5 percent of the seats, while in the State Senate it was as low as 25.5 percent.[9] However, in addition to assuring minority representation in the legislature, they also very nearly succeeded in eliminating two-party competition for election to the House. Over the 1900–1960 period, there was no contest for election to the Illinois House in over half of the state's legislative districts in most elections, and the defeat of an incumbent legislator was even rarer than competition for the seats.[10]

Competition was rare under the cumulative voting system because a minority party could almost always win one seat if all their votes were cast for a single candidate. Similarly, the majority party could almost always win two seats if all their votes were cast for just two candidates. However, if the minority party votes were spread out more thinly to two or three candidates, they would lose everything; and similarly, if the majority party votes were spread out to include three candidates and the minority party votes were concentrated on two candidates, then the minority party might win two seats to only one for the majority party.

The practical effect of cumulative voting in Illinois was to institutionalize noncompetition. In each Illinois district the state representative district committee for each party had the authority to determine the number of candidates to be offered by the party in the district. In most cases the decision was to offer no

---

[8] George S. Blair, *Cumulative Voting: An Effective Electoral Device in Illinois Politics* (Urbana, Ill.: University of Illinois Press, 1960), p. v.
[9] Gilbert Y. Steiner and Samuel K. Gove, *Legislative Politics in Illinois* (Urbana, Ill.: University of Illinois Press, 1960), p. 8.
[10] *Ibid.*, pp. 5–6.

competition to the opposing party. Consequently, the only electoral battles in Illinois in most legislative districts were within the parties for nomination rather than between the parties for election. Further, cumulative voting encouraged collusion between the parties because they were not at odds. Victory in elections depended on nomination on a party's ticket and an agreement between the parties concerning the division of the seats within the district. There was no reason for disputes concerning the division of the spoils, let alone public policy.

Legislative malapportionment was another feature which encouraged Democratic and Republican bipartisan collusion. Prior to the 1955 reapportionment, the population of Illinois' legislative districts varied from 39,000 to more than 700,000. Cook County, in particular, suffered from the malapportionment. The county had half the state's population and only nineteen of the state's fifty-one senatorial districts. The 1955 reapportionment provided for a relatively minor improvement in the apportionment of districts (the range in the Senate districts was from 54,000 to 384,000 population). Downstate Democrats as well as Republicans benefited from malapportionment. Consequently, the downstate members of both parties united to defeat or dilute reapportionment.[11]

In 1964, after the state Supreme Court voided Illinois' apportionment system, the legislature was elected at large rather than by cumulative voting, and the two parties competed for two-thirds of the 177 House seats. The result was the election of 118 Democrats (exactly two-thirds) to 59 Republicans in the 1964 Democratic landslide, and, possibly, a permanent rearrangement of the politics of the state.

Party Primaries

Now that we have examined the seamier side of Illinois politics, let us look at the effect of political organization on the results of primaries, in which the rank and file of the parties select their candidates for office. The 1956 Democratic and 1960 Republican primaries for the gubernatorial nomination provide instructive examples of the effect of organization on primary results in Illinois.

The central issue in the 1956 Democratic gubernatorial primary was the "ins" versus the "outs," or the downstate Demo-

---

[11] See Steiner and Gove, *Legislative Politics in Illinois*, pp. 86, 115.

crats (the "outs") versus the Cook County Democrats (the "ins").[12] Herbert C. Paschen was the organization choice for the nomination. Sachs was the candidate of the "outs" for governor and was supported by powerful downstate Democrats, including the powerful Representative Paul Powell of Vienna, Illinois. Powell and the downstate Democrats were particularly concerned about the 1956 election because they feared that reapportionment would result in Cook County domination of the Illinois House of Representatives. Powell said, "Downstaters will have to fight to protect their share of the gas tax, school aid, and other state grants."

The organization choice won the hardfought primary by 475,813 votes for Paschen to 347,458 for Sachs. Sachs won most of the downstate counties, but Paschen carried Cook County by a wide enough margin to win the primary. Further inquiry, however, indicates that the formula for the Paschen victory was not so uncomplicated as this implies. Paschen carried the low-income downstate counties and won by an enormous margin in the Chicago low-income organization wards. Sachs, on the other hand, won handily in the high-income downstate counties and narrowly in the middle-income downstate counties. In Cook County, Sachs received a majority of the vote in the high-income suburbs.[13]

In the 1960 Republican gubernatorial primary, the voting pattern was remarkably similar to the 1956 Democratic gubernatorial primary. In 1960 Republican Governor William G. Stratton sought renomination (the "ins"), whereas Hayes Robertson, his

---

[12] After winning the 1956 primary, Paschen withdrew as Democratic candidate for governor because of disclosures that he had put pressure on Chicago bankers to contribute to a "flower fund" in return for deposits made in their banks. This was particularly embarrassing to Democrats because they were hoping to capitalize on the Orville L. Hodge scandal. Hodge was a Republican state auditor who was imprisoned for stealing at least $1,612,639 in state funds. See George Thiem, *The Hodge Scandal* (New York: St. Martin's Press, 1961), for an account of the incident.

[13] In the 1956 Democratic gubernatorial primary, Paschen received an average of 53 percent of the vote in the eleven low-income counties (30 percent or more of the population with incomes less than $3000), 48 percent in the forty-nine middle-income counties (15–29 percent under $3000), and 45 percent in the thirty-eight high-income (excluding Cook County) counties (0–14 percent under $3000). In Cook County, Paschen won the organization wards (Wards 1, 2, 3, 20, 21, 24, 25, 27, 28, 29, 31, 42) with 83 percent of the vote (108,219 votes for Paschen to 21,771 for Sachs), carried the remainder of Chicago with 57 percent of the vote, and lost suburban Cook County, where he received 49 percent of the primary vote.

Republican opponent, ran as an anti-organization candidate (the "outs"). Robertson's battle cry was opposition to "dictation by party bosses." Robertson also ran as a conservative Republican, but this was unimportant as an issue because Stratton was also conservative. Governor Stratton's vote sources in the 1960 Republican primary were almost identical to Paschen's vote strongholds in the 1956 Democratic primary. Stratton, like Paschen, won by large margins in the Cook County organization counties and in the low-income downstate counties and received dwindling percentages of the vote as the income of the people in the counties increased.[14]

The central issue in both the Democratic and Republican primaries was the "ins" versus the "outs" or the organization versus the rebels. The question, then, is the reason for the tendency of low-income people to vote for the organization in both parties. There was no very apparent reason for low-income people to vote for either Paschen or Stratton on public policy questions because there was little difference between them and their opponents on such questions. In fact, if the low-income downstaters had voted their economic self-interest, their ballots would have been cast for Sachs against Paschen because they benefited from the disproportionate allocations of state taxes to downstate counties. However, the low-income downstate counties tended to cast a majority of their ballots for the Chicago organization candidate, Paschen.

The tendency of voters in low-income areas in Illinois to vote for organization candidates is not unique to that state. In a study of Kentucky politics it was observed that "the political leaders of the less wealthy counties of the state are much more dependent upon the Administration [or organization] for their political power than are leaders in wealthier communities. In a county where per-capita income payments to individuals are only 15 or 25 or 35 percent of the national average, a position with the State Highway Department or a contract for the delivery of office equipment or a thousand dollars for use on election day assumes an importance of truly heroic proportions. The wise use of these emoluments of power in low income counties can result in the creation of a political machine of considerable potency."[15]

---

[14] In the 1960 Republican gubernatorial primary, Stratton received an average of 74 percent in the Chicago organization wards and 69 percent in the downstate low-income counties; 60 percent in the middle-income counties and 69 percent in the rest of Chicago; and 50 percent in the state's high-income counties and 52 percent in suburban Cook County.

[15] Fenton, *Politics in the Border States*, pp. 35–36.

The use of money and jobs for political purposes was carried about as far in Illinois as American political morality permitted, and the "lean and hungry" recipients of the political patronage crumbs voted en masse for the organization candidates in both parties' primaries. The Cook County organization wards, in particular, provided massive support for the organization candidates. As a result of this voting pattern, the organization candidate almost always won in Illinois. The only exception to the rule in the memory of living man was in 1936, when Henry Horner, the incumbent Democratic Governor, defeated the Cook County organization by winning renomination against the Cook County Democratic candidate in the primary. However, even in this instance the Governor's organization defeated the rebel Cook County organization and in a sense proved the rule, for only the Cook County Democratic organization was wealthy enough to buck the Governor in the lean depression years, and it lost.

When the Republicans were out of power in the state, there was no "boss." The Republicans lacked any central source of power and votes in the absence of a Republican governor, in which case the intraparty struggles tended to break down into factional fights between a number of leaders who controlled small political baronies.[16] On the other hand, the Illinois Democratic party was dominated by the Cook County Democratic organization whether there was a Democratic or Republican governor, because of the organization votes at its command.

In the light of the corruption that attends Illinois politics, the number of able and well-known political figures produced by the system, including Adlai Stevenson, Everett Dirksen, and Paul Douglas, is puzzling. One explanation offered by an Illinois politician for the presence on the party tickets of able candidates is borrowed from Boss Plunkett of Tammany Hall, but applies to Illinois as well. According to the story, a candidate for lesser office complained to Jake Arvey that his name never appeared on campaign posters or on radio and television, but that Stevenson monopolized the publicity. "Look," said Arvey, "have you ever watched a boat dock along the lakefront?" "Yes," was the reply. "And did you notice the garbage and trash that was drawn into the dock by the boat?" "Uh, huh," said the candidate. "Well," Arvey concluded, "Stevenson is the boat and you are the garbage."

---

[16] See Clayton D. Ford, "The Republican Party in Illinois," in *Illinois Political Parties*, University of Illinois Bulletin, pp. 69–70, for discussion of the weakness of Republican party organization save when a Republican governor was in power.

Political Change in Illinois

The judicious employment of jobs and contracts can affect the results of an individual election when the voters are narrowly divided between the parties. But political change that endures is never the product of patronage but develops out of events and the reactions of political parties and their officeholders to the crises that confront them. It is the enduring type of political change that has accompanied war and depression, peace and prosperity, to which our attention is now directed.[17]

In the presidential elections, 1920–1960, tens of thousands of Illinois' voters cast their ballots in one election for the Democratic candidate and in the next switched to the Republican presidential candidate. At the time of their vote decision, each of the voters thought that he was acting as an independent judge of the qualifications of the candidate. In fact, though, he was affected by the culture in which he lived and the reaction of that culture to policies and personalities of the candidates. The political change that occurred in Illinois, 1920–1960, is not random in nature as would tend to be the case if each of the voters were an independent agent. The improvements in the percentage of the votes received by Republicans and Democrats over the 1920–1960 period assumes a distinctly sectional cast. Pronounced plus-Democratic change was registered in every northern Illinois county in the presidential elections, 1920–1960, while all of the counties in which the Republican party enjoyed significant increases in their proportion of the vote were located in southern Illinois. Examination of the distinctive characteristics of the two categories of counties reveals that plus-Democratic change tended to occur where there were large proportions of people who were foreign-born or native with foreign parents, while plus-Republican change tended to be concentrated in areas where the native American population was undisturbed by an admixture of foreign elements. There were other variables which were also significantly related to plus-Democratic or plus-Republican change, including the place of residence (urban or rural), the percent of the population that was non-white, the proportion of Catholics in the population, and whether the county was Democratic- or Republican-inclined at the time of the Civil War.[18]

[17] The political change in presidential elections (1920–1960) discussed in the following pages was measured along a line of regression for each county and thus is a product of all the elections in the time series rather than the first and last elections.

[18] The simple coefficient of correlation of percentage-point Democratic change along a line of regression in presidential elections, 1920–1960, with

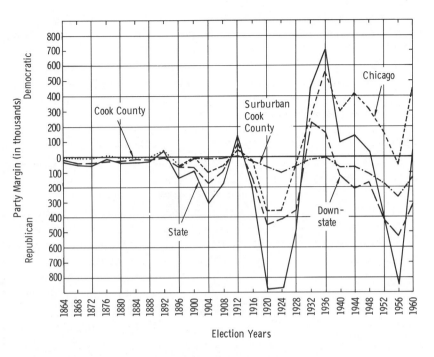

Election Years

FIGURE 7.2   THE WAY ILLINOISANS DIVIDED THEIR VOTES, 1864–
1960 by state and sections in presidential elections

Explanatory Note: The major components of Illinois' vote margins are
traced on the graph. The dominant impression taken from it is the great
and growing gulf between the Democratic pluralities registered by Chicagoans and the Republican pluralities returned by suburbanites and downstate voters. The sum of the votes equals a sharply competitive state politics.

The statistics indicate very strongly that in Illinois as in Ohio
and Indiana the principal political event of the 1920–1960 political period was the influx of urban, Catholic, foreign-born, children of foreign-born, and Negro elements into the Democratic
party, followed by the departure from the Democratic ranks of

the percentage of foreign-born and children of foreign-born by counties is
.65; and (−).62 with percent rural-farm by counties, .52 with percent
urban, (−) .40 with percent Democratic of two-party vote in 1860 (traditional vote), .36 with percent non-white, and .32 with percent Catholic. Thus
the Democratic party gained ground, 1920–1960, in counties which were
predominantly urban and contained substantial proportions of people who
were Catholic, foreign-born or children of foreign-born, and Negroes. The
Republicans gained ground in counties which were predominantly rural-
farm and contained people who were largely farmers, native, white, and
whose forebears voted Democratic at the time of the Civil War.

its native, white, rural, Protestant adherents.[19] Figure 7.2 shows graphically the vote payoff of Illinois' political trends. Before 1896 the state was narrowly Republican, going Democratic only in 1892. Cook County (Chicago) was somewhat more Democratic than the remainder of the state, casting a plurality of its vote for the Democratic presidential candidate in 1876 and 1892. Downstate Illinois (or the remainder of the state) never went Democratic over the 1864–1892 period. In 1896 and until 1928, Chicago, suburban Cook County, and downstate Illinois became increasingly Republican. The only Democratic victory in Illinois between 1896 and 1928 occurred in 1912, when the Republican party split between the Theodore Roosevelt, or progressive, elements and the Taft, or old-guard, elements. After 1932 political divisions in Illinois changed dramatically. Chicago became a Democratic stronghold, returning large Democratic pluralities in every election, 1932–1960, with the single exception of 1956. However, Democratic fortunes in downstate Illinois suffered a decline, 1932–1936, that seemed to be a continuation of the erosion of Democratic downstate strength that began in 1896. In suburban Cook County, Democratic pluralities fell off after the 1936 election.

In every Illinois presidential election following 1936 and through 1960, the central political question was whether the Democratic margins out of Chicago would be large enough to outweigh the Republican pluralities from suburban Cook County and downstate Illinois. In 1940, 1944, 1948, and 1960 the Democratic vote in Chicago was large enough to carry the state for the Democratic presidential candidate. However, the ever-widening Republican margins from downstate Illinois and suburban Cook County narrowed the Democratic margins of victory to the near-vanishing point. In 1960, for example, John F. Kennedy carried Chicago by 456,312, a margin exceeded only by Franklin Roosevelt's victory margin of 555,492 votes in 1936. But Kennedy won the state by only 8858 votes in 1960, compared to Roosevelt's 1936 statewide margin of 714,606 votes. The differences between the 1960 and 1936 election results were due in part to the steady lessening of Democratic strength in the less urban portions of the state.

[19] The multiple correlation of percentage-point Democratic change, 1920–1960, with percent rural-farm, 1960 plus the 1860 percent Democratic vote (−).68; and with percent urban, 1960, plus percent foreign-born and native with foreign parents (.71) provides statistical evidence of the dimensions of the big-city immigrant flood into and the native rural flight out of the Democratic party in the presidential elections, 1920–1960.

Two-party Competition and Governmental
Expenditures in Illinois

The political changes that occurred in Illinois, 1920–1960, made it a sharply competitive two-party state. Among the states it ranked twelfth in terms of the narrowness of its margins in the gubernatorial elections and in its legislature, 1946–1958. Its rank among the states in terms of expenditures for state services was also generally high, although not as high as its income level would seem to warrant. In 1960 the state ranked seventh among the states in per-capita income compared to seventeenth in its per-recipient payments for old age assistance, fifteenth in aid to the blind, and twelfth in aid to dependent children per-recipient expenditures. The state and local expenditures for education were somewhat higher, relatively, than for welfare programs. In 1960 Illinois ranked eighth in expenditures per pupil in average daily attendance and tenth in the estimated average salary of its instructional staff. However, it ranked twenty-third in the percent of its college-age population attending college. Its tax and expenditure program seemed relatively modest for a state with its wealth. In terms of effort devoted to governmental expenditures (the percent per capita state and local tax revenue from own sources of per-capita income), Illinois ranked a low forty-fourth among the states in 1959.

Thus, the Illinois job-oriented two-party competition produced a government which spent a relatively modest amount of money in relation to the wealth of the state. The reasons are implicit in the state's political organization. Illinois' politicians were not crusaders. They were not issue-conscious. For them, issues were a means of getting the government jobs. The result was a government which tried to do something for everyone but did not try too hard.

Summary and Conclusions

Predictions are notoriously hazardous in the field of politics. Another major depression or a hot war could work radical changes in the state's political trends. However, if no major catastrophe overtakes the nation, such as depression or war, the prospects for the Republican party in Illinois in the 1960s appear bright and those for the Democrats correspondingly dim.

The erosion of Democratic strength in downstate Illinois was secular from 1936 to 1956. The nomination of a Catholic Democrat in 1960 probably accelerated the separation of native white

Protestants from their Democratic loyalties. To these traditional Democrats their party seemed less and less the party of the common man. Rather, for them it appeared increasingly to be the party of metropolitan Illinois and to be dominated by elements to which they were at best indifferent and at most actively antagonistic.

The Democratic gains in Chicago which occurred from the nomination and election of John Kennedy were unlikely to offset the losses. Much of the Catholic community in the Midwest was integrating into the greater community. The Germans and the Irish Catholics increasingly perceived politics through eyeglasses colored by the same prejudices as those of the white Anglo-Saxon Protestants. They felt just as threatened by the newly arrived immigrants from eastern Europe and the white and Negro South as the native white Protestants (perhaps more threatened). They increasingly were part of the "have"vote rather than the "have not" vote. Taxes concerned them more than employment, and few of them experienced any dramatic improvement in their economic well-being as a result of the election of a Catholic President. True, there were certain psychological returns incident to the election of a Catholic President, but the long-run result of the psychological returns was likely to be an increased identification with the "have" portion of the community.

The only portion of the Democratic vote that appeared to be "safe" was that of the people who lived in cultural ghettoes either out of choice or necessity. The largest part of the "safe" Democratic vote was cast by the Polish and Negro residents of the metropolitan centers, supplemented by a relatively small Jewish vote. These people had failed or had been unable or refused to integrate with the greater society. Consequently, they indentified with the political party that was the slum refuge of the disinherited.

However, this left the Democratic party peculiarly vulnerable politically. In many ways Democratic party support in the 1960s resembled the vote it received after 1860. After 1860 the Democratic party was supported by elements outside the main thrust of American society. Its vote came from those unhappy with the results of the Civil War and after 1896 from those discontented with the power shifts coincident with the industrial revolution. Similarly, the Democratic party in the 1960s was increasingly the party of those who lived in the ghettoes of the cities or were disturbed by the results of automation.

Chapter **8**

Conclusions

The Midwest is both a geographical location and a state of mind. It is neither East nor West, neither South nor North. It is the population center of America and in many respects it is the heart of the nation. The people are heterogeneous in their origins, but perhaps more homogeneous in their Americanism than the residents of other sections of the nation. Unlike the citizens of Texas, Mississippi, or Vermont, who identify strongly with the Lone Star State or the South or New England, most Midwesterners think of themselves as Americans. They do not live in the Midwest. Rather, they live in America, for the Midwest is America.

Given the heartland character of the Midwest, the findings concerning two-party politics in Ohio, Indiana, Illinois, Michigan, Wisconsin, and Minnesota have a significance that transcends regional lines. In the past, the two-party job-oriented politics that typified the American party system was rooted most firmly in the villages of Ohio, Indiana, and Illinois. The two-party issue-oriented politics of the post-World War II period, similarly, is nationally identified with developments in Michigan, Wisconsin, and Minnesota.

The foregoing inquiries into the politics of six Midwest states largely revolved around assessments of the degree to which the theoretical benefits of two-party competition are realized in issue-oriented as opposed to job-oriented political systems. An eminently practical reason for the inquiry was to assess the desirability of the turn taken by American politics after World War II. The notion or hypothesis around which the studies of the states' politics revolved was that two broad aspects of two-party competition must be present before the theoretical benefits of two-party competition (discussed in the opening chapter) may be realized: (1) a fairly equal division of the electorate between the two parties roughly along the lines of contemporary problems; and (2) a leadership of the parties which makes them distinct entities, competes at every level of government, advocates alternative approaches to issues, and attempts to carry through after election by translating the programs into public policy. In the following pages we will review the findings concerning the degree to which the two requisites of two-party competition were present in the six states studied, the reasons for their presence or absence, and the consequences on the governments of the states.

(1) A Fairly Equal Division of the Electorate between the Two Parties along the Lines of Contemporary Problems

In the six Midwest states studied, the electorate was rather narrowly divided between the Democratic and Republican parties. Although some of the states tended Republican and others tended Democratic, there was little difference between them in the competitiveness of their state politics when competitiveness is defined to mean the narrowness of the vote division between the two parties. There were important differences, however, in the nature of the divisions between the parties. In Ohio, Indiana, and Illinois, the Democratic party was an alliance of rather conservative rural people, whose Democratic loyalties dated from their great grandparents' pro-Southern inclinations during the Civil War, and the more recent immigrants to the cities from eastern Europe and the American South.

The Republican parties in Ohio, Indiana, and Illinois consisted largely of the white, Protestant, more prosperous Americans. The traditional centers of Republican strength in the three states were the areas settled by New Englanders. The Yankee Republican voting strength was supplemented by the votes of people who prospered in the cities and the corn belts. The Republicans in the three states were largely people who had invested their blood and sweat and money in their lands and enterprises and had prospered. They resisted the demands of more recent immigrants for a larger share of the material goods of the state.

In summary, the voters of Ohio, Indiana, and Illinois were rather evenly divided between the Democratic and Republican parties. However, in all three states the division was, in part, along lines which had little or no relationship with twentieth-century issues.

The dominant political trend, 1920–1960, in the three states was for urban disadvantaged elements (foreign, non-white, urban) to enter the Democratic party and for traditional rural Democrats to leave the party.[1] As a result, voters were more and more likely to take political sides for reasons related to twentieth-century problems, but the Civil War continued to exert an important influence on voting habits.

In contrast to Ohio, Indiana, and Illinois, the two-party divisions of voters in Minnesota, Wisconsin, and Michigan were closely related to differences of opinion on twentieth-century issues. The lines along which the Democratic and Republican parties divided were remarkably similar in Minnesota and Wisconsin. In the two states there was a history of issue-oriented divisions of the voters within the dominant Republican party. In Minnesota the intraparty Republican division between liberals and conservatives was institutionalized by the creation of a Farmer-Labor party which competed with the Republican party in state elections. Following the New Deal and World War II, the Farmer-Laborites joined the urban disadvantaged groups in a Democratic-Farmer-Labor party. Similarly, in Wisconsin the Republican intraparty division between liberal La Follettes and conservatives was institutionalized during the 1930s in a Progressive party which competed with the Republican party in statewide elections. The Progressive party disbanded in 1946; and with the defeat of Robert La Follette by Joseph McCarthy in the 1946 Republican U.S. senatorial primary, the Wisconsin Pro-

---

[1] Simple coefficients of correlation (r) of percentage-point political change in presidential elections by counties along a line of regression with demographic variables provides convincing support for the statement that the dominant voting trend in Ohio, Indiana, and Illinois was the exodus of traditional Democrats from their party and the entrance into it of urban, disadvantaged elements. The relationships (r) of Democratic political change with percent foreign-born and natives of foreign parents, 1960, was .75 for Ohio, .39 for Indiana, and .65 for Illinois; with percent urban, 1960, it was .52 for Ohio, .44 for Indiana, and .52 for Illinois; with percent Catholic it was .21 in Ohio and .36 in Illinois; with percent non-white it was .52 in Ohio and .36 in Illinois. The coefficients of correlation bearing on the exodus of traditional elements were the relationships of Democratic political change, 1920–1960, with the 1860 percent Democratic vote in the presidential election which was (−).68 for Ohio, (−).38 for Indiana, and (−).40 for Illinois; and with percent rural-farm, 1960, which was (−).75 in Ohio, (−).45 in Indiana, and (−).62 in Illinois.

gressives tended to join the urban immigrants in a liberal Democratic party.

Therefore in both Minnesota and Wisconsin the affiliation of groups to the Democratic and Republican parties was related to twentieth-century issues. In large part, the immigrants of Milwaukee and Minneapolis and St. Paul cast their lot with the Democratic party because of Franklin Roosevelt's New Deal. Similarly, the Farmer-Laborites and Progressives of the two states left the Republican party in the 1920s and 1930s because they felt that its approach to social and economic problems was overly conservative. The merging of these groups in the Democratic party brought together farmers, laborers, immigrants, and liberals, all of whom demanded positive governmental action to redress their grievances, mainly in the form of a more egalitarian distribution of goods and opportunities. This left the Republican parties of Minnesota and Wisconsin with most of the people who felt relatively comfortable with the given distribution of goods and opportunities and who felt threatened by the demands of the urban and rural disinherited; that is, the native, Protestant, non-Scandinavian, stalwart or conservative Republicans.[2]

Michigan is the sixth of the Midwest states studied, and the divisions of people between the two parties in Michigan breaks more markedly along urban disadvantaged versus less-urban advantaged group lines than in any of the other five states. The combined impact of the New Deal plus the "Soapy" Williams administration, 1948–1960, drew into the Democratic party large numbers of Negro and eastern European immigrants, most of whom lived in the cities. At the same time, the liberal Democratic policies at both the national and state levels drove most conservative Democrats into the Republican party.[3] Urban eastern

[2] Statistical verifications of the generalizations concerning party affiliation in Wisconsin and Minnesota are provided by coefficients of correlation of the two states' 1962 percent Democratic gubernatorial vote with the 1946 La Follette vote in Wisconsin (.41), and the Farmer-Labor vote in the 1942 gubernatorial election in Minnesota (.50), and particularly with the Scandinavian adherents of these parties (.48 in Minnesota and .41 in Wisconsin). It was also positively related to the foreign-born or natives with foreign parents (.20 in Minnesota and .47 in Wisconsin), and Catholic variables (.17 in Minnesota and .35 in Wisconsin). There is little relationship between urban or rural-farm and the Democratic vote in Minnesota and Wisconsin because both rural and urban disadvantaged are in the same party. This tends to "flatten out" all the relationships.

[3] The bipolarization of groups of people in Michigan produced extremely high coefficients of correlation of percent Democratic in the 1962 gubernatorial election with demographic variables. The relationships (r) of the

European Catholic and Negro people in Michigan voted over-whelmingly Democratic and the less-urban western European Protestant white people voted Republican. The result was a division of groups along the lines of problems that currently faced them. Michigan's urban disadvantaged sought improved job and educational opportunities, along with a greater share of the good things of life, and they were largely in the Democratic party; on the other hand, the more well-to-do native white elements were relatively content with the given share of goods and opportunities or wanted an even larger share, and resisted the attempts of the disadvantaged to chip away at their privileges through progressive taxes and generous welfare and public education programs.

In summary, the Ohio, Indiana, and Illinois electorate were divided along both Civil War lines and along urban disadvantaged versus advantaged lines. This resulted in populations which, in large part, adhered to a political faith for reasons which were irrelevant to the problems that confronted them. The Minnesota and Wisconsin voters divided between the Democratic and Republican parties along cleavages marked out by the La Follette Progressive and the Farmer-Laborites, as well as along the urban disadvantaged versus advantaged "faults" which were exploited by the New Deal. In most cases, the Progressive and New Deal lines dividing the electorate paralleled or supplemented one another. The outcome was a division of the electorate along issue lines which were relevant to the problems the people of the states faced in mid-twentieth century America. Some of these issues were, conservation, welfare, employment, tax policies, parks, education, mental health, and farm programs. In Michigan the division between the two parties tended to be along the urban disadvantaged versus advantaged lines marked out by the New Deal. The Republican party maintained a strong grip on the traditional political loyalties of the sons and daughters of the settlers of the state, regardless of their economic status. The result was the division of the electorate between parties roughly along the lines of contemporary problems. The political trends in Ohio, Indiana, and Illinois were in the direction of a Michigan-type division of the electorate.

We turn next to a summary of the effects of the nature of the

1962 vote with percent foreign-born and native with foreign parents, 1960, was .64; with percent Catholic, 1957, it was .73; with percent urban, 1960, it was .47; and with percent rural-farm, 1960, the relationship was $(-)$.57.

vote divisions in the six states on the style of their political leadership. The discussion will be in terms of the second condition for effective party government.

(2) Leadership of the Parties
Which Makes the Parties Distinct Entities,
Competes at Every Level of Government,
Advocates Alternative Approaches to Issues,
and Attempts to Carry Through after Election
by Translating Their Programs into Public Policy

The analyses of political organization in the six Midwest states dealt largely with political leadership in the traditional two-party states of Illinois, Indiana, and Ohio, as opposed to the programmatic party leadership in Minnesota, Wisconsin, and Michigan. Perhaps the most interesting finding was the process by which programmatic political leadership emerged in Minnesota, Wisconsin, and Michigan. The dates and occasions for the emergence of issue-oriented politics in the northern tier of states were as follows: (1) In Minnesota it occurred in 1944 with the merger of the Democratic and Farmer-Labor parties; (2) in Wisconsin, the key date was 1946, when the Progessive party disbanded and Robert La Follette, Jr., was defeated by Joseph McCarthy in the Republican senatorial primary; and (3) in Michigan, programmatic politics developed out of the formal entrance into the Democratic party of the United Auto Workers and the capture of the Democratic party organization by an alliance of labor and liberals in 1948.

In each of the three states the pattern of events and the dynamics of transition to a programmatic type of two-party politics was similar. First, the Democratic party was an empty shell. Many of the traditionally Democratic but relatively conservative German and Irish Catholic voters had deserted the Democratic party in the 1930s and early 1940s because of the liberal economic policies pursued by Franklin Roosevelt and because of their disapproval of American involvement in World War II. In company with the desertion of their party by traditional Democrats, job-oriented politicians in the three states lost interest in political activity because of the adoption of strict civil service laws and the outbreak of World War II, which dimmed the luster of political jobs and appointments by providing better-paying employment opportunities elsewhere.

Therefore, the Democratic party was weak and disorganized

in the three states in the early 1940s. However, the party retained a substantial untapped vote base which voted for Franklin Roosevelt and the New Deal, but ignored the state Democratic party's candidates because of their conservatism and corruption. In Minnesota and Wisconsin these liberal votes were cast for the Farmer-Labor and Progressive party candidates in state elections, leaving the Democratic party a weak third party. In Michigan much of the liberal vote was not cast at all.

The moribund condition of the Democratic parties attracted the attention of astute political and interest-group leaders. In every instance the kind of political leadership which moved to fill the vacuum in the three state Democratic parties was issue-oriented rather than job-oriented. In Minnesota, many professors moved into positions of political leadership; in Wisconsin the new programmatic-oriented leaders were largely labor leaders, ex-Progressives, and Socialist leaders; and in Michigan the new issue-oriented leadership came largely from the ranks of labor, from liberals in business, and from the professions. In all three states women also played an important part in providing new political leadership.

The professors, women, labor leaders, Socialists, and liberals who captured the three state Democratic parties encountered little opposition, because of the disinterest of traditional job-oriented politicians in an activity that promised little in the way of jobs or other traditional perquisites of political power after the enactment of civil service laws. The key to the successful exploitation of the situation and seizure of the Democratic party by issue-oriented people was the existence of organized groups of liberals in the three states who were in a position to provide direction, lend luster to, and in some instances financially support the efforts of liberals. In Minnesota the most important organized group of liberals was the Farmer-Labor party; in Wisconsin the key liberal groups were the Progressive party, labor unions, and Socialists in Milwaukee; and in Michigan it was the United Auto Workers. In each state, then, liberals had an institutionalized power base from which to operate. They were not lonely and atomized. Rather, they interacted frequently through the Farmer-Labor party, Progressive party, Socialist party, the United Auto Workers, or through tangential groups such as Americans for Democratic Action, where leaders from all these segments of liberalism came together and in turn interacted with otherwise atomized liberals in business and the professions.

Once installed, this new Democratic leadership provided a

distinctly different face from the Republican leadership. The differences derived basically from the motives which impelled people to desert the Republican party and join the Democratic party. Fundamentally, the motive was dissatisfaction with the existing power structure and the distribution of goods and opportunities which accompanied it. Consequently, the leadership which precipitated the move into the Democratic party was also most firmly committed to policies and programs which would alter the status quo by providing a larger share of goods and opportunities for the less privileged members of the society. Often these people were white, native, privileged, Protestant Anglo-Saxons. Nevertheless, they were committed by reason of ideology to alterations in the power structure.

The Republican party was largely left with the people who were relatively happy with the existing power structure. These tended to be the more successful farmers, professional people, and businessmen. Frequently, as in Minnesota, the wives of the businessmen belonged to the League of Women Voters and interlarded their conservatism with a desire for improvements in the existing political, economic, and social systems (for example, civil rights, honest government, public education, and mental health). In the Republican party, as in the Democratic party, the traditional job-oriented politician tended to disappear in the 1940s, to be replaced by businessmen, as in Wisconsin and Michigan, and the wives of businessmen, as in Minnesota.

The outcome was the development of parties which were distinct entities. There was none of the mutual esteem that Republican and Democratic "pros" professed for one another in Ohio, Indiana, and Illinois. After all, the Democratic and Republican "pros" in traditional two-party states wanted the same thing—jobs! But in Minnesota, Wisconsin, and Michigan the political leaders sought different ends and the result was meaningful competition at every level of government and an absence of the bipartisan collusion that characterized the politics in other states. After election, no urging was required to persuade the issue-oriented politicians of Minnesota, Wisconsin, and Michigan to earnestly attempt to translate their programs into public policy. Their only reason for participation in politics was commitment to issues. The businessmen left good-paying jobs with American Motors or General Motors because they felt that their notions concerning the proper role of government would best serve the interests of the nation. Similarly, wealthy liberals, such as Neil Staebler, or university professors, such as Hubert Humphrey, were not attracted to government by patronage jobs but rather by a commitment to certain ideals and a desire to see them incorporated into the day-to-day activities of government.

In Indiana and Illinois the traditional job-oriented politicians held sway in the 1960s. Their continued organizational dominance was due to the presence in the Republican and Democratic parties of people whose party allegiance was unrelated to contemporary problems. In addition, both parties contained large numbers of adherents whose allegiance represented a response to the policies of Franklin Roosevelt and Dwight D. Eisenhower. The job-oriented politician emerged out of the traditional segment of the party but found a useful niche in the parties in mediating conflicts between the factions of the party and by nominating candidates who were acceptable to conservatives and liberals alike. In these states neither party was an empty shell and the job-oriented politician was rewarded by patronage for his activities. Consequently, the leadership of both parties sought jobs through political activity rather than public policy ends. Therefore, the parties were not distinct entities, but rather they were engaged in bipartisan collusion for corrupt ends. They often failed to compete, as in the Illinois legislature. And after election they seldom made an earnest attempt to translate their election programs into public policy.

Ohio political organization or disorganization was substantially different from that of the issue-oriented states or the traditional two-party states. In a sense, Ohio's political organization was similar to Michigan's before the UAW—liberal seizure of the Democratic party in 1948. There was no statewide Democratic party in Ohio. Rather, there were many city-based and county-based Democratic machines which were sustained through patronage at the local level. Each resisted the development of a strong state party because it would threaten their independence. Why was it then that issue-oriented groups did not seize the Ohio Democratic party as in Minnesota, Wisconsin, and Michigan? The answer is that there was no institutional base for Ohio liberals comparable to the UAW in Michigan, the Farmer-Labor party in Minnesota, or the Progressive party in Wisconsin. Ohio's liberals were atomized and seldom interacted with one another.

Ohio's Republican party was well organized under the direction of the very able Republican State Chairman Ray Bliss. One explanation for the existence of a cohesive Republican party in Ohio was the concentration of Republican votes, money, and jobs in the Cincinnati area, which enabled the Cincinnati Republican leaders to dominate and provide guidance for the party. In addition, Republicans in Ohio were well organized out of necessity. Lou Harris' polls indicated that the Democrats enjoyed an advantage in the stated party preferences of Ohioans. However, the Republicans were ahead in numbers of registered voters due to good organization.

The end product of Ohio's political disorganization was that the parties' candidates did not consistently advocate alternative approaches to the problems of government and were not distinct entities. For example, Senator Frank Lausche, Democrat of Ohio, was more conservative than most Republican candidates. In addition, because of Democratic disorganization little was done to translate into public policy the programs advocated in the election campaigns. The Republican party deliberately attempted to keep "divisive" issues out of elections for fear that they would activate urban Democrats.

In summary, the issue-oriented two-party states of Minnesota, Wisconsin, and Michigan had a fairly even division of voters along the lines of twentieth-century issues and an issue-oriented leadership of the two major political parties which competed at every level of government, advocated alternative approaches to problems facing the people of the states, and attempted to translate their political programs into law after election. These conditions for meaningful two-party competition were not met in Ohio, Indiana, and Illinois. We now turn to comparisons between the actual performance of government as a result of two-party issue-oriented politics as practiced in Minnesota, Wisconsin, and Michigan, and government performance where the more traditional job-oriented politics was practiced, as in Ohio, Indiana, and Illinois.

Comparative State Programs

In the opening chapter it was pointed out that the more competitive two-party states tend to spend more on welfare and education than the less competitive states. Inquiry also led to the hunch that another important determinant of the amount and direction of state expenditures is the degree to which the politics of the state is issue-oriented. It remains now to pull together some of the material concerning job-oriented and issue-oriented political systems in order to test the validity of the hypothesis that states with programmatic political parties tend to spend more on government, and especially on welfare and education, relative to the wealth of the people than do states with traditional job-oriented political parties.

Data concerning the total amount spent on state government and on welfare and education programs relative to the amount of money earned by the people of the state show that in every instance the governments of the three states with programmatic parties made a greater effort (spent more relative to income) than the governments of the three states with traditional job-oriented two-party competition (see Table 8.1 for the comparative figures for the six states). The dollar expenditures per pupil in average daily attendance and the per-capita welfare expenditures also tended to be higher in the three issue-oriented states than in the three traditional two-party states (not included in Table 8.1).

There were no profound differences between the states with respect to their two-party competition scores, 1946–1958; per-capita income, 1959; per cent urban, 1960; and per cent rural-farm, 1960. Therefore, the hypothesis that issue-oriented two-party politics encourages a diversion of resources from private to public expenditures in order to divide goods and opportunities more equitably has been strengthened by the results of the study. Six equally competitive two-party states were studied, and the governments of the states where issue-oriented politics prevailed invariably levied higher taxes and spent more on welfare and education relative to the wealth of the state. The study does provoke some questions concerning the social utility of traditional two-party competition where the divisions of the voters are partially along Civil War lines. The traditional parties would seem to serve few of the theoretical ends of two-party competition and to exact a rather large price for their services. In addition, they tend to institutionalize divisions of the voters along lines which have no relationship to the problems the people face.

The people of Minnesota, Wisconsin, and Michigan were found to be in the enviable position of owning state governments which were genuinely responsive to the public will. The question that remains is whether political conditions in the three states represent aberrations from the two-party norm or a trend in a new direction for American politics. The data on the six Midwest states clearly indicated that the development of issue-oriented political parties in the 1940s in the northern Midwest was no accident. It was the result of forces that were in operation throughout American society. In the states of Ohio, Indiana, and Illinois it was observed that the traditional conservative Demo-

Table 8.1

COMPARATIVE GOVERNMENTAL PROGRAMS, DEMOGRAPHIC AND POLITICAL DATA FOR SIX MIDWEST STATES

	TWO-PARTY COMPETITION SCORE 1946–1958*	TOTAL EFFORT % PER-CAPITA STATES LOCAL TAX REVENUE, 1959, OF PER-CAPITA INCOME 1959	WELFARE EFFORT % PER-CAPITA PUBLIC WELFARE EXPENDITURES LESS FEDERAL, 1959, OF PER-CAPITA INCOME, 1959	EDUCATION EFFORT % PER-PUPIL EXPENDITURES IN AVERAGE DAILY ATTENDANCE 1959–1960, OF PER-CAPITA INCOME, 1959	PER-CAPITA INCOME 1959	% URBAN 1960	% RURAL-FARM 1960
Traditional Two-Party States							
Ohio	77	6.9	0.55	15.7	$2328	73.4	5.4
Indiana	83	8.0	0.34	16.9	2102	62.4	10.4
Illinois	89	6.7	0.45	15.4	2610	80.7	5.6
Issue-oriented States							
Minnesota	—	10.3	0.76	20.6	1962	62.2	17.2
Wisconsin	73	9.3	0.62	18.2	2116	63.8	14.0
Michigan	80	8.7	0.60	18.9	2253	73.4	5.6

* The two-party competition score is derived from the average percentage divisions between the two parties in the gubernatorial elections and in the two houses of the state legislature, 1946–1958. For example, if the average percentage division in all the gubernatorial contests, 1946–1958, were *55–45*, and if the average two-party division of seats in the state Senate were 70–30 and in the state House of Representatives 60–40, leaving an average division in the state legislature of *65–35*, 1946–1958, the two-

crats were deserting their party in opposition to disadvantaged urban elements in the Democratic party. Outside Michigan, Wisconsin, and Minnesota this redivision of the electorate along issue lines was furthest advanced in Ohio. However, no catalyst had appeared in Ohio to transform the state's politics into an issue-oriented form.

The division of voters along lines related to twentieth-century problems appeared to be working to the long-run advantage of the Republican party. The Republicans benefited by this division because the flow of immigrants from eastern Europe was reduced to a trickle by discriminatory immigration laws, and the new immigrants to the cities were either Negroes who voted Democratic (but were less likely to vote than other groups) or people from neighboring farm areas who often brought with them rather strong pro-Republican biases. The outcome was a gradual plus-Republican trend concentrated especially in the medium-sized cities where the rural-farm immigrants to the cities often settled. If the Republican party responded to this opportunity with sensitivity, it would almost inevitably return to majority party status. However, if it pursued reactionary policies it would frighten its urban adherents into the Democratic party, as in 1964.

In any event, the future holds the prospect of continuing two-party competition in all the Midwest states with a growing tendency for the electorate to divide between the parties along issue lines. The result should be healthy for the future of American democracy.

Selected Bibliography

Books

Banfield, Edward C., and James Q. Wilson. *City Politics*. Cambridge, Mass.: Harvard University Press and MIT Press, 1963.

Berelson, Bernard R., Paul F. Lazarsfeld, and William N. McPhee. *Voting*. Chicago: University of Chicago Press, 1954.

Billington, Ray. *Westward Expansion: A History of the American Frontier*. New York: The Macmillan Co., 1949.

Blair, George S. *Cumulative Voting: An Effective Device in Illinois Politics*. Urbana, Ill.: University of Illinois Press, 1960.

Blegen, Theodore C. *Minnesota: A History of the State*. Minneapolis: University of Minnesota Press, 1963.

Bogue, Donald J., and Calvin L. Beale. *Economic Areas of the United States*. New York: The Free Press of Glencoe, Inc., 1961.

Campbell, Angus, *et al. The American Voter*. New York: John Wiley and Sons, Inc., 1960.

Chaddock, Robert E. *Ohio Before 1850* ("Columbia University Studies in History, Economics, and Public Law," vol. 31.) New York: Columbia University Press, 1908.

Derthick, Martha. *Cleveland*. Cambridge, Mass: Joint Center for Urban Studies of MIT and Harvard University, 1963.

Eldersveld, Samuel J., *et al. Political Affiliations in Metropolitan Detroit* ("Michigan Governmental Studies," No. 34 [Ann Arbor, Mich.: University of Michigan Press, 1957]).

Epstein, Leon D. *Politics in Wisconsin*. Madison: University of Wisconsin Press, 1958.

Fenton, John H. *Politics in the Border States*. New Orleans, La.: Hauser Press, 1957.

Gara, Larry. *A Short History of Wisconsin*. Madison: The State Historical Society of Wisconsin, 1962.

Gray, Kenneth E. *A Report on Politics in Cincinnati*. Cambridge, Mass.: Joint Center for Urban Studies of MIT and Harvard University, 1959.

Heard, Alexander. *The Costs of Democracy*. Chapel Hill, N.C.: University of North Carolina Press, 1960.

Key, V. O., Jr. *American State Politics*. New York: Alfred A. Knopf, Inc., 1956.

————. *Southern Politics*. New York: Alfred A. Knopf, Inc., 1950.

Marshall, Thomas. *Recollections of Thomas R. Marshall: Vice-President and Hoosier Philosopher*. Indianapolis: The Bobbs-Merrill Co., Inc., 1925.

Martin, John B. *Indiana: An Interpretation*. New York: Alfred A. Knopf, Inc., 1947.

Mayer, George H. *The Political Career of Floyd B. Olsen*. Minneapolis: University of Minnesota Press, 1951.

Mitau, G. T. *Politics in Minnesota*. Minneapolis: University of Minnesota Press, 1960.

Murray, Robert K. *Red Scare*. Minneapolis: University of Minnesota Press, 1955.

Porter, George H. *Ohio Politics During the Civil War Period* ("Columbia University Studies in History, Economics, and Public Law," vol. 40.) New York: Columbia University Press, 1911.

Sarasohn, Stephen B., and Vera H. Sarasohn. *Political Party Patterns in Michigan*. Detroit: Wayne State University Press, 1957.

Sawyer, Robert L., Jr. *The Democratic State Central Committee in Michigan*. Ann Arbor, Mich.: Institute of Public Administration, University of Michigan, 1960.

Sherman, John. *Recollections*. vol. I. New York: The Werner Co., 1895.

Steiner, Gilbert Y., and Samuel K. Gove. *Legislative Politics in Illinois*. Urbana, Ill.: University of Illinois Press, 1960.

Straetz, Ralph A. *P.R. Politics in Cincinnati*. New York: New York University Press, 1958.

Thiem, George. *The Hodge Scandal*. New York: St. Martin's Press, Inc., 1963.

White, Theodore. *The Making of the President, 1960*. New York: Atheneum Publishers, 1961.

Articles

Arneson, Ben A., and William H. Ellis. "Voting Behavior in 1948 as Compared with 1924 in a Typical Ohio Community," *American Political Science Review*, vol. 44 (1950), p. 432.

Baggaley, Andrew R. "Patterns of Voting Change in Wisconsin Counties, 1952–1957," *Western Political Quarterly*, vol. 12 (1959), p. 141.

Becker, Robert W., *et al*. "Correlates of Legislative Voting: Michigan House of Representatives, 1954–1961," *Midwest Journal of Political Science*, vol. 6 (1962), p. 384.

Campbell, Angus, and Henry Valen. "Party Identification in Norway and the United States," *Public Opinion Quarterly*, vol. 25 (1961), p. 505.

Christenson, Reo M. "The Power of the Press: The Case of the Toledo Blade," *Midwest Journal of Political Science*, vol. 3 (1959), p. 227.

Epstein, Leon D. "Party Activism in Wisconsin," *Midwest Journal of Political Science*, vol. 1 (1957), p. 291.

————. "Size of Place and the Division of the Two-Party Vote in Wisconsin," *Western Political Quarterly*, vol. 9 (1956), p. 138.

————. "A Two-Party Wisconsin," *Journal of Politics*, vol. 18 (1956), p. 427.

Fenton, John H. "Ohio's Unpredictable Voters," *Harper's* (October 1962), p. 61.

Flinn, Thomas A. "The Outline of Ohio's Politics," *Western Political Quarterly*, vol. 13 (1960), p. 702.

Glantz, Oscar. "The Negro Voter in Northern Industrial Cities," *Western Political Quarterly*, vol. 13 (1960), p. 999.

Jewell, Malcolm. "Party Voting in American State Legislatures," *American Political Science Review*, vol. 49 (1955), p. 773.

Key, V. O., Jr. "Secular Realignment and the Party System," *Journal of Politics*, vol. 21 (1959), p. 198.

————. "A Theory of Critical Elections," *Journal of Politics*, vol. 17 (1955), p. 3.

MacRea, Duncan, Jr., and James A. Meldrum. "Critical Elections in Illinois: 1888–1958," *American Political Science Review*, vol. 54 (1960), p. 669.

Masters, Nicholas A., and Deil S. Wright. "Trends and Variations in the Two-Party Vote: The Case of Michigan," *American Political Science Review*, vol. 52 (1958), p. 1078.

Miller, Warren E. "One-Party Politics and the Voter," *American Political Science Review*, vol. 50 (1956), p. 707.

Mitau, G. T. "The Democratic-Farmer-Labor Party Schism of 1948," *Minnesota History*, vol. 34 (Spring 1955), p. 187.

Salisbury, Robert H. "St. Louis Politics: Relationship Among Interests, Parties, and Government Structure," *Western Political Quarterly*, vol. 13 (1960), p. 498.

Sorauf, Frank J. "Extra Legal Political Parties in Wisconsin," *American Political Science Review*, vol. 48 (1954), p. 692.

Unpublished Materials

Adamany, David W. "The 1960 Election in Wisconsin." Master's thesis, University of Wisconsin, 1962.

Crane, Willard W., Jr. "The Legislative Struggle in Wisconsin: Decision-Making in the 1957 Wisconsin Assembly." Dissertation, University of Wisconsin, 1959.

Kessel, John H. "Road to the Mansion: A Study of the 1956 Gubernatorial Campaign in Ohio." Dissertation, Columbia University, 1958.

Munger, Frank. "Two-Party Politics in the State of Indiana." Dissertation, Harvard University, 1963.

Naftalin, Arthur. "A History of the Farmer-Labor Party in Minnesota." Dissertation, University of Minnesota, 1948.
Patterson, Samuel C. "Toward a Theory of Legislative Behavior." Dissertation, University of Wisconsin, 1958.

Other Sources

The presidential election data in the study were drawn from Walter D. Burnham, *Presidential Ballots, 1836–1892*, Baltimore: Johns Hopkins Press, 1955; Edgar E. Robinson, *The Presidential Vote, 1896–1932*, Stanford, Cal.: Stanford University Press, 1947; ————, *They Voted for Roosevelt*, Stanford, Cal.: Stanford University Press, 1947; and Richard Scammon, *America Votes*, vols. 1–5, Washington, D.C.: Governmental Affairs Institute, 1954, 1956, 1958, 1960, 1962.

The state election data were obtained from the States' Bluebooks; James R. Donoghue, *How Wisconsin Voted, 1848–1960*, Madison, Wis.: Bureau of Government, University of Wisconsin, 1962; John P. White, *Michigan Votes*, Ann Arbor, Mich.: Bureau of Government, University of Michigan, 1958; Samuel K. Gove, (ed.), *Illinois Votes*, Urbana, Ill.: Institute of Government and Public Affairs, University of Illinois, 1959; Wayne L. Francis and Sharron E. Doerner, *Indiana Votes*, Bloomington, Ind.: Bureau of Research, Indiana University, 1960.

Demographic data, except where otherwise indicated, were obtained from the United States Census or from the *World Almanac*.

During the study, scores of political, labor, business, and civic leaders were interviewed in addition to university and college professors in each of the Midwest states. The results of the interviews provided the bulk of the data on which the study is based.

Index